Leading Improvements in Student Numeracy

Edited by
Michael Gaffney
and Rhonda Faragher

ACER Press

First published 2014
by ACER Press, an imprint of
Australian Council *for* Educational Research Ltd
19 Prospect Hill Road, Camberwell, Victoria, 3124, Australia

www.acerpress.com.au
sales@acer.edu.au

Edited by Susan Keogh
Cover design, text design and typesetting by ACER Creative Services
Cover image © Shutterstock.com/bloomua
Indexed by Russell Brooks
Printed in Australia by BPA Print Group

National Library of Australia Cataloguing-in-Publication data:

Author: Gaffney, Michael (Michael Francis), author, editor.

Title: Leading improvements in student numeracy /
               Michael Gaffney (author/editor);
               Rhonda Faragher (author/editor).

ISBN: 9781742860459 (paperback)

Notes: Includes index.

Subjects: Numeracy--Study and teaching--Australia.
               Mathematics--Study and teaching--Australia.

Other Authors/Contributors:
               Faragher, Rhonda, author, editor.

Dewey Number: 372.720994

CONTENTS

Contents

FIGURES

TABLES

PREFACE

What does it take to achieve lasting improvement in student numeracy achievement? Our view is that the combination of high-quality teachers of mathematics and highly capable educational leaders working in close collaboration is the key foundational element. Yet in researching the background for *Leading improvements in student numeracy*, we found that there is a significant gap in the educational leadership and mathematics education research and practice literature. While there are many books about the links between educational leadership and learning, and on mathematics teaching, curriculum, assessment and student achievement, there are few that link these two domains. *Leading improvements in student numeracy* is designed to make that link. Moreover, it includes a systemic dimension, dealing with the issues, factors and strategies involved in supporting numeracy development at classroom and school level.

Leading improvements in student numeracy honours the contributions of teachers, principals and system officers to the Leading Aligned Numeracy Development (LAND) project. The LAND project was funded by the Australian Government as a National Literacy and Numeracy Pilot initiative to investigate how to develop and sustain higher levels of student numeracy achievement in low socioeconomic communities. The educators involved in the LAND project at school and central office level were a rich source of professional expertise and insight about ways to improve student numeracy achievement. The research and development work that we undertook with these colleagues through the LAND project forms the basis of the themes, ideas, principles and guidelines explored in this book. Our aim is to provide practical and strategic advice for those charged with the responsibility of leading numeracy improvement at school and system level.

Leading improvements in student numeracy is a book for teachers, principals and other school executives, teacher educators, education authority officers and policy advisers with the desire and responsibility for student numeracy achievement. It comprises four sections. The first section sets out the context and challenge for improving student numeracy achievement. It introduces a framework for numeracy development that highlights the value of combining educational leadership with quality teaching, and the need to appreciate and build links between what happens in classrooms, schools, and education authority offices and government to bring about sustained systemic improvement in student learning.

The second section focuses on the core areas of professional knowledge, attributes and practices necessary to support students' numeracy development. It draws upon research into characteristics of effective mathematics teaching and the associated leadership capabilities required of principals and teachers at school level to encourage such teaching.

Aligning the efforts of teachers and principals and others, and encouraging coherence in perspectives, policies and programs is the theme of the third section. The importance of networking is highlighted. The use of digital technology is investigated as a means of supporting collaboration within and among school communities and education authorities, and with university and government partners. The distinctive and complementary roles of university researchers, education authority project officers, and government personnel are explored.

The final section of the book is devoted to defining the key principles to sustain numeracy development. These are based on the characteristics of effective teaching and educational leadership, and how these should be brought together within and across schools in planning, monitoring and evaluating numeracy programs to realise sustained development in individual schools and across the system.

We trust that you will find the insights, research findings and advice in this book helpful, and wish you every success in leading numeracy improvement in your schools and education systems!

Michael Gaffney and Rhonda Faragher
January 2014

ABOUT THE LEADING ALIGNED NUMERACY DEVELOPMENT PROJECT

The Leading Aligned Numeracy Development (LAND) project took place over the period 2009–2011. It was co-directed by Professor Michael Gaffney, Professor of Educational Leadership, and Professor Doug Clarke, Professor of Mathematics Education, at the Australian Catholic University (ACU). The project coordinator was Dr Rhonda Faragher, Senior Lecturer in Mathematics Education at ACU, while strategic support was provided by Associate Professor Michael Bezzina, Director of the Centre for Creative and Authentic Leadership at ACU. Professor Chris Branson from the University of Waikato and Associate Professor Charles Burford from ACU assisted with workshop design and delivery. Craig Ashhurst and Matt Skoss shared their expertise in the project design, delivery and evaluation as consultants in the areas of policy analysis and effective mathematics teaching respectively. Dr Megan Poore played a leading role in the design and support of the LAND wiki used by project participants as a social networking tool to share their ideas and insights.

The project was a partnership involving the Catholic Education Office of Western Australia, Catholic Education South Australia, the Northern Territory Catholic Education Office and a sample of schools in communities with low socioeconomic status in each of these jurisdictions. Each participating education authority appointed officers to provide project liaison and management services and ongoing specialist support to schools. In Western Australia, this role was performed by Julie Southwell; in South Australia by Christelle Plummer, Athina Folopoulos and Jane Buhagiar; and in the Northern Territory by Jacqui Langdon and Chris Pollard.

For further information about the LAND project contact:

Professor Michael Gaffney, University of Canberra
Email: Mike.Gaffney@canberra.edu.au

Dr Rhonda Faragher, Australian Catholic University
Email: Rhonda.Faragher@acu.edu.au

HOW TO USE THIS BOOK

Leading numeracy improvement is a multifaceted task. It requires attention to identifying, disseminating and developing effective teaching practice in mathematics; making adjustments to organisational arrangements and curriculum and assessment programs and priorities; gathering, analysing and using evidence about mathematics teaching and student numeracy levels; and building alignment between what happens within and across various levels of education systems (classrooms, schools and central offices). Most of all, the achievement of widespread, sustainable improvement in numeracy requires teachers and principals with the school leadership capability and professional expertise in mathematics teaching and student numeracy learning to make a real and lasting difference.

In other words, achieving better numeracy outcomes requires principals and teachers who exhibit the highest standards of professional practice. This is where *Leading improvements in student numeracy* can help. We have deliberately designed the content and sequence of the chapters to assist school-based educators to consider, reflect upon and develop their standards of professional practice.

The book is divided into four sections. These are linked to current professional standards frameworks for Australian schools, including the Standards for Excellence in Teaching Mathematics in Australian Schools (Australian Association of Mathematics Teachers, 2002); the Australian Professional Standards for Teachers and the Australian Professional Standard for Principals (Australian Institute for Teaching and School Leadership, 2012a, 2012b).

For teachers, *Leading improvements in student numeracy* provides guidance to assist their career progression to becoming Highly Accomplished and Lead Teachers across the three domains of professional knowledge, practice and engagement. The links between these domains of teaching and the book chapters and their related content focus areas are summarised in Table 0.1.

For principals, *Leading improvements in student numeracy* is designed as a practical reference to assist in leading numeracy improvement in their school. The ideas and approaches that are presented emphasise the crucial role of principals in working with and through their teacher colleagues and other members of their school communities to raise student achievement, as well as the uniqueness of each school within its community (Australian Institute for Teaching and School Leadership, 2011a). The relationship between various aspects of professional practice, drawn from the Australian Professional Standard for Principals (Australian Institute for Teaching and School Leadership, 2011a), the chapters and their associated content focus areas are outlined in Table 0.2.

Table 0.1: Links to professional standards for Highly Accomplished and Lead Teachers

Professional standards for teachers	Chapter	Content focus area
Professional knowledge • know students and how they learn • know the content and how to teach it	1	The challenge of improving numeracy in diverse school contexts, including national and international trends and comparisons
Professional practice • plan for and implement effective teaching and learning • create and maintain supportive and safe learning environments • assess, provide feedback and report on student learning	2 3 4 9 10	A framework for numeracy school-based development that incorporates research-based characteristics of effective teaching of mathematics, along with articulating and embedding teaching purposes and practices through the use of evidence
Professional engagement • engage in professional learning • engage professionally with colleagues, parents/carers and the community	5 6 7 8	Engaging school communities with numeracy, and networking and supporting numeracy development

Table 0.2: Links to the Australian Professional Standard for Principals

Professional practices of principals	Chapter	Content focus areas
Leading teaching and learning	1 2	The context, need and strategic framework for improvement in student numeracy achievement
Developing self and others	3 4	Areas of leadership capability (personal, professional, relational and organisational) necessary to bring about numeracy improvement
Leading the management of the school	2 4	A strategic framework and set of leadership capabilities, themes and actions to manage numeracy improvement processes
Engaging and working with the community	5 6 7	Involving parents/carers in their child's numeracy development; and networking with other school communities, central education authorities, university researchers and others in supporting numeracy development
Leading improvement, innovation and change	8 9 10	Taking a systemic view to promote and sustain numeracy improvement, including consideration of creative and strategic ways of articulating effective evidenced-based practice and embedding numeracy development

For teachers, school executive members or principals with an interest in improving the numeracy achievement of their students, we suggest that the ideas and information in *Leading improvements in student numeracy* is used to consider existing practices and school contexts. See how they align with the ideas and strategies for improving numeracy in your setting, and then share your insights with colleagues within and beyond your school. We encourage you to use this book to try new approaches to numeracy improvement, to contribute to the pool of knowledge about numeracy research and development, and to model and promote the highest standards of professional practice.

A related purpose for writing *Leading improvements in student numeracy* is to provide practical and strategic guidance for those educators and policy-makers working in the central offices of education authorities. If you are one of those individuals, we encourage you to read the sections on school leadership and teaching practice carefully, and to enhance your appreciation of what is required – not just by the teachers in classrooms or the principals in your schools, but also what you need to do with and through your school-based colleagues to help create the conditions for mathematics teaching and numeracy learning to flourish across your education system.

To support readers, an accompanying webpage has been developed and is hosted at <www.acer.edu.au/leading-improvements-in-student-numeracy>. This webpage includes important detail about the themes and topics covered in the text, along with the Appendix material and related resources to support improvements in numeracy achievements at the local and system level.

Schools cannot improve numeracy outcomes by working in isolation. Networks and partnerships with parents and families, other schools, education authority central offices and governments are vital. Those of you with education system responsibility need to look to yourselves – to your mindsets, your policy-making practices, and the ways you develop, monitor and evaluate your efforts in working with schools. You need to realise that what you do is intimately connected to the students, staff and school communities you serve. Chapter 7 on supporting numeracy development and Chapter 8, dealing with numeracy improvement as a 'wicked policy problem', are especially focused on making such connections. What is more, the consequence of such realisations may well involve doing things differently at central office and – yes – even at ministerial level. After all, it takes a whole system to bring about lasting improvements in student numeracy.

Michael Gaffney and Rhonda Faragher (editors), on behalf of the contributing authors

THE EDITORS

Michael Gaffney is Professor of Education in the Faculty of Education, Science, Technology and Mathematics at the University of Canberra. He is also a University Professorial Fellow at Charles Darwin University, and Adjunct Professor and Former Chair of Educational Leadership at the Australian Catholic University. Michael has wide experience as a teacher, as an education system senior executive and as a researcher, consultant and policy adviser to Australian schools, education authorities and governments. His work is focused on supporting teachers, principals, central office staff and policy-makers to develop their capability to lead sustainable, worthwhile and systemic improvement in student achievement.

Rhonda Faragher, PhD, is Head of Education (Canberra Campus) and Senior Lecturer in Mathematics Education in the Faculty of Education at the Australian Catholic University. Rhonda is an experienced teacher and researcher and is a recipient of a number of awards, including the Vice-Chancellor's award for Excellence in Teaching and a Commonwealth of Australia, Endeavour Executive Award.

THE CONTRIBUTORS

Doug Clarke is Professor of Mathematics Education and Director of the Mathematics Teaching and Learning Research Centre, Australian Catholic University. Doug is internationally recognised for his research in mathematics education and for his work as an expert adviser to schools, education systems and governments on teacher professional learning and student numeracy improvement.

Michael Bezzina is Director of Teaching and Learning at the Catholic Education Office, Archdiocese of Sydney, New South Wales. Michael was previously Director of the Centre for Creative and Authentic Leadership and Head of the School of Educational Leadership at the Australian Catholic University. He is an experienced teacher, researcher and education system senior executive with interests and expertise in the role of values and ethics in educational leadership.

Chris Branson is Professor of Educational Leadership at the University of Waikato, New Zealand. Chris is an experienced teacher and school principal with research interests in the areas of values and ethics in the practice of school leadership. His book, *Leadership for an age of wisdom*, was voted by members of the International Leadership Association as one of the top three leadership texts in 2012.

Megan Poore, PhD, is an instructional designer specialising in the use of emerging digital technologies and the use and implications of social networking for education. Megan has a background in social anthropology and has undertaken academic appointments at the Australian National University, the Australian Catholic University and the University of Canberra.

Julie Southwell is a school support consultant with the Catholic Education Office of Western Australia, specialising in whole-school improvement through building teacher efficacy. Julie is an experienced teacher with research interests in educational leadership within the early years.

Craig Ashhurst is the Managing Director of Niche Thinking Pty Ltd. Craig is an experienced teacher, instructional designer and consultant to educational, business and government organisations. Craig's consultancy work has included a variety of projects with a focus on identifying and developing learning systems in large organisations, with clients including the Commonwealth Attorney General's

Department, BHP Billiton Indonesia and Fairfax. He is currently engaged in PhD research at the Australian National University into 'wicked problems'.

Matt Skoss is a teacher of mathematics and ICT at Centralian Middle School in Alice Springs, Northern Territory. Matt combines his regular teaching work with consultancy and facilitation roles with rural and remote schools across Australia. His particular interests include working with teachers to integrate ICT into their instructional practice and to amplify and extend student thinking about mathematical ideas. Making mathematical ideas accessible, enjoyable and memorable for all students is his aim.

SECTION 1
LEADING TEACHING, IMPROVING NUMERACY

CHAPTER 1

THE NUMERACY CHALLENGE: STUDENT ACHIEVEMENT, TEACHER QUALITY, SCHOOL LEADERSHIP AND SYSTEM POLICY

Michael Gaffney, Doug Clarke and Rhonda Faragher

Once there were two Year 5 students – Joseph and Rebecca. Both attend schools on the edge of town. Most mornings Joseph bounces out of bed and can't wait to get to school. This is one of those mornings. For the past few weeks, his teacher Ms Rushton has been doing measurement. She has been taking the whole class out into the playground and they have been developing and testing out their long-jump skills. Joseph jumped further than ever yesterday, and what's more – his team's overall score (calculated by the total distance that everyone jumped) is accelerating! They are starting to close the gap between themselves and the other teams ahead of them. The practice they are doing is starting to pay off. His classroom has lots of displays and charts as well as photos of himself and his classmates in midair, taking off, landing, measuring, and smoothing out the sand. They have also learnt how to use iPads to film and measure their velocity – and even how long the length of their stride is just before take-off! When Joseph gets to school, his friends and classmates are already at the long-jump pit.

A couple of suburbs away, Rebecca is starting the day by making her own breakfast. She has already helped a couple of her younger siblings get ready for school. She'll make her own way to school once she sees them off safely. This morning, like most other mornings, her class will have mathematics just after the morning recess. The sessions usually go for about 30 minutes or so – less if there is an assembly. Her teacher, Mr Banks, seems to like using worksheets. This week the worksheets are coloured green – which can be a bit frustrating as her pencils and markers tend to change their tone when she and her friends are colouring in the squares or joining the dots. Anyway, Mr Banks has said that once you finish your worksheet, you can go on the computer and practise Mathletics. Sometimes, in fact most times, Rebecca doesn't get the point. Why is she doing this?

Introduction

Every student has the right to be numerate. Making sure that they become numerate is the numeracy challenge. Meeting this challenge is a multifaceted undertaking. For students to develop the knowledge, skills and attitudes in numeracy that will continue to serve them over their lifetime, they need to be engaged and feel confident in their learning. Engaged, confident numeracy learners are a consequence of quality teaching, of teachers who know their mathematics and know how to teach it. These teachers understand where their students are likely to experience difficulty, and have the repertoire of teaching strategies (that is, the 'pedagogical content knowledge') to help their students over the hump. In fact these are teachers who are able to educate and enthuse their students about mathematics and assist them in developing the numeracy capabilities they need to flourish, not only in their future studies and occupations but also in their everyday life.

So meeting the numeracy challenge involves having teachers who are knowledgeable, skilled and confident in teaching mathematics and who foster a productive learning environment by providing appropriate and engaging tasks for their students. But quality teaching across a school does not just happen. While there are talented teachers and classroom-based pockets of effective practice in every school, getting widespread agreement and shared principles about effective teaching of mathematics requires something more. It requires school leaders who value teachers and their professional learning, inspire shared understandings and vision, engage the school community (especially parents) in numeracy development, and organise the resources and infrastructure to support teachers' work with their students.

But meeting the numeracy challenge across an entire school system requires even more than the efforts of students, teachers, principals and parents in individual school communities. It requires well-designed, carefully monitored and thoroughly evaluated system policies. Such policies cover areas of curriculum, assessment and reporting, staffing and professional development of teachers, and resourcing based on hard evidence about levels of student need and performance. Good policies are informed by research on effective practice within and external to the system, and involve collaboration between students, teachers, parents, principals, education authority officers and governments in their development, implementation and review.

In this chapter, these different aspects of the numeracy challenge are considered. They are designed to provide a basis for the chapters that follow.

Raising numeracy achievement – A local, national and international challenge

Defining numeracy

In 1997, the Ministerial Council for Education, Employment, Training and Youth Affairs (MCEETYA, now known as the Standing Council on School Education and Early Childhood – SCSEEC) in its *National report on schooling in Australia* defined numeracy as follows:

> Numeracy is the effective use of mathematics to meet the general demands of life at school and at home, in paid work, and for participation in community and civic life. (1997, p. 30)

This built on the work of Willis (1992, p. 5) who defined numeracy as 'being able to use mathematics – at work, at home, and for participation in community or civic life'. The Australian professional association for teachers of mathematics (Australian Association of Mathematics Teachers – AAMT) described numeracy as including

> the disposition to use, in context, a combination of: underpinning mathematical concepts and skills from across the discipline (numerical, spatial, graphical, statistical and algebraic); mathematical thinking and strategies; general thinking skills; [and] grounded appreciation of context. (1997, p. 15)

In attempting to elaborate differences between numeracy and mathematics (while not claiming they are mutually exclusive), the AAMT further noted:

> Numeracy is not a synonym for mathematics, but the two are clearly interrelated. All numeracy is underpinned by some mathematics; hence school mathematics has an important role in the development of young people's numeracy. The implemented mathematics curriculum (i.e. what happens in schools) has a responsibility for introducing and developing mathematics, which is able to underpin numeracy. However this 'underpinning of numeracy' is not all that school mathematics is about. Learning mathematics in school is also about learning in the discipline – its structure, beauty and importance in our cultures. Further, while knowledge of mathematics is necessary for numeracy, having that knowledge is not in itself sufficient to ensure that learners become numerate. (1997, pp. 11–12)

In whatever manner these two terms are defined and related by professional associations, education authorities and curriculum documents, it is clear that for full participation in an increasingly technological society, students need a strong background in mathematics including a positive disposition to the subject.

Assessment in mathematics classrooms: Some issues

Nobody ever got taller by being measured. (Professor Wilfred Cockroft, UK)

You don't fatten a pig by weighing it. (American saying)

The two related aphorisms might remind us that assessment divorced from subsequent action is unlikely to lead to improved learning. Sometimes, politicians and other educational policy-makers believe that it is *the act* of assessment that will lead to improved learning, when in fact it is the *action*, using the information gained from the assessment, that follows that is potentially most powerful.

In the 1980s, an increasing consensus emerged among classroom teachers that traditional forms of assessment were inadequate in meeting all the revised goals that teachers held for assessment. The argument was that, if we value genuine understanding, problem-solving and group skills, and the ability to use what has been learned in 'real' situations, then we need to broaden the repertoire of assessment techniques from the classic pen-and-paper test, combining 'informal' assessment with a greater range of formal methods of assessment.

David Clarke (1988) claimed that we communicate most clearly to students those things that we value by the ways we assess them. Both the educational and wider communities have considerable faith in the pen-and-paper test as a form of assessment, but we all know students for whom the pressure of the test leads to performance that is not representative of their knowledge and understanding. In addition, students whose background in English is not strong may also find it difficult to demonstrate what they know and can do using this assessment format.

Research in mathematics education has generated data that suggests that students who give correct answers to pen-and-paper mathematics items sometimes have little or no understanding of the concepts and relationships that the tests were designed to measure. The work of Clements and Ellerton (1995) with students in three Australian states produced data that indicated that around one-quarter of students' responses to multiple-choice and short-answer mathematics items could be classified as either correct answers given by students who did not have a sound understanding of the relevant knowledge, skills, concepts and principles; or incorrect answers given by students who had partial or full understanding.

The late 1980s saw an increased emphasis on the use of anecdotal records, check-lists, portfolios, student self-assessment and so on. These assessment alternatives continue today, with teachers refining them in light of experience.

> Not everything that counts can be counted. Not everything that can be counted counts. (Claimed to be posted on Albert Einstein's wall)

This aphorism reminds us that, just because we can easily assess memory of procedures and facts, this does not necessarily mean that such procedures and facts should be the major focus of our assessment attention. Unfortunately, for the busy teacher, it remains true that the easier a given form of assessment is to use, the less useful the information it is likely to provide.

An important issue is whether we are teaching for short-, medium- or long-term understanding. Most secondary teachers will recall the horror that greets an announcement that the end-of-term exam will cover the entire term's content. A common response is, 'You mean I have to learn it all over again?' In these students' minds, there is no expectation that any understanding of the assessed content will be retained for more than a few weeks, let alone well into the future. The 'teach it/test it/teach it/test it' process may actually be creating the illusion of learning.

One interesting development in assessment in recent years has been the use of scoring 'rubrics' (or marking sheets with explicit criteria and standards for assessment) with a greater emphasis on making more 'holistic' judgements of students' work, with less emphasis on counting up 'rights' and 'wrongs'. Such an approach can enable attention to 'big ideas', rather than simply facts and procedures.

Educational and assessment policies come and go, but the major purpose of assessment should continue to be *to inform teaching*. Such an orientation will have an effect on the kinds of tasks and processes we use for assessment, the timing and use of such tasks and processes, the ways in which students view assessment, and the subsequent quality of our teaching. The most effective teachers are likely to be those who approach assessment as an opportunity for students to show what they know and can do, who link assessment and teaching (making these links clear to students), and regard assessment as a prelude to action.

In the 1990s and 2000s, issues of accountability at classroom, school and system level brought a greater emphasis on nominating desired outcomes and ways of collecting, documenting and reporting students' growth of understanding over time. These issues of accountability have led to a greater interest in data on mathematics performance from international and national testing. In the next section, we discuss evidence from international and national assessments on the performance of Australian students in mathematics.

Performance of Australian students on TIMSS, PISA and NAPLAN

There are two major international school assessments in mathematics: TIMSS and PISA. TIMSS is the Trends in International Mathematics and Science Study, which is conducted every four years with Year 4 and Year 8 students. TIMSS studies the intended, implemented and attained curriculum in mathematics and science. As well as a range of demographic, pedagogical and technological information, TIMSS assesses student achievement. In 2011, 63 countries participated, and a stratified random sample of 280 primary schools and 290 secondary schools was involved in Australia. The mathematics test involved a mixture of multiple-choice items and constructed response items. Australia's performance at Year 4 level was significantly higher than 27 countries, similar to 6 countries, but below that of 17 countries. Australia's 2011 score was significantly higher than the result for TIMSS 1995. In Year 8, performance was greater than that of 27 countries but lower than that of 6 countries (Thomson et al., 2012).

In 2007, 49 countries participated, and a stratified random sample of 230 primary schools and 230 secondary schools was involved in Australia. The mathematics test involved a mixture of multiple-choice items and constructed response items. Australia's performance at Year 4 level was significantly higher than 20 countries, similar to 3 countries, but below that of 12 countries. In Year 8, performance was greater than that of 31 countries, similar to 8 countries and less than that of 9 countries (Thomson & Buckley, 2009).

Australian Year 4 students performed well compared to other countries on items involving understanding of shapes, but more poorly for items involving fractions, multiplication and area. In Year 8, students' understanding of algebra was found to be relatively poor at the international level.

The TIMSS 1999 video study (Hollingsworth, Lokan & McCrae, 2003) revealed some concerns about teaching practice in Year 8. The researchers videotaped and analysed in great detail a total of 638 Year 8 lessons from seven participating countries, including Australia. Altogether, 87 Australian schools and one teacher in each school were randomly selected in a way that was representative of all states, territories, school sectors, and metropolitan and country areas. Each teacher was filmed for one complete lesson.

Although the report detailed the international findings, the findings for Australia included some concerning aspects:
- More than three-quarters of the problems used by teachers were rated as low in procedural complexity (requiring four or fewer steps to solve).
- The majority of problems involved emphasis on correct use of procedures to solve them.

- One-third of problems per lesson, on average, were solved publicly by giving the answer only. Only 8 per cent of the 15 per cent of problems intended to be solved by making mathematical connections were actually solved that way publicly.
- Just over a quarter of problems were set up with use of real-life connections (42 per cent in The Netherlands).
- More than 90 per cent of problems were presented to students as having only one solution. (See Hollingsworth et al., 2003, pp. xviii–xxi)
- The authors recommended that 'Australian students would benefit from more exposure to less repetitive, higher-level problems, more discussion of alternative solutions, and more opportunity to explain their thinking' (Hollingsworth et al., p. xxi). They explained that

  > there is an over-emphasis on 'correct' use of the 'correct' procedure to obtain the correct answer. Opportunities for students to appreciate connections between mathematical ideas and to understand the mathematics behind the problems they are working on are rare.

- This had the consequence of creating 'a syndrome of shallow teaching, where students are asked to follow procedures without reasons' (Hollingsworth et al., p. xxi).

PISA is the Programme for International Student Assessment and comprises a survey that measures reading, mathematics and science literacy skills. It was established to determine the capabilities of 15-year-old students at applying their skills and knowledge to real-life problems and situations, and also to measure their ability to analyse, reason and communicate their ideas effectively (Thomson, De Bortoli & Buckley, 2013). In this way, PISA has a greater emphasis on applying mathematics than does the TIMSS assessment.

Since 2000, PISA has been conducted every three years, with 65 countries involved in 2012, the latest survey administered. In the area of mathematical literacy, Australian students performed above the OECD average in 2012 with 30 countries achieving lower scores than Australia and 7 countries achieving at the same level. Sixteen countries scored significantly higher than Australia. Of note, the gap between the lowest and highest achieving students in Australia was significantly wider than the OECD average. Australia's performance has shown a statistically significant decline between 2003 and 2013 with this decline being observed across all performance levels (that is top performers, average performers and low performers). The gender gap in mathematics, which had appeared to be closing over recent decades, emerged again in 2009. The difference increased in the most recent results, with boys performing significantly better than girls on PISA in 2012. Results for Indigenous students continue to be a concern, with differences equating to around two-and-a-half years of schooling between Indigenous and non-Indigenous students. In addition, the gap between Indigenous and non-Indigenous performance widened between 2003 and 2012.

One reason for the decline in performance of Australian students appeared to be the decrease in the number of high achievers. Thomson (2011) noted the important finding that 'in an increasingly global economy and workforce, Australian students appear to be losing ground on students from nations they may find themselves competing with jobs for in the future' (p. 5).

In Australia, a National Assessment Program – Literacy and Numeracy (NAPLAN) has recently been introduced across the country (Australian Curriculum, Assessment and Reporting Authority, 2011). To give an example of the style of the test, the 2010 Mathematics NAPLAN test for Year 3, for example, was made up of a total of 35 questions; 8 of these required a one-number answer and the remaining questions were multiple choice, with options A, B, C or D.

The benefit of large-scale mathematics assessments being in the form of pen-and-paper tests is that they are relatively simple to administer and marking can be completed by a computer, which is time efficient. This allows for various reports to be generated for the different stakeholders. The most publicised repository for reports on the NAPLAN results is the My School website, a website where 'you can quickly locate statistical and contextual information about schools in your community and compare them with statistically similar schools across the country' (Australian Curriculum, Assessment and Reporting Authority, 2013). As part of the compliance and accountability arrangements associated with school funding from the Australian Government to state and territory government and non-government education authorities, individual reports for parents, school data for principals and reports for state or territory governments are also produced. Results of these tests can measure the progress over time and compare schools and students across the nation. Interventions with particular students or schools can then be put in place.

Issues remain of drawing unjustified conclusions from such tests. In multiple-choice tests where students are not asked to explain their choices, one can never be sure of the basis of choice, and whether students have chosen the right alternative for the wrong reason. If ACARA reports, for example, that 34 per cent of Victorian Year 7 students made the successful choice in the task shown in Figure 1.1, there are at least two things to note. First, the capacity of most Year 7 students to apply their understanding of fraction equivalence and addition is quite limited. Secondly, and even more sobering, is that even if everyone sitting the test guessed on this item, one would expect at least 25 per cent to get it correct!

So, recent data from international and national assessments provide evidence of a considerable challenge for Australian teachers in achieving the aim of a

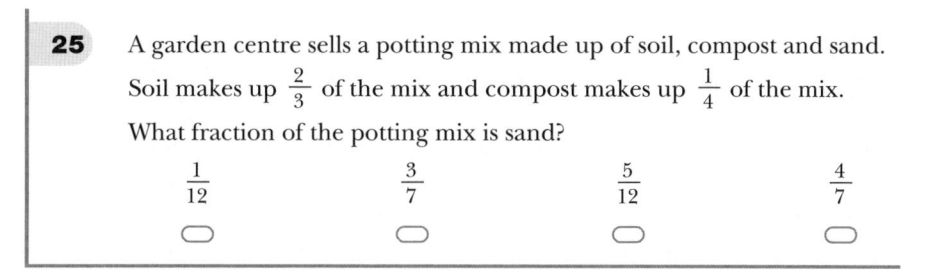

25   A garden centre sells a potting mix made up of soil, compost and sand. Soil makes up $\frac{2}{3}$ of the mix and compost makes up $\frac{1}{4}$ of the mix. What fraction of the potting mix is sand?

$\frac{1}{12}$ $\frac{3}{7}$ $\frac{5}{12}$ $\frac{4}{7}$

Source: Ministerial Council on Education, Employment, Training and Youth Affairs (2008a), p. 9

Figure 1.1: Sample multiple-choice question – NAPLAN 2008 numeracy test

confident and capable group of mathematics graduates from our Australian schools.

Effective policy and programs for numeracy development

Australian teachers cannot meet the numeracy challenge on their own. Raising the achievement of students across the board requires the encouragement and support of education authorities and governments. At her address to the National Press Club in Canberra on 3 September 2012, prime minister Julia Gillard (2012) announced that she would be introducing a Bill to the parliament:

> to enshrine our nation's expectations for what we will achieve for our children, our vision of the quality of education to which our children are entitled and our preparedness to put success for every child at the heart of how we deliver and fund education.

The prime minister made an impassioned plea for the Australian community, families and business to join her in working to achieve the following goals:

> By 2025, I want Australian schools to be back in the top five schooling systems in the world. By 2025, Australia should be ranked as a top 5 country in the world in Reading, Science and Mathematics – and for providing our children with a high-quality and high-equity education system.

Ms Gillard explained that the Bill – to become the Australian Education Act, would establish the country's support for a child's education as one of the entitlements of citizenship. She invited the Australian community to commit to a National Plan for School Improvement that would involve asking the states and territories, and Catholic and independent schools to sign up to new requirements including the following:

- the lifting of the quality of teachers, including requiring more classroom experience before graduation and higher entry requirements for the teaching profession
- more power for principals, including over budgets and staff selection
- more information for parents through the My School website.

The prime minister explained that the practical implications of these requirements would be that mathematics, along with reading and writing, would remain one of the foundation stones of children's education; that those students falling behind would be supported by personalised learning plans and access to extended school activities such as breakfast clubs and after-hours activities; and that principals, teachers and parents would be enabled and encouraged to exercise more local initiative in concert with system authorities to develop and sustain improvements in students' learning outcomes. Exactly how these intentions will play out in the years ahead is hard to say, but they constitute a continuation of the increasing importance that leaders in government, and politicians more generally, are placing on school performance as measured by student achievement in areas such as numeracy.

This government interest was certainly apparent in the *National numeracy review report* commissioned by the Human Capital Working Group of the Council of Australian Governments or COAG (2008a). This report foreshadowed several of the themes highlighted above by prime minister Gillard (2012). For example, in making reference to Australia's ambitions to be one of the 'very high-performing countries' and retain its economic wellbeing in the face of global economic, technological and social changes, the Review Panel (Council of Australian Governments, 2008a) made several recommendations:

- teacher educators should recognise and prepare all teachers as teachers of numeracy
- educational authorities should give more time to mathematics as a discipline and to numeracy as a general capability in the school curriculum
- increased resources (including specialist teachers) should be directed to support teachers in regular classrooms to provide intervention for students at risk (especially in the early years).

The *National numeracy review report* made a timely impact on the shape of forthcoming government programs, in particular the Literacy and Numeracy Pilots in Low SES [socioeconomic status] School Communities designed to inform the development of the National Partnership Agreement on Literacy and Numeracy between the federal, state and territory governments. The total funding under the National Partnership was $540 million from 2008–09 to 2011–12. The reforms were to achieve the following goals:

- effective and evidenced-based teaching of literacy and numeracy
- strong school leadership and whole-school engagement with literacy and numeracy
- monitoring student and school literacy and numeracy performance to identify where support was needed.

While the programs funded under the partnership were administered through the Commonwealth Department of Education, Employment and Workplace Relations, the COAG Reform Council had the role of assessing and publicly reporting the achievement against performance benchmarks agreed between the Commonwealth and the states and territories.

The most recent report of the National Partnership program was released by COAG in June 2012. It indicated that there had been improvement in particular areas. For example, the number of Indigenous Year 3 students performing below the national benchmarks in participating schools had dropped from 53 per cent in 2008 to 12.9 per cent in 2011. But the partnerships were yet to make a statistically significant improvement on the average NAPLAN results of schools that received funding under the program. The author of the report, Auditor-General Ian McPhee, was reported as stating that national literacy and numeracy achievement had mostly been stable since the program was introduced, including for low-performing and Indigenous students (Milburn & Hall, 2012).

Other findings from the report were that students with high socioeconomic status performed about the same across the country, but the achievements of students with low socioeconomic status varied between the states and territories. COAG Chair Paul McClintock expressed particular concern at these results noting that 'This means that students who are disadvantaged by their socio-economic status may be further disadvantaged because of where they live' (Milburn & Hall, 2012).

The report also found Indigenous student school attendance rates have continued to fall in almost every jurisdiction, especially in the upper high-school years. In the Northern Territory, just 61 per cent of Year 10 Indigenous students attended school. This had fallen from almost 70 per cent attendance in 2007. McClintock warned that this trend had implications for state and territory governments in meeting their targets, while Federal Schools Minister Peter Garrett indicated that the responsibility to improve these attendance rates needed to shared between the schools and the parents – saying that 'schools have to support and better accommodate Aboriginal and Torres Strait Islander students, and that parents ensure the importance of schooling is communicated very clearly to their children' (Milburn & Hall, 2012).

This synopsis of recent government policy and program initiatives shows the complexity of bringing about large-scale systemic change in student numeracy achievement, yet the moves already taken and those planned in new legislation are just part of the overall picture of current school reform in Australia. Along with the National Partnerships, NAPLAN, and My School, Australian schools and system authorities have also been asked to engage with the development of the Australian Curriculum.

'Meeting the numeracy challenge' in this regard means coming to terms with the content, form and the underlying philosophy of the *Australian Curriculum: Mathematics* document. Like past attempts to create greater national coherence, this most recent endeavour has its critics. For example, Atweh and Goos (2011) expressed their concern that the *Australian Curriculum: Mathematics* failed to give sufficient priority to the development of active citizenship, which, they explained, includes the ability to participate in work and manage the demands of everyday life. They also argued:

> The focus on content would lead to privileging knowledge of content and basic skills at the expense of making sense of mathematics and its use for creative problem-solving in complex real-world problems. (Atweh & Goos, 2011, p. 225)

Regardless of the extent to which these claims are valid, the fact remains that the shape of the curriculum in the classroom, that is, 'the enacted curriculum' compared with what is written as policy as 'the intended curriculum', depends on the capability of teachers to interpret what is called for and then to develop and customise their teaching strategies and assess their students' learning in light of their context, their school's systemic requirements and accountabilities, and their own professional philosophy and outlook. This is sophisticated work and requires thorough preparation, collegial interaction and support, and timely access to quality professional learning opportunities. These are areas that highlight the connection between quality teaching and school leadership.

Quality teaching and school leadership for numeracy development

One of the major and most consistently critiqued factors influencing student achievement in numeracy is teacher quality. The attraction, retention and development of high-quality teachers of mathematics have been the subject of numerous reviews over recent years (Australian Academy of Science, 2006; Australian Association of Mathematics Teachers, 1997, 2002; Australian Council for Educational Research, 2003; Australian Council of Deans of Science, 2006;

Commonwealth Department of Education, Science and Training, 2004; Council of Australian Governments, 2008a). Despite this plethora of activity, issues of teacher quality remain.

The latest effort to deal with this issue is the Senate Inquiry on Teaching and Learning (maximising our investment in Australian schools) that began in 2012. In his submission to this inquiry, Professor Geoff Masters, Chief Executive of the Australian Council for Educational Research, argued that international research suggests that governments can enhance the quality of teaching and learning in the following ways:

- restricting and raising the quality of student intakes to teacher education
- setting and confirming the achievement of minimum standards for registration
- recognising and rewarding the development of specialist knowledge and skill.

Each of these strategies deserves further consideration. With regard to the first, Masters (2012) argued that this should involve more than the blunt approach of selecting the 'top 30%'; instead, the task involves developing clarity about the attributes sought in future teachers and then testing for those as part of the selection process. The second and third strategies focus attention on the value of teachers demonstrating their areas of knowledge and skill, and being professionally and appropriately recognised. These are complex areas of policy and practice, and cannot be effectively solved without careful attention to teacher professional development.

The *National numeracy review report* (Council of Australian Governments, 2008a, p. xiv) found that exemplary professional development programs shown to enhance numeracy outcomes are based on these principles:

- enhancing pedagogical content knowledge (that is, knowledge about teaching specific mathematical content)
- providing teachers and support staff with approaches for accessing the thinking of individual students
- the premise of high expectations of all students and providing conceptually rich strategies for tackling the needs of those not achieving well
- a strong theory–practice link including partnerships between schools, systems and universities
- providing sustained opportunities for teacher learning and reflection and collegial and/or specialist support.

The report went on to make two further recommendations of particular significance for this book, and for the LAND research project on which it is based:

- pedagogical content knowledge (that is, knowledge about teaching specific mathematical content) be a prime focus of both pre-service and in-service programs for teachers of mathematics across all the years of schooling

- structured programs be implemented to support teachers to develop the knowledge and skills necessary to exercise effective leadership roles in numeracy and mathematics within schools (Council of Australian Governments, 2008a, p. xiv).

The first recommendation underscores the view of the AAMT (2002) that excellent teachers have a thorough knowledge of the students they teach, a sound and coherent knowledge of the mathematics appropriate for their students and a rich knowledge of how their students learn mathematics – and, what's more, they know how to put this knowledge into practice! (For more detail on the nature of effective mathematics teaching, see AAMT, 2006, and Chapter 3.)

With regard to the second recommendation, while emphasising the role and central place of the classroom teacher in numeracy improvement, the *National numeracy review* also noted from a research perspective that 'there has been little attention paid to the organisation, structure, and activities of the group of teachers in any school who teach mathematics' (Council of Australian Governments, 2008a, p. 76). In other words, there appeared to be a gap in the thinking about how to go about whole-school and system-wide development in numeracy. The focus on the individual teacher was welcomed and important, but it had taken the spotlight away from what needs to happen to support (and sometimes challenge) teachers. The report sought to remedy this deficiency by highlighting the value of professional learning teams and recommending that teachers be supported in becoming mathematics curriculum leaders. Interestingly, at a time when the role of the principal as a 'leader of learning' was beginning to gain prominence (Fink & Resnick, 2001; Fullan, 2005; Robinson, 2007), the COAG (2008a) report made no mention of the role of the principal in numeracy improvement.

In the years since the release of the *National numeracy review report* (COAG, 2008a), interest in the role of principals in influencing student learning has continued to gather momentum. One example is the recently developed Australian Professional Standard for Principals (Australian Institute for Teaching and School Leadership, 2012a) that cites the professional practices of principals in leading teaching and learning, and the contribution they make to raising student achievement and creating and sustaining the conditions under which quality teaching and learning thrive (see Chapter 4 for more detail).

Systemic leadership and numeracy development

The traditional way of thinking about system-wide development in education (including numeracy development) has been to employ a 'top-down' approach. A recent example was the McKinsey report of Barber and Mourshed (2007), *How the world's best- performing school systems come out on top*. They concluded that the experience of these 'top school systems', as identified through the type of national and international comparisons described earlier in this chapter, suggests that three things matter most:

- getting the right people to become teachers
- developing them into effective instructors
- ensuring that the system is able to deliver the best possible instruction for every child.

One of the premises underpinning the McKinsey report is that governments and education authorities need to make sure that 'the things that matter most' actually happen! In other words their role is to act *from the top down* – at least as far as enacting legislation and providing the appropriate funding, infrastructure and program designs are concerned. Whether in fact, *those things that matter most* do actually happen depends of course on what happens during the implementation phase – as T. S. Eliot wrote in *The hollow men* (1925):

> Between the idea and the reality
> Between the motion and the act,
> Falls the shadow.

On a related note, one of the authors of the McKinsey report – Sir Michael Barber – was also one of the chief architects of the National Numeracy Strategy (Department for Education and Employment, 1999) developed by the Blair Government in the UK in the late 1990s. This initiative was studied closely by Australian governments as a means designed to lift the numeracy achievement of Australian school students. It was based on the following principles:

- intervention should be in inverse proportion to success, that is, leave successful schools alone, and instead, focus on the ones seen to be 'failing'
- set ambitious standards in curriculum and assessment
- accountability should be evident through inspection and publication of school performance
- teachers should have access to 'best practice' and high-quality professional development
- decisions should be made on the basis of good data and clear statutory targets
- schools as the unit of accountability should have devolved responsibility to make decisions in light of their local context.

Through applying these principles, the Blair Government sought to create a 'high challenge – high support' environment for improving student numeracy achievement. The Numeracy Strategy (Department for Education and Employment, 1999), like its predecessor Literacy Strategy, was driven 'from the centre'. The newly elected Blair Government had a strong mandate to do something about the quality of schooling – riding as it did on the wave of its 'three' electoral campaign priorities of 'education, education and education'. In the years immediately after its election, the results began to improve. Through the late 1990s and into the early 2000s, there were steady increases in student numeracy levels across the UK (Hopkins, 2008).

But the results began to plateau from 2003. Fullan (2009) put this down to an absence of 'change knowledge', by which he meant an understanding by those involved of the key drivers for successful change. His findings showed that the top-down approach has its limits. While the scale and complexity of the Blair Government reforms were generally appreciated and supported, and the structural elements such as the provision of professional development, and mandated hours for numeracy (and literacy) were seen as valuable, school-based educators and those in local authorities and government began to realise that any further improvement needed to rely upon principals and teachers taking a more proactive role in reform efforts and exercising more professional judgement and discretion. Over more recent years, we have hence seen greater focus upon systemic reform from the bottom up, or as Elmore (2004) prophesied, more educational change being undertaken 'from the inside out'. In the current Australian context, it is timely to examine these top-down and bottom-up perspectives in more depth. This includes consideration of whether they can in fact be integrated and, if so, how, so that sustainable worthwhile educational opportunities and learning improvement in numeracy for *all students in all settings* are realised (Caldwell & Spinks, 2008).

Accompanying this change in thinking about systemic reform has been the emerging notion of what is meant by an 'education system leader'. UK researcher David Hopkins has described these types of individuals as those who care about and work for the success of other schools as well as their own. In his book, *Every school a great school*, he put the view:

> If our goal is to have *every school a great school* then policy and practice has to focus on system improvement … Sustained improvement of schools is not possible unless the whole system is moving forward. (2008, p. 3)

Harris takes a similar position:

> System level change can only be achieved by changing the way people connect, communicate and collaborate. To be successful, leaders at the school and local authority levels need to create the structural and cultural conditions where professional learning cultures can thrive, survive and excel. (2010, p. 204)

Her comments highlight that having 'system leaders' emerging from and engaged with others at the school level is only part of the challenge of bringing about sustained systemic improvement. System leaders also need to come from other places, including from government and the central offices of education authorities. In this way, the different perspectives, experiences and areas of expertise of educators in different parts of the system can be brought together to tackle the complex problems associated with achieving sustainable improvement in student numeracy achievement.

In short, we are talking about a different way of going about education reform, where what binds system leaders is not their position in the organisational hierarchy. Rather it is five characteristics:

- their commitment to improving teaching and learning
- their desire to measure success in terms of student outcomes that both raise the bar and decrease the gap
- their priority on professional development and the support of professional learning communities
- their focus on personalising learning for all their students
- their appreciation that the classroom, school and central office levels of the system affect each other and that, in order to change the larger system, you have to engage with it in a meaningful way (Hargreaves, 2008; Harris, 2010; Hopkins, 2008).

Examples of the kinds of actions that system leaders take include the following:

- encouraging partnerships across school communities
- acting as curriculum and pedagogic innovators who develop and disseminate effective practice
- brokering communication and collaboration across and between school communities and central office
- giving advice and being change agents in system policy and program discussions.

In essence these are educators who take a systemic view. They base their actions on working for the common good (that is, what is in the interest of all – rather than on self or sectarian interest), and work from 'the inside out' – from the local level (whether this be a school or central office) to the system level. They operate in networks rather than in bureaucratic hierarchies and define themselves by something other than their roles on organisational charts.

The numeracy challenges facing teachers and principals, schools and school systems, and governments require system leaders: that is, educators who are able to build links between what happens in the classroom, the school and the central office. Fullan (2005, 2009) has referred to this as 'tri-level reform', although he applied it to the context of the school, the school district or authority and the government. Nevertheless, the thrust of his thinking is the need not only to create stronger alignment but also to have greater interaction, communication and mutual influence within and across the levels of the system. The role of system leaders is to do just that: to combine the top-down and bottom-up approaches to reform in order to provide powerful learning experiences for all students (Hopkins, Munro & Craig, 2011).

Recent international research (Mourshed, Chijioke & Barber, 2010) has highlighted that the associated challenge of how to combine top-down and bottom-up approaches to reform has some common foundational elements but also depends on the stage of the development of the school system involved. In this second McKinsey report (after the one by Barber and Mourshed, released in 2007), Mourshed et al. (2010) found that six areas of intervention were evident in all 20 selected school systems that they studied as making sustained progress in student achievement between 1995 and 2007:

- building the instructional skills of teachers and the management skills of principals
- assessing students
- improving data systems
- facilitating improvement through the introduction of policy documents and education laws
- revising standards and curriculum
- ensuring an appropriate reward and remuneration structure for teachers and principals.

The way that these interventions manifested themselves differed according to the 'performance journey' of that particular system (from poor to fair, fair to good, good to great, great to excellent). In particular, Mourshed et al. (2010) argued that school systems further along the journey sustain improvement by balancing school autonomy with consistent teaching practice – or, put more simply, systems that are 'doing poorly to fairly' are more likely to be operating on top-down principles and maintaining tight central control of just about everything, whereas those who are 'going great' are more likely to have schools with the autonomy to engage in more locally grown, bottom-up and networked approaches to improving student achievement. The findings of the McKinsey report by Mourshed et al. (2010) are useful in that they raise questions about the extent of control that 'the centre' – whether this be government or another relevant education authority – should have over what happens in schools in the light of the performance of the system as a whole.

In applying the thinking of the McKinsey report (Mourshed et al., 2010) to the problem of how to bring about the sustained systemic improvement in student numeracy achievement, it would be important that system leaders consider the evidence of student numeracy achievement in their system over time – what Mourshed et al. (2010) referred to as their system's 'improvement journey'. In these times of national and international league tables, their work is likely to involve at least some comparison with other systems, but it also needs to incorporate serious consideration based on their expectations, aspirations and understandings of their local system context. Their consequent numeracy challenge is to decide how to go about the types of professional development, assessment, curriculum and other interventions identified by Mourshed et al. (2010) in light of that evidence and their related comparisons and considerations.

Questions and implications for meeting the numeracy challenge

Achieving sustainable improvement in student numeracy requires that teachers, principals and officers of education authorities and governments appreciate the multiple factors that affect numeracy development and have the complementary expertise to make better numeracy outcomes a reality for all students, regardless of the socioeconomic or geographical circumstances of their school community.

The numeracy challenge is both an individual and collective one. At an individual level, those educators working in schools, for education authorities and in government departments have a professional responsibility to develop their capability to lead improvement in student numeracy.

For teachers this means asking questions such as: what are my strengths as a teacher? What do I know about the characteristics of effective teaching in mathematics, and how do I engage my students to promote their numeracy learning? How confident am I about my knowledge of mathematics and my ability to develop key concepts in my students? How do I know how my students are going? What assessment practices are most appropriate for what purposes? What evidence do I need to collect and how do I use this evidence to inform my teaching practice? What are my areas for development as a teacher, and what forms of professional learning are appropriate and available to me?

For principals, meeting the numeracy challenge involves many of the same questions that apply to their teachers. For example: what do I know about effective teaching of mathematics? How confident am I in talking with teachers and students in my school about what is being taught and learnt in mathematics? What types of evidence should be collected and used to make decisions about teaching practices, curriculum choices, forms of assessment and reporting of student learning? And, also like teachers, principals need to reflect on their areas for development as a school leader and the forms of professional learning that would meet those needs.

Principals of course have particular responsibilities for whole-school performance. Some relevant questions for them might include: how do I go about developing a shared understanding and vision for numeracy achievement in my school? How do I monitor the quality of teaching practice to ensure more effective practice is supported and disseminated and less effective practice is improved? How do I manage the resourcing and related organisational arrangements (staffing, curriculum, timetabling, physical and digital infrastructure) to produce the best possible outcomes for my students? How should I engage parents and the wider community in school life, and how might this improve student learning in numeracy? How do I represent and promote the interests of my school community – and other school communities – to education authorities and governments to ensure appropriate compliance and accountability, as well as recognition and support for our achievements?

For those working in education authorities, the numeracy challenge takes on a particular systemic dimension. These educators might ask: how do we develop, monitor and evaluate numeracy policies and programs for the diversity of school communities in our education system? What is the appropriate balance between central control and local autonomy when it comes to designing and implementing numeracy initiatives in schools? How do we work with principals and teachers through a combination of pressure and support to build the collective capacity and will to make real and sustainable improvements in numeracy outcomes for students across the system? And from the viewpoint of their relationship with government, how do we, in education authorities, negotiate the appropriate funding and forms of evidence, compliance, and accountability necessary to ensure sustainable systemic improvement in student numeracy achievement? These negotiations clearly have a political as well as a professional dimension, and strong cases need to be put to convince resource providers of the value of the proposed courses of action.

Finally, for those responsible for numeracy policies and programs at the government level, the questions relating to the numeracy challenge are similar to those asked at the education authority level. They also have a political as well as a professional dimension, and might include: what forms of evidence about numeracy performance are understood and acceptable to their minister, to other ministers, and to those in the departments of treasury and finance? What levels of numeracy performance actually constitute a 'policy success' and provide a rationale for continuance, or indicate a 'policy problem' and establish a need for further action? These are questions that can only be answered by a thorough understanding of the local school, central office and systemic issues involved in numeracy development – and such understanding can only arise by working closely with educators working at classroom, school and central office level.

We began this chapter by stating that meeting the numeracy challenge is a multifaceted undertaking. Not only does it involve each of 'the players' noted previously in dealing with the questions related to their particular sphere of influence, it also requires those in schools, central offices and government departments to develop an appreciation of each other's roles and contexts, and to work to ensure effective and creative alignment of their collective efforts: in other words, to be 'system leaders'.

We conclude with this question: how do teachers, principals, and education authority and government officers understand their own and each other's roles, and how can they work individually and collectively to meet the numeracy challenge of sustaining higher levels of student achievement for all students in all school settings?

The following chapters are designed to consider this question and support the efforts of those in schools and systems leading developments in student numeracy.

CHAPTER 2

IMPROVING STUDENT NUMERACY: A FRAMEWORK FOR DEVELOPMENT

Michael Gaffney and Rhonda Faragher

Rokhshana and Tjandamurra attend school in very different parts of Australia.

Rokhshana is a student from a non-English-speaking background in Year 3 at St Algebra Primary School on the outskirts of Capital City in south-eastern Australia. Her parents arrived from Afghanistan by boat three years ago.

Tjandamurra is an Aboriginal student in Year 5 at Central Community School in remote north-western Australia. His ancestors walked overland from Asia some tens of thousands of years ago.

Today is Tuesday, the day of the NAPLAN test. Students with backgrounds similar to Rokhshana and Tjandamurra do not tend to do as well as their peers in schools in places with higher socioeconomic status. NAPLAN results over recent years indicate that St Algebra Primary is generally below the national average on most indicators, but is performing relatively well compared to schools with similar student background characteristics. Last year there were some noticeable and encouraging gains in some areas.

Rokhshana's and Tjandamurra's teachers have spent time over the past six weeks helping students to prepare for the test. Both teachers, like most of their school colleagues, are on their first appointment and classified as 'early career' teachers.

The principals and staff at St Algebra's and the Central Community School work in challenging contexts. Both schools are in low socioeconomic status communities with high unemployment (and underemployment). At St Algebra's, 60 per cent of the children have non-English-speaking backgrounds, and they come from more than 20 countries. The Central Community School has a 95 per cent Indigenous enrolment, with children from more than 20 tribal and kinship groups.

The NAPLAN test is in English.

For the past two years, each principal along with two of their teachers have worked as a school numeracy development team on an Australian Government–funded project designed to improve the numeracy achievement of students from schools in low socioeconomic communities. Their work has involved them in research and development activity with a university team with specialist expertise in mathematics teaching and school leadership, along with ongoing support from central office consultants from their local education authorities. This activity involved a series of workshops – collaboratively designed and delivered by the university team, central office consultants and the school numeracy development teams; school visits by the university team members and central office consultants; and online participation and contributions to the project wiki website.

Rokhshana's and Tjandamurra's teachers participated in professional learning community activities led by members of their schools' numeracy development team. Over the period of the project, they learnt from these team members about research on effective teaching practice in mathematics; they demonstrated strategies that worked with their students; they were exposed to different ways of teaching mathematics, and they worked with colleagues to develop shared understandings of student numeracy development and teaching practice. One tangible outcome of each school's involvement in the project was a statement of agreed practice about effective mathematics teaching at their school. The teachers referred to this as their Charter for Effective Teaching of Mathematics.

Along the way, the principals at St Algebra's and the Central Community School developed their ability to lead numeracy development as well as their understanding of effective teaching and how to develop and support it. The teacher members of the school numeracy development teams developed their understanding and repertoire of effective teaching strategies in mathematics, as well as their knowledge, skills and determination to lead numeracy development at the school level.

As Rokhshana and Tjandamurra sit down with their classmates to do the NAPLAN numeracy test, their teachers expect them to do their best. These teachers, their principals and teaching colleagues are more informed and hopeful about their students' performance than in previous years. Above all, they are more confident they can work with the results to find evidence of growth and areas for further improvement. After all, NAPLAN is just one source of data. And from there, they are determined to continue to work together to refine and design strategies that will give their students the best opportunity to develop their knowledge, skills and attitudes in numeracy. Improving student numeracy achievement is a team effort at St Algebra's Primary and the Central Community School, and the teachers and principals and the supporting staff at central office and the university realise the complexity but also the need to sustain their efforts and the promise of better outcomes for their students.

Introduction

The scenes described above reflect the story of the schools involved in the Leading Aligned Numeracy Development (LAND) project. LAND was a collaborative research and development project between the Australian Catholic University

(ACU) and Catholic Education Offices of South Australia, the Northern Territory and Western Australia, designed to identify ways of improving the numeracy achievement of students in low socioeconomic status school communities. It involved teachers and principals from participating schools, central office consultants, and university researchers in a combined search to investigate what it takes to bring about sustained improvement in student numeracy achievement in these communities. LAND was a multi-site project involving 17 schools in four school clusters from remote parts of the Northern Territory (5 schools) and the Kimberley (4 schools), as well as from metropolitan Perth (4 schools) and Adelaide (4 schools). The project was funded by the Australian Government as a Literacy and Numeracy Pilot initiative to inform its Smarter Schools National Partnership agreements with state and territory education authorities (Commonwealth Department of Education, Employment and Workplace Relations, 2008; Council of Australian Governments, 2008b).

In this chapter, the research base to the LAND project and its framework for numeracy development is presented. Subsequent chapters explore various aspects of the LAND approach based on this framework.

The LAND research base for improving student numeracy

The LAND project was underpinned by the idea that numeracy development not only requires effective teaching but also effective leadership. The project hence had two major themes:

- *numeracy development* – the characteristics of effective teaching of mathematics, and the development of teacher pedagogical content knowledge and school-wide pedagogy for teaching mathematics
- *educational leadership* – the development and sustainability of quality teaching and student achievement in numeracy, including building alignment in the thinking and actions of those working within and across classrooms, schools and central offices of education systems.

Each of these themes has a research base. The areas of the literature associated with the research base for each theme are explained in the following sections.

Characteristics of effective teaching of mathematics

The Early Numeracy Research Project (McDonough & Clarke, 2003) identified highly effective teachers of mathematics in the early years of schooling. The key measure of effectiveness was growth in student mathematical understanding as revealed in student interview assessment data from over 11 000 students. Extensive lesson observations and interviews with these teachers by the research team identified the characteristics of effective teaching of mathematics in the early years of schooling (Clarke & Clarke, 2004). These characteristics are treated in more detail in Chapter 3. A number of themes are associated with the effective teaching of mathematics (Clarke & Clarke, 2004):

- mathematical focus
- purpose and choice of tasks
- materials, tools and representations
- adaptations, connections and links
- organisational style(s) and teaching approaches
- learning community and classroom interaction
- expectations
- reflection
- assessment methods
- personal attributes of the teacher.

The LAND project investigated the application of this research to the teaching of mathematics in the participating schools. Fifteen of the 17 schools were primary schools; the remaining two schools were remote area community schools predominantly comprised of primary classes with small numbers of secondary enrolments. All schools were situated in low socioeconomic status communities.

The purpose in working with these characteristics of effective teaching of mathematics was twofold. The first was for teacher and principal participants to examine their practice and experience with mathematics teaching in light of the various characteristics, and consider areas of strength and importance as well as priorities for development. The second purpose was to examine the validity and application of the characteristics to schools in low socioeconomic status communities. In other words, the purpose of using the characteristics was to develop and recognise the professional knowledge of the teacher and principal participants in the LAND project, and to validate and refine the listing of characteristics of effective teaching.

Development of teacher pedagogical content knowledge and school-wide pedagogy in numeracy

Research into numeracy development and whole-school improvement in teaching practice indicates that there are significant numbers of Australian primary teachers who would benefit from professional development in pedagogical content knowledge (Council of Australian Governments, 2008a); the widespread adoption of effective teaching practice, based on validated pedagogical content knowledge, requires the development of shared principles for teaching and collective responsibility for promoting student learning achievement across the school.

The former finding regarding the significance of professional development was a recurrent theme in the *National numeracy review report* (COAG, 2008a). In fact the report highlighted that professional development programs should be focussed on building teachers' pedagogical content knowledge, providing ways to access students' thinking, allowing time and space for teacher learning and reflection, underpinned by a strong theory–practice link, and premised on high expectations for all students (see page 15 for the listing of principles of exemplary professional development programs from this report).

The design of the LAND project was developed with these features in mind. The last finding, regarding the adoption of effective teaching practice across a school, has been a feature of international school improvement research (Andrews et al., 2004; Crowther et al., 2012; Crowther et al., 2002). This research presents a view of pedagogy that has three dimensions: teachers' 'personal pedagogy' (that is, practices that are innate or come naturally to the individual concerned), 'authoritative pedagogy' (practices that are informed by research) and 'school-wide pedagogy' (the principles and practices that teachers share with one another).

While personal pedagogy and authoritative pedagogy have a rich heritage in educational research and practice (Dewey, 1916; Gardner, 1993), the concept of school-wide pedagogy is relatively recent, having been developed through the IDEAS process of school capacity building over the past ten years (Crowther, 2012). The concept of school-wide pedagogy draws on earlier work by Fred Newmann and Associates (1996) at the University of Wisconsin-Madison, who developed the notion of 'authentic pedagogy' from research findings that indicated that student achievement can be improved when teachers work collaboratively to develop a common pedagogical philosophy and support each other in their teaching practices through intensive shared professional learning (Crowther et al., 2012). While each of these dimensions has value in its own right, it is the combination of these components that is regarded as having the most significant effect on student achievement. This combination is referred to as 'three-dimensional pedagogy', as shown in Figure 2.1.

The LAND project recognised teachers' personal pedagogy as well as their need to expand their pedagogical content knowledge and teaching repertoire. Moreover, it sought to support teachers in the participating schools to develop shared principles of mathematics teaching at their school, or what Andrews et al. (2004) might have considered as a school-wide pedagogy for the teaching of mathematics. The three-dimensional pedagogy model was hence implicit in the LAND project. This focus on teacher professional growth meant that careful thought and planning needed to be given to the development and exercise of educational leadership, especially at the school level, to help bring it about.

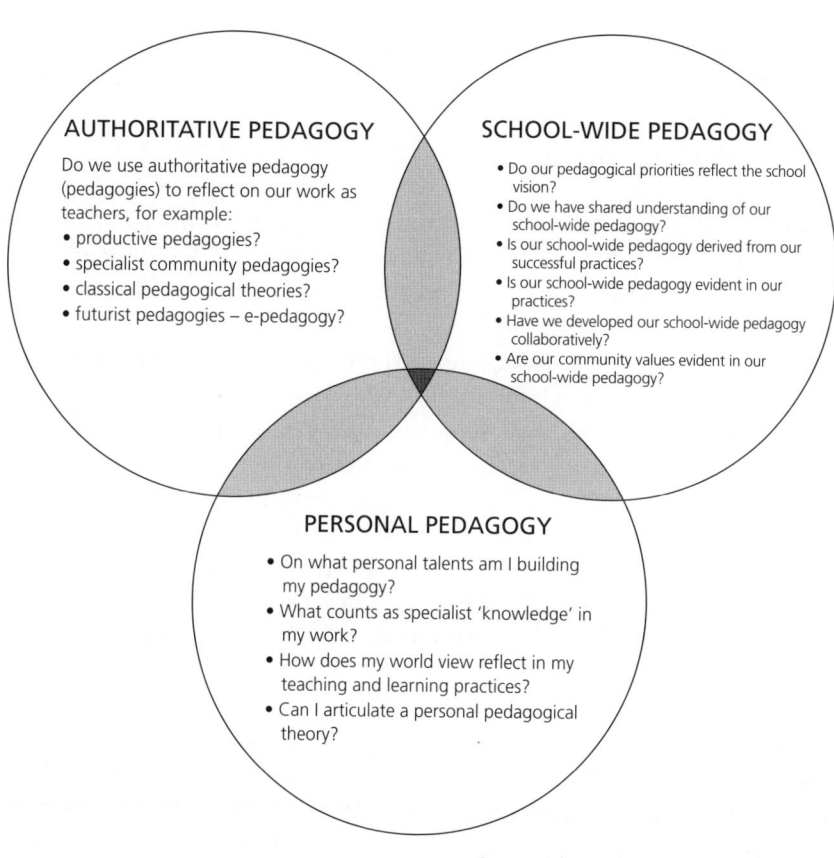

Source: Adapted from Andrews et al. (2004), p. 15

Figure 2.1: Three-dimensional pedagogy

School-level development of quality teaching and student achievement

School improvement, in the final analysis, is judged by increases in student achievement. No matter what funding is received, no matter what buildings are constructed, no matter what new programs are put in place, no matter what principal or teachers are appointed – in the end, it is the learning outcomes of students that determine whether or not a school has truly 'improved'. While some writers are critical of using 'the school' as the sole focus for improvement and unit for analysis (Harris, 2010; Levin, 2009), recent meta-analyses of international research (Barber & Mourshed, 2007; Hattie, 2009) point to high-quality teaching as the most significant 'within school' factor affecting student achievement. But quality teaching does not 'just happen'. For quality teaching and student learning to be developed, teachers require a school learning environment with these characteristics:

- clear goals and expectations
- strategic resourcing
- informed and coordinated planning and evaluation of teaching and curriculum
- promotion of and participation in teacher learning and development
- orderly and supportive policies and organisational structures (Robinson, 2007).

Similarly, the creation and sustaining of these types of environments does not 'just happen'. It requires school leaders who have the knowledge, skills and understanding to promote and support quality teaching, foster appropriate organisational arrangements and build effective community relationships. These features were evident in the background paper commissioned by the Ministerial Council on Education, Employment, Training and Youth Affairs (2008b – now known as the Standing Council on School Education and Early Childhood, SCSEEC) underpinning the LAND project. They are also reflected in the models of school improvement developed by Caldwell (2007), Caldwell and Spinks (2008) and Crowther et al. (2012).

Over recent years, the thinking on school improvement has evolved to a point where it is seen as a complex phenomenon, requiring the recognition and alignment of important features of the school organisation. These features have their origin in the various schools of organisational thought. For example, the emphasis on efficient processes and the production of measurable outcomes is linked to the idea of schools as machine-bureaucracies. The focus on personal relationships and community highlights the powerful human and informal elements that are part of organisational life, as well as the need for school organisations to be in touch with their environment in order to 'survive'. The importance of vision, shared values and how these are lived out in day-to-day behaviour and reflected in organisational processes is associated with the view that schools have distinctive organisational cultures. Finally, the view that the design of organisations is contingent on the type of work (or technology) that is involved puts the spotlight on the nature of the core technology of schools, that is teaching and the extent to which it is seen as a 'profession' or as 'organised labour' or as 'social work' or as 'cultural transmission' (or possibly 'cultural transformation') – or possibly as some hybrid combination of all four concepts, depending on the knowledge, skills and attributes of the teacher and the school context in question.

In fact, contemporary approaches to school development such as those mentioned (Caldwell, 2007; Caldwell & Spinks, 2008; Crowther et al., 2012) require that schools are 'imagined' in terms of each of these schools of thought *simultaneously*, and that furthermore the elements of each need to be brought together in ways that serve the needs of the student, their parents, their community, business and industry, government and society at large. It is a big ask! Nevertheless, the models put forward by Caldwell and Spinks (2008) and Crowther et al. (2012) pick up these ideas in similar but distinctive ways. Let's see what is involved.

The Caldwell and Spinks (2008) model is designed to explain what is involved in the process of 'school transformation', which they define as effecting sustainable worthwhile learning improvements for 'all students in all settings'. The model refers to four kinds of 'capital' that are centred on the student (as shown in Figure 2.2). These need to be aligned through governance processes for transformation to take place. The four kinds of capital are the following:

- *intellectual capital* – the level of knowledge and skill of those who work in the school
- *social capital* – the level of esprit de corps and good will, and the strength of relationships and partnerships in the school community
- *financial capital* – the monetary resources (and associated infrastructure) available to support the school
- *spiritual capital* – the strength of moral purpose and coherence of values, beliefs and attitudes of members of the school community.

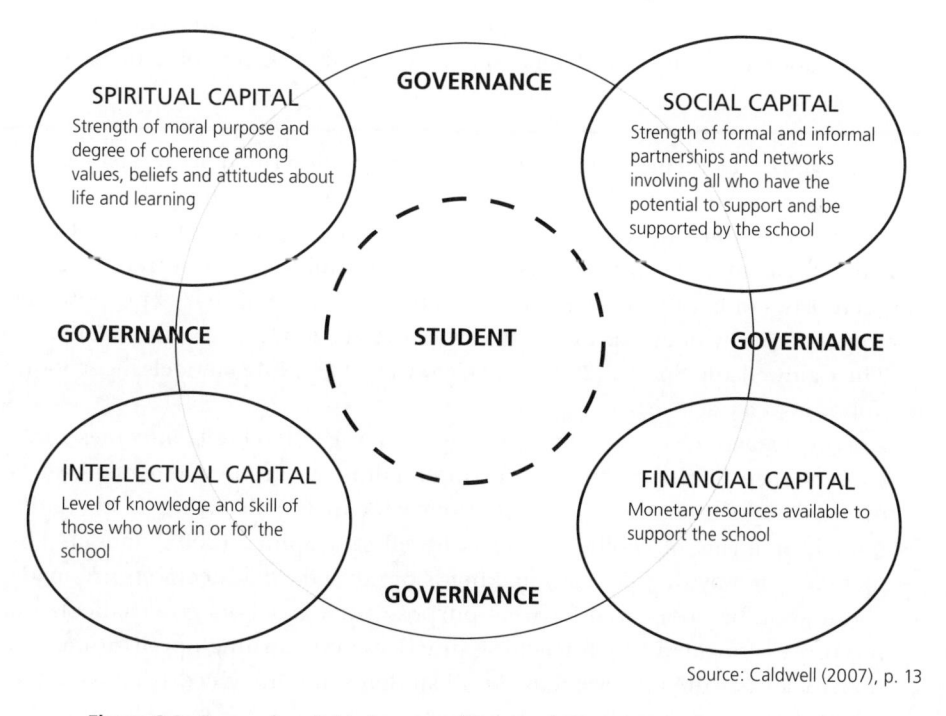

Source: Caldwell (2007), p. 13

Figure 2.2: Forms of capital to be strengthened and aligned through governance to achieve school transformation

The model developed by Crowther et al. (2012) also conceives the successful school as an aligned organisation. Over the last 15 years, Frank Crowther, Dorothy Andrews and their colleagues at the University of Southern Queensland, in partnership with teacher leaders, school principals and education authorities across Australia and internationally, have developed an approach to school development that they refer to as IDEAS. They describe IDEAS as a means of school revitalisation that values the work and professionalism of teachers (Andrews et al., 2004). In essence, it is a strategy to assist schools to work with change, and can be understood as a 'meta-strategy of school improvement' in that it provides a framework or way of approaching the process of school improvement. It is distinguished by the use of four interdependent constructs (Andrews et al., 2004):

- the IDEAS research-based framework for enhancing school outcomes, producing an image of a successful school as an aligned organisation (shown in Figure 2.3)
- the IDEAS process of professional inquiry – initiating, discovering, envisioning, actioning and sustaining
- three-dimensional pedagogy (shown in Figure 2.1) – an authentic school-based pedagogical framework
- parallel leadership, referring to teacher leaders and principal leaders working in collaborative and complementary ways to enhance school processes and outcomes.

This fourth element of parallel leadership is described as a 21st-century leadership construct that engages teacher leaders and principal leaders in collaborative action while at the same time encouraging the fulfilment of their individual capabilities, aspirations and responsibilities. The three essential characteristics of parallel leadership are mutualism, sense of shared purpose and allowance for individual expression (Crowther et al., 2002).

The Caldwell and Spinks (2008) and Crowther et al. (2012) models incorporate the following characteristics:

- *a focus on outcomes* – student learning and related school outcomes are a consequence of the influence and interaction of various elements: that is, dimensions of the research-based framework in the Crowther et al. (2012) model, or forms of capital in the Caldwell and Spinks (2008) model. This includes the way that decision-making is organised, what decisions are made, about what, by whom, and for what purpose (that is, school governance); and the process through which teaching practices and learning opportunities are shaped so that the achievements of all students are enhanced (that is, school transformation and professional supports).

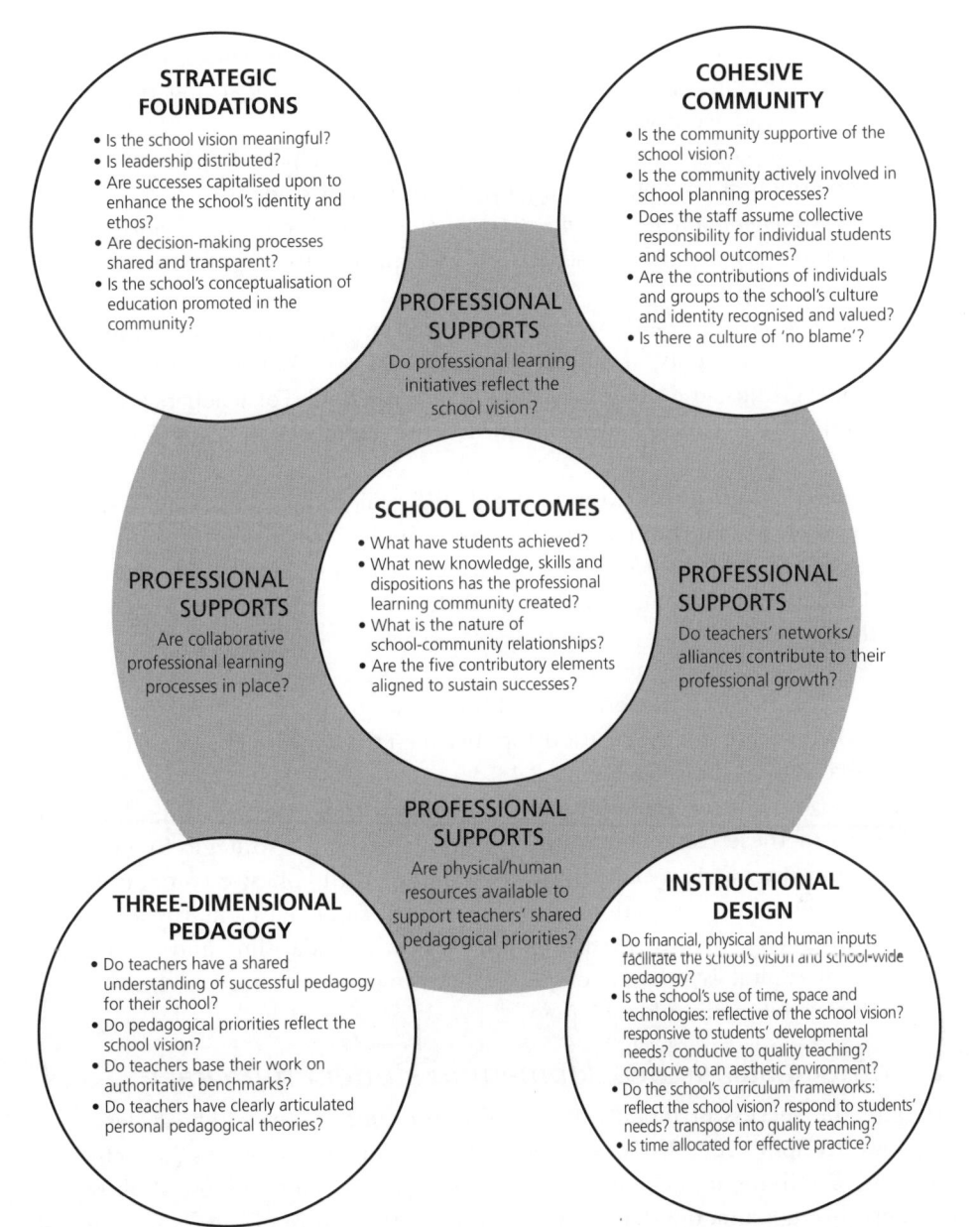

STRATEGIC FOUNDATIONS
• Is the school vision meaningful?
• Is leadership distributed?
• Are successes capitalised upon to enhance the school's identity and ethos?
• Are decision-making processes shared and transparent?
• Is the school's conceptualisation of education promoted in the community?

COHESIVE COMMUNITY
• Is the community supportive of the school vision?
• Is the community actively involved in school planning processes?
• Does the staff assume collective responsibility for individual students and school outcomes?
• Are the contributions of individuals and groups to the school's culture and identity recognised and valued?
• Is there a culture of 'no blame'?

PROFESSIONAL SUPPORTS
Do professional learning initiatives reflect the school vision?

SCHOOL OUTCOMES
• What have students achieved?
• What new knowledge, skills and dispositions has the professional learning community created?
• What is the nature of school-community relationships?
• Are the five contributory elements aligned to sustain successes?

PROFESSIONAL SUPPORTS
Are collaborative professional learning processes in place?

PROFESSIONAL SUPPORTS
Do teachers' networks/ alliances contribute to their professional growth?

PROFESSIONAL SUPPORTS
Are physical/human resources available to support teachers' shared pedagogical priorities?

THREE-DIMENSIONAL PEDAGOGY
• Do teachers have a shared understanding of successful pedagogy for their school?
• Do pedagogical priorities reflect the school vision?
• Do teachers base their work on authoritative benchmarks?
• Do teachers have clearly articulated personal pedagogical theories?

INSTRUCTIONAL DESIGN
• Do financial, physical and human inputs facilitate the school's vision and school-wide pedagogy?
• Is the school's use of time, space and technologies: reflective of the school vision? responsive to students' developmental needs? conducive to quality teaching? conducive to an aesthetic environment?
• Do the school's curriculum frameworks: reflect the school vision? respond to students' needs? transpose into quality teaching?
• Is time allocated for effective practice?

Source: Andrews et al. (2004), p. 8

Figure 2.3: The IDEAS research-based framework for enhancing school outcomes

- *an informed, agreed and shared approach to teaching* – the understandings that teachers develop and come to share and to practise regarding the art and science of effective teaching
- *a vision and purpose* – the reason teachers and principals do what they do, to provide the best possible learning opportunities for students
- *supportive organisational arrangements* – the school policies, priorities and programs, organisational structure and procedures, infrastructure and resources support
- *an engaged community* – the respect and involvement of members of the school community (students, teachers, parents, school executive, community and business groups, and others) in the life of the school. For teachers and school executives, the concept also includes being members of their professional learning community.
- *alignment* – the correct positioning of different components with respect to each other, so that they perform properly, that is, to achieve integration
- *principal* and *teacher leadership* – how teachers and principals work distinctively and collaboratively to make a positive difference to student learning outcomes at their school.

In addition to these characteristics, Caldwell and Spinks (2008) and Crowther et al. (2012) also represent the relationships between the key elements of their models in a similar way, as shown in Figure 2.4.

In fact you can see the alignment in their thinking through the placement and focus of these elements. Spiritual capital links with strategic foundations, identity and direction; social capital corresponds with cohesive community and shared stakeholder expectations and aspirations; financial capital is associated with infrastructure features (such as use of IT, curricula, time and space); and intellectual capital is related to quality teaching as evidenced and supported through three-dimensional pedagogy.

Leading systemic development in student numeracy

Despite the success of models of school improvement such as those described (Caldwell & Spinks, 2008; Crowther et al., 2012) in single schools or school clusters, decades of well-intentioned effort trying to bring about reform across whole school systems through a model that puts the school at the centre of the reform process have simply not delivered (Harris, 2010). This is not because the ideas, the efforts made or the funding expended have been inadequate, but because there has been a preoccupation with school-level change by those in government and education authorities that has been reinforced by decades of school effectiveness and school improvement research (Harris & Chrispeels, 2008). The consequence has been that many of the basic features of schooling, including how schools are funded,

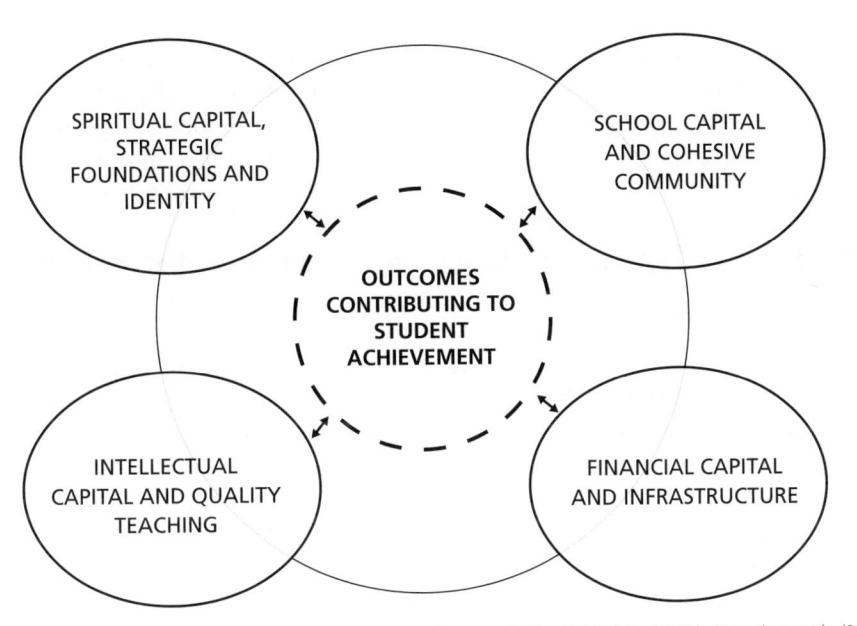

Sources: Caldwell & Spinks (2008); Crowther et al., (2012)

Figure 2.4: School capacity building and transformation framework

governed, structured and staffed, have remained unaltered (Levin, 2009). This focus on schools with a corresponding neglect of other players and factors in the education reform scene is now considered to have had a negative impact on the implementation and sustainability of reform – even the most promising of reform initiatives. They just run out of puff, staff move or are promoted, support falters, other priorities emerge and the initiatives fade. Critics of this essentially school-centred, initiative-reliant approach to education reform are calling for a different way of going about the complex professional and moral challenge of ensuring quality teaching and learning outcomes for all students (Crowther, 2012; Hargreaves & Fullan, 2012). In this sense, they are 'not suggesting that schools should not be a focus of change – but rather that they should not be the *only* focus for change' (Harris, 2010, p. 197).

Over recent years, there has been a noticeable shift in thinking and focus among policy-makers and researchers regarding school-system reform. Contemporary policy and research literature (Fullan, 2010; Levin, 2009; Barber & Mourshed, 2007; Mourshed et al., 2010) are commonly advocating that widespread and lasting improvement in student achievement requires change in the system itself: that is, in the way that *all* the major players (schools, governments, statutory authorities, employing authorities, teacher unions, professional associations, parent and community organisations, and universities) operate individually and collectively. This change in perspective has also had implications for the way in which educational leadership is understood, developed and practised at the system level. This thinking was also incorporated in the design of the LAND project.

The LAND framework for leading developments in student numeracy

The approaches to school capacity building and transformation pioneered by Brian Caldwell, Jim Spinks, Frank Crowther, Dorothy Andrews and their colleagues provided the inspiration and the conceptual foundation for the research framework that underpinned the LAND project. The philosophy and key elements of their models were distilled and applied to the problem of how to develop and sustain improved student numeracy achievement. The LAND project deliberately focused on bringing the characteristics of their models to life in the school communities and school systems with whom the researchers worked.

The design and purpose of the LAND project was based on the framework, shown in Figure 2.5. The form of the diagram is similar to those adopted by Caldwell and Spinks (2008) and Crowther et al. (2012): the elements have been given broader titles, and the outcomes related to student numeracy development have been given priority.

The logic of the LAND framework is that student numeracy development is a consequence of the influence and effective interaction of certain key elements. Quality teaching practice is understood to have a direct and powerful positive effect on student learning outcomes (Hattie, 2009). Applying the LAND framework, this effect is enhanced by organisational arrangements and community characteristics that closely align with the vision that the members of the school

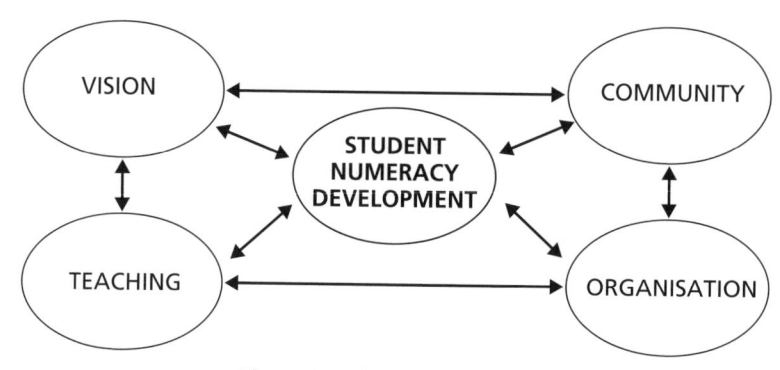

Figure 2.5: The LAND framework

community share for student numeracy development. Student numeracy development, teaching practice, organisational processes and structures, community engagement and vision were hence the major elements for investigating numeracy development through the LAND project. The particular aspects associated with each key element are listed in Table 2.1.

Table 2.1: School-level aspects associated with key elements of the LAND framework

Key element	School-level aspects
Student numeracy development	Evidence of student numeracy achievement including the following: • school-based (internal) assessment • standardised testing (e.g. NAPLAN) • other externally developed or delivered assessment (e.g. SENA – the Schedule for Early Number Assessment)
Teaching	Teacher confidence and sense of efficacy Teaching repertoire Understanding and use of the characteristics of effective mathematics teaching Appreciation and practical alignment with the school's charter for effective mathematics teaching
Organisation	Program funding and infrastructure (including access and use of LAND project resources and professional support) Curriculum and teaching resources Use of time and space School policies and procedures School organisational structure – staff roles, accountabilities and responsibilities
Community	Teacher professional learning community Engaged parent community Home–school communication
Vision	Expectations and aspirations for student numeracy development in terms of: • the target (i.e. vision of the end point) • how to get there (i.e. vision of the process)

The LAND framework served as a vehicle for identifying and analysing the factors that contribute to student numeracy development, and as a basis for planning, implementing and evaluating project activity at the school level. But sustained development in student numeracy across a school system cannot happen through school-based actions alone. Something more is required. The answer lies in the way education reform is thought about and the model of change that needs to be employed when *systemic* development is the priority.

The LAND project took a systemic approach to numeracy development. It was based on the idea that classroom and school-level change is vital but also that, for this to occur, there needs to be a corresponding focus on what happens at central office level to support it. Schools do not and cannot be expected to change when central offices do not or are not prepared to also review and adjust how they go about their work in related policy and program areas. For numeracy development to be widespread and sustained, a systemic approach to change incorporating both school and central office is needed. As a consequence, the LAND project focused on building the alignment necessary between what is desired and what is actually happening at classroom, school and central office level in regard to numeracy teaching and learning.

Developing and sustaining reforms for higher quality teaching and levels of student achievement in numeracy require leadership that is exercised with a multi-level perspective. This means having educators at classroom, school and central office levels with the capability to understand and appreciate the relationships between teachers' work with students in classrooms, the organisational design, culture and effectiveness of the school, and the demands and support offered by the central office. This type of leadership is being increasingly described as 'system leadership' (Fullan, 2005; Hopkins, 2008). It refers to leaders who are able to work within, between and across schools and central offices to broker, support, challenge and make connections across the system (Harris, 2010). They identify, develop and disseminate effective practices, form networks (rather than rely on bureaucratic chains of command) and influence upward, downward and sideways to bring about worthwhile change in system priorities, policies, programs, practices and overall performance (see also Chapter 1).

The LAND framework was applied to the systemic context by considering how the thinking and practice of those working in numeracy development at classroom, school and central office level were aligned across the key elements of student numeracy development, teaching, organisation, community and vision. The systemic application of the LAND framework is shown in Figure 2.6. It is designed to focus attention on the links between the levels and the nature of the alignment in views and actions of people working at each level.

Taking a systemic perspective, as reflected in Figure 2.6, raises questions about the vision for numeracy development held by those working at different levels in the system, how they see the nature and importance of quality teaching, what they regard as appropriate organisational arrangements, how they value and support community engagement, and what constitutes evidence of numeracy development. Given their different responsibilities and experiences, it might be expected that those working in these different parts of the system hold some similar and some different views about such questions. Their views and the techniques used to investigate the alignment between them are discussed in Chapter 8.

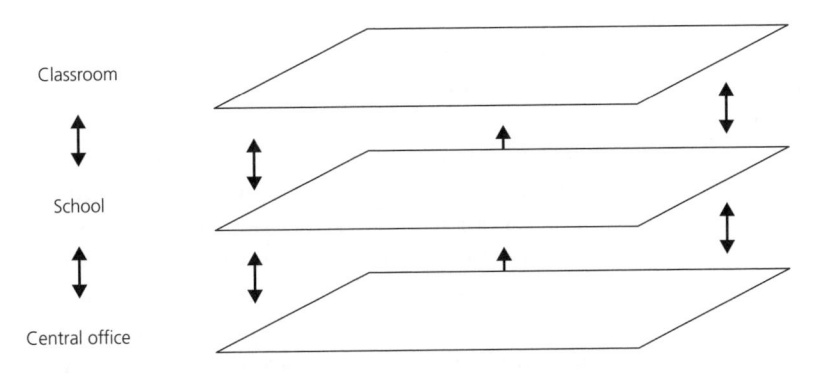

Figure 2.6: Multi-level LAND framework

The LAND project design for improving student numeracy

The LAND project was aimed at improving the numeracy of children in low socioeconomic status school communities, and was based on the premise that attention to both numeracy and educational leadership is needed to bring this improvement about. Accordingly, the project had two main areas of focus:

- the identification, development and support of effective teaching of mathematics
- the educational leadership exercised by teachers, principals and central office personnel to develop and sustain effective practices in teaching and learning.

This dual focus was set in the context of systemic development – that is, what needs to happen at classroom, school, and central office levels to develop and sustain higher levels of student learning in numeracy. Consequently, the project design stressed the importance of two kinds of alignment:

- *alignment of thinking:* the level of professional consensus among teachers, principals and central office staff regarding their goals, assumptions, and understandings about numeracy and numeracy development
- *alignment in policies, programs and administrative processes:* the level of integration associated with the functioning and coordination of numeracy development activity across the system – the classrooms, schools and central offices.

Such alignment is evidenced in a number of ways:

- teachers who have high levels of pedagogical content knowledge in numeracy, confidence in their ability to teach mathematics, and a shared approach with colleagues to teaching mathematics in their school

- school leaders (principals and teacher leaders) who understand pedagogy and the organisational and community factors that support effective numeracy teaching, and can strengthen and explain the connection between these factors and the school vision for student numeracy achievement
- central office staff (executive, officers and consultants) who appreciate the context of teachers' and school leaders' work and are able to support and challenge them accordingly. These staff are also aware of the expectations and opportunities offered by colleagues working in other areas of central office as well as external stakeholders (including governments and other agencies), and they structure and adjust their work practices accordingly – in collaboration with those colleagues and stakeholders.
- teachers, school leaders, and central office staff who have a shared vision for numeracy development and a common understanding of each other's roles. This is demonstrated by the collective responsibility and the distinctive and complementary leadership contributions of these educators for promoting student achievement in numeracy.
- systemic integration and efficiency in the development, implementation and evaluation of policies, programs and administrative processes relating to numeracy development.

Allied with the purpose and the importance placed on alignment, and the proposed benefits for schools of participating in the LAND project were improved teaching quality and student numeracy outcomes, more informed school community understanding of numeracy development strategies, and better system policies and programs to support numeracy. These were described in a flyer headed by the question 'Why should your school community be involved in the LAND project and what benefits might be expected', with the answers provided:

> The LAND project provides opportunity for your school community to:
> - share effective teaching and learning practices in numeracy
> - develop agreed school-wide principles for effective teaching of mathematics
> - align these practices and principles with your school's vision, organisation, community characteristics and expectations in order to strengthen numeracy outcomes
> - inform system-wide policy and program development for sustaining higher levels of student numeracy achievement.
>
> The major benefits of involvement in the LAND project for your school are:
> - increased teacher capability to bring about sustainable, high levels of student numeracy achievement

- deeper understanding among school community members of how these outcomes and teaching practices are supported by the school's vision, organisation and community relationships
- enhanced leadership capability of school community members to develop and align the key elements of vision, teaching practices, organisation and community needed to sustain higher levels of student numeracy achievement.

On the basis of the proposed benefits, schools were either invited by their central office to express an interest in being involved in the LAND project (as was the case with the Western Australian and South Australian Catholic education authorities) or nominated to participate (as happened with the Northern Territory Catholic Education Office). The schools that participated in the LAND project are listed in Appendix 2.

Each school participating in the project was required to form a LAND school leadership team. These teams always included the principal and at least one or two teachers, depending on the size of the school. For example, the constraints facing some of the smaller and remote schools meant that they had fewer team members. The LAND school leadership teams were responsible for leading numeracy development in their school communities, and were supported by central office personnel and the research team throughout the two years of the project.

There were the following expectations for those who participated in the LAND project:

- teachers and school leaders are valued for their knowledge, skills and other professional attributes as well as their capacity and willingness to engage in professional learning
- central office staff reflect about how their roles, policies, programs, organisational structures and processes of central offices affect schools and classrooms
- teachers, school leaders and central office staff learn to exercise leadership in ways that have a meaningful and positive influence on the 'system' as a whole: that is, in ways that demonstrate their 'system leadership' responsibility across classroom, school and central office levels
- teachers, school leaders and central office staff build a shared understanding of the principles of effective teaching and exercise collective responsibility for student outcomes.

To realise these expectations, the LAND project employed a mix of traditional and innovative methods of educational research and development. The project took the form of a multi-site case study and employed a range of data collection instruments including surveys, interviews, focus groups, causal mapping and observations conducted during workshops and school visits. The stages of the LAND project are described in Appendix 2.

Each pilot site consisted of a cluster of schools together with a central office (a Catholic Education Office). Educators in the schools and central office worked with the Australian Catholic University research team to analyse the nature and issues surrounding student achievement in numeracy at each site. They advised and collaborated with the research team in trialling programs designed to develop their professional capabilities, the organisational capacity of their workplaces and the system *as a whole* to sustain improvement in numeracy achievement.

A series of cluster-based workshops were organised and delivered by the Australian Catholic University in collaboration with the schools and their central office. These were attended by the LAND school teams in each cluster. The workshops were designed to deepen participants' understanding of the nature and relationship between quality teaching in mathematics, the exercise of educational leadership and numeracy outcomes. The focus of these workshops was developing participants' pedagogical content knowledge in mathematics and numeracy, and their capabilities to lead numeracy development. The workshop topics also included the design, implementation and evaluation of numeracy interventions. The ideas, strategies and techniques treated in the workshops were trialled and further developed by the LAND school teams back in their school communities. This follow-up work was supported through school site visits from the project officers and the university research team.

Along with this follow-up work was the establishment and trialling of the LAND wiki website. The LAND wiki enabled workshop material and related follow-up work at school level to be stored in digital form, and then accessed, shared, modified and customised to local school contexts by the participating schools and their communities. In this way, it acted as a vehicle for networking the professional learning experiences of LAND project participants (see Chapter 6 for more detail).

A LAND project officer was appointed by each of the participating education authorities. LAND project officers played a key liaison role between the schools, their central office, the Australian Catholic University as the university partner, and the Commonwealth Department of Education, Employment and Workplace Relations as the funding agency. Their responsibilities were to support LAND school teams, monitor their progress, collaborate in the design and refinement of the project with researchers, link LAND project activity with education system priorities and programs, and manage project administrative, accountability and compliance requirements (see Chapter 7 for more detail on the role of the LAND project officer).

Two kinds of outcomes were envisaged from the LAND project. The first set of outcomes related to improvements in student numeracy learning and the quality of mathematics teaching, and greater community engagement of students, staff and parents in numeracy. The second kind of outcome was a set of principles that can be used to inform and sustain systemic improvement in numeracy achievement. This involved ways of achieving greater clarity in goals, processes and accountabilities related to numeracy achievement, and better policy and program design and integration at school and central office level.

In this chapter an explanation of the LAND framework as a model for improving student numeracy has been provided. The research base for the framework has been explained as it applies to both individual schools and to school systems interested in numeracy development. The foundational understandings that underpinned the LAND project were that sustained improvement in numeracy achievement requires attention to both quality teaching and educational leadership, and to the notion of 'alignment'. At the school level, 'alignment' refers to how the components of the LAND framework (vision, teaching, organisation and community, and student numeracy development) are integrated. At the system level, 'alignment' focuses attention on the fact that sustained improvement in numeracy achievement is only possible if there is change at the central office level as well as at school level, and that those working in different parts of 'the system' understand each other's roles and work together to achieve their shared vision.

The LAND project was designed to incorporate these key elements and understandings about the relationship between leadership, effective teaching of mathematics and student numeracy achievement. The importance of linking the perspectives and actions of those working at classroom, school and central office level was highlighted through collaboratively designed and delivered workshops, regular school visits and ongoing school support, a virtual communication network (the LAND wiki), and the project partnership involving principals and teacher leaders from the LAND schools, project officers and their central office colleagues, and the research team. The manner and extent to which the LAND project achieved its objectives and the implications of the research findings for developing better alignment and sustainable system-wide gains in student numeracy achievement are detailed throughout the remaining chapters of this book.

SECTION 2
BUILDING CAPABILITY, CHANGING PRACTICE

CHAPTER 3

TEACHING MATHEMATICS EFFECTIVELY

Rhonda Faragher and Doug Clarke

'I was never any good at maths', remarked Linda. 'I gave it up as soon as I could – after Year 10.'

'Yes, same story for me', replied Marie. 'I just didn't get it.'

Linda and Marie are teachers at Cold Heart Primary School, located in a suburb with low socioeconomic status in Capital City. As they shuffled in their scarves, gloves and coats to the staff room for the weekly 'professional learning' session, Linda complained, 'It's too cold for a meeting this afternoon'.

'You're right about that', agreed Marie. 'I need a coffee – quick.'

As they entered the room they saw the new mathematics teaching resources on display – student games and worksheets, teacher manuals and lots of colourful animated software. Dr Parabola, a former university academic, smiled as he greeted them, saying: 'Welcome. Feel free to check out what's on the table. I think you'll find it really interesting and useful. I have developed a range of teaching resources with a highly regarded international educational research and development company based in Finland. The resources have been customised for the Australian Curriculum, your local system's scope and sequence documents, and best of all – they contain sample assessment items similar to those used on recent NAPLAN tests. Please, grab a coffee and a muffin, we'll be starting in about five minutes.'

'Whoopee', thought Linda. 'Just what I need – step-by-step approaches that make sure I can cover the material, do the assessments and keep my students occupied.'

'Here we go again', thought Marie. '"Maths Teaching for Dummies" – the resources sure look good, but how will they suit my particular students and the way I teach?'

Linda and Marie feel that they don't really understand the key concepts of mathematics; they are uncertain about how their students understand the big ideas around numeracy; and they have a limited teaching repertoire on how to help their students build their knowledge and understanding of mathematics and their numeracy skills. Over their careers, they preferred spending time on helping their students to learn to read rather than learn about numbers, measurement or spatial relationships – or even 'thinking mathematically'.

As they made their way to their chairs in the back corner of the staff room, the principal rose to welcome his teachers and introduce Dr Parabola, adding that 'unfortunately he had to leave in a few minutes to attend an urgent principals' meeting at Central Office'.

Meanwhile on the other side of town, at Warm Heart Primary School, the principal and several teachers were just finishing their discussions about existing effective practice in maths teaching at their school and what characteristics seemed to be most in evidence. They had been reading recent research on the topic, had considered what areas of maths teaching could do with a boost, and had begun to check out approaches to build on existing strengths of their staff and colleagues. They had done an audit of existing teaching resources. At the staff meeting the next week, they planned to have some structured planning and discussion time about what was working well and why, different ways of organising staffing and the timetable, and inviting teachers to express interest in what they would like to work on in their maths teaching.

The principal at Warm Heart Primary headed to that afternoon's meeting at Central Office.

Introduction

Most teachers have a sense of what good mathematics teaching looks and feels like. Most could list features of the physical environment, the style of the teacher, the actions of the students and so forth that would exemplify effective practice. Similarly, most mathematics teachers have aspects of their practice that they know to be effective in assisting learners, while being aware of aspects they would like to develop. In the LAND project, from the beginning, we focused on effective teaching practice and encouraged project participants to identify areas to develop over the life of the project. In this chapter, you will read about the development of this aspect of the LAND project. We look at the literature on effective mathematics teaching and the development of the 25 characteristics that were the main framework of this part of the project. We also review what we learnt about applying this framework over two years of the project and the subsequent refinements that were made.

What is effective mathematics teaching?

In his seminal work, *Critical variables in mathematics education*, Begle (1979) noted:

> if we agree that the focus of our educational enterprise is student learning (in the broad sense, including affective as well as cognitive learning), then we should

base our definition of teacher effectiveness on the degree to which the teacher's students learn, or, at the very least, we should validate any other kind of definition that we might adopt against measures of student learning. (p. 29)

But, until the last 15 years or so, evidence linking teaching practices with learning outcomes in mathematics has been relatively limited (Askew, 2004).

Brophy and Good (1986) conducted the so-called 'process-product' research. In these studies, the dependent variable was performance on standardised achievement tests. Most of these studies occurred in classrooms where the curriculum and classroom organisation were designed to support the teacher in direct instruction. Not surprisingly, most of the effective teacher variables involved teacher behaviours associated with this style of teaching, including clarity of presentation, teacher wait-time and whole-class questioning strategies.

Such research therefore is limited in what it offers of assistance to teachers seeking to operate in a classroom where meaning and understanding are the focus (Hiebert et al., 1997; Skemp, 1976), although clarity of explanation and appropriate wait-times are, of course, still desirable. In what follows, the research that is reviewed is focused specifically on mathematics classrooms.

Given the success of particular Asian countries in the Third International Mathematics and Science Study (TIMSS), there was considerable interest in describing commonalities between classrooms of particularly effective countries. In particular, much interest focused on Japanese primary classrooms. Through observation and videotape, Stigler and Stevenson (1991) conducted a study of 120 classrooms in Taipei (Taiwan), Sendai (Japan) and Minneapolis (USA). They characterised the classrooms in Japan and China as consisting of:

> coherent lessons that are presented in a thoughtful, relaxed, and non-authoritarian manner. Teachers frequently rely on students as sources of information. Lessons are oriented toward problem solving rather than rote mastery of facts and procedures and utilize many different types of representational materials. The role assumed by the teacher is that of knowledgeable guide, rather than that of prime dispenser of information and arbiter of what is correct ... There is frequent verbal interaction in the classroom as the teacher attempts to stimulate students to produce, explain, and evaluate solutions to problems. (p. 14)

It was not uncommon for these lessons to be organised around a single problem. Asian teachers tended to use short, frequent periods of the students being seated, alternating between group discussion of problems and time for children to work through problems on their own. Reflection was a major feature of classrooms.

Brown (1998, p. 2) noted that international observational studies seem to agree on some aspects of teacher quality that correlated with attainment, including the following:

- the use of higher order questions, statements and tasks that require thought rather than practice
- emphasis on establishing, through dialogue, meanings and connections between different mathematical ideas and contexts
- collaborative problem-solving in class and small group settings
- more autonomy for students to develop and discuss their own methods and ideas.

International comparisons can be difficult to interpret. As Askew et al. (2010) noted, 'teaching is a minor factor compared to the matching between curriculum and test items in explaining international differences' (p. 16). In what follows, we will focus not on data arising from international comparisons but rather on studies within given countries that sought to explain why the growth in understanding of students in one country might be different from one classroom to the next.

Clarke (1997, p. 280) summarised research on the role of the teacher from studies in early years and middle school mathematics classrooms where problem-solving was a major focus. He identified seven components of the role of the teacher that were common to these various settings:

- the use of non-routine problems, without the provision of procedures for their solution, as the starting point and focus of instruction
- the adaptation of materials and instruction according to local contexts and the teacher's knowledge of students' interests and needs
- the use of a variety of classroom organisational styles (individual, small group, whole class)
- the development of a 'mathematical discourse community', with the teacher as a 'fellow player' who values and builds on students' solutions and methods
- the identification and focus on the big ideas of mathematics
- the use of informal assessment methods to inform instructional decisions
- the facilitation of student reflection on activity and learning.

In a major study of effective primary school mathematics teaching in the UK, Askew et al. (1997) studied the practices of a number of different teachers with varying levels of effectiveness. A specially designed oral mathematics test, 'tiered' for different age ranges, was administered to the classes of 90 primary teachers at the beginning and end of the school year. Two thousand children were assessed. The researchers considered relative learning gains, and accordingly grouped teachers as 'highly effective', 'effective' and 'moderately effective'. Data were then collected (using interviews, questionnaires and observations) from 18 case-study teachers (six in each category), providing information on teachers' beliefs, pedagogical and mathematical subject knowledge, professional development experiences and practices. This study found these characteristics in the teaching practices of the highly effective teachers:

- they connected different ideas of mathematics and different representations of each idea by means of a variety of words, symbols and diagrams
- they encouraged students to describe their methods and reasoning, and used these descriptions as a way of developing understanding through establishing and emphasising connections
- they emphasised the importance of using whatever mental, written or electronic methods are most efficient for the problem at hand
- they particularly emphasised the development of mental skills.

Possibly just as importantly, there were some characteristics of teaching practice that didn't enhance student learning.

> Teachers who gave priority to pupils acquiring a collection of standard arithmetical methods over establishing understanding and connection produced lower numeracy gains . . . Teachers who gave priority to the use of practical equipment rather than developing effective methods, and delayed the introduction of more abstract ideas until they felt a child was ready for them, also produced lower gains. (Askew et al., 1997, pp. 2–3)

Highly effective teachers of mathematics had knowledge and awareness of conceptual connections between the areas of the primary mathematics curriculum. There was no particular association between the amount of formal mathematics studied by teachers and student gains. Highly effective teachers were much more likely than other teachers to have undertaken mathematics-specific continuing professional development over an extended period. Elsewhere, Askew (2004) commented:

> perhaps the thing that most distinguished the connectionist teachers was the ways in which they tried to make their classrooms 'communities of learners', in which everyone learned from everyone else. (p. 181)

Brown (1999) noted:

> quality teaching is more important than class organisation . . . it's not whether it's whole-class, small group or individual teaching but rather what you teach and how you interact mathematically with children that seems to count. (p. 7)

The New South Wales Department of Education and Training, the Catholic Education Commission New South Wales and the Association of Independent Schools of New South Wales (2004) studied the practices of 25 high-performing schools across New South Wales, determined by state mathematics test data. Two sets of case studies in 45 schools focused on factors and strategies within the classroom. They summarised their 14 strategies under three factors: language as a focus for learning; assessment to identify and accommodate difference; and purposeful pedagogy.

Kilpatrick and Silver (2000), in exploring challenges for mathematics education into the future, described various ways that good mathematics teaching had been seen during the 20th century:

> giving learners clear explanations, identifying clear instructional objectives, prefacing instruction on complex knowledge and skills with hierarchical sequences of purported prerequisites, breaking instruction into small steps learners can easily take on their own, immersing learners in dilemmas with which they must struggle, helping learners resolve one another's confusions, tailoring instructional activities to individual learners' perceived ways of learning. (p. 226)

Kyriacou and Issitt (2008) reviewed 15 studies in order to characterise effective teacher-initiated teacher–pupil dialogue to promote conceptual understanding of mathematics. Although these studies advocated practices – such as going beyond traditional initiation–response feedback and working collaboratively with pupils – they noted that few studies provided evidence that advocated strategies actually led to the promotion of pupils' conceptual understanding. In a more widespread review, Hiebert and Grouws (2007) noted that teaching that promotes conceptual development has two clear features: teachers and students attend explicitly to concepts; and students struggle with important mathematics.

Kieren (1997), in a reflection on the relationship between mathematics education research and practice, noted that, because so much research today occurs in classrooms, its potential direct relevance to practice is raised. He argued that research has pointed to alternative effective teaching practices and to new emphases:

- listening to rather than simply listening for
- acting with students in doing mathematics rather than simply showing students how to do mathematics
- establishing effective discourses of mathematical argument or mathematical conversation rather than simply the discourse of telling, interrogating and evaluating
- the mechanisms of students' mathematical thinking rather than simply on students' answers

- the teacher and student as fully implicated by their actions, each in the learning of the other
- the teacher as co-developer of a lived mathematics curriculum not just the recipient of, or a conduit for, a pre-decided curriculum (p. 33).

It is clear that the research by different scholars in relation to the characteristics of effective teaching provides some similarities and some differences in the lists they develop. The differences can be accounted for by the varying methodologies, the different contexts in which the research took place and the choice of the dependent variable in each case. In the next section, we outline the approach developed from a study of effective teachers in Victorian schools. This approach formed the basis of our professional development and research work in the LAND project and involved groups of primary school teachers and principals in three Australian states and territories.

Background to the LAND approach to effective teaching of mathematics

The LAND project built on understandings of effective mathematics teaching as explained in the previous section. In addition, the development of the project was heavily influenced by the findings of a large-scale research project previously undertaken by some of the research team in Victoria, Australia: the Early Numeracy Research Project (ENRP). The ENRP was a collaborative venture between Australian Catholic University, Monash University, the Victorian Department of Employment, Education and Training, the Catholic Education Office (Melbourne) and the Association of Independent Schools Victoria. The project was funded in 35 project ('trial') schools and 35 control ('reference') schools.

As part of the ENRP, 354 junior primary teachers in 35 schools participated in a three-year research and professional development project, exploring the most effective approaches to the teaching of mathematics in the first three years of school. (For a full description of the ENRP, see Clarke, 2001.) The project had three key components:
- a research-based framework of 'growth points' in young children's mathematical learning (in number, measurement and space)
- a 40-minute, one-on-one interview, used by all teachers with all children at the beginning and end of the school year
- extensive professional development at central, regional and school levels, for all teachers, coordinators and principals.

Over the course of the ENRP, the assessment interview was used with more than 11 000 students on a total of around 36 000 occasions. During each interview, teachers completed a four-page record sheet. The information on these sheets was then coded by a trained team of coders, assigning achieved growth points to each child for each domain. This process, including statistical measures to convert the growth-point data to an interval scale, is discussed in detail in Rowley and Horne (2000).

Given that the project took place over three years, it was possible to use student interview data from the first two years to identify particularly effective teachers for intensive study in the third year. In identifying effective teachers, the interest of the ENRP team was in growth in student understanding across the school year (as with Askew, 2004; Askew et al., 1997). The emphasis on growth allowed the researchers to choose teachers who made a considerable difference to the students they taught, in terms of 'adding value'. By aggregating data on children's growth in terms of movement through the ENRP growth points, the first two years' data were used to identify particularly effective teachers – the ones whose students showed the greatest growth over two years for each of the two cohorts of children.

Using these data, six teachers were chosen for case studies and were studied intensively through use of the following data sources:

- five lesson observations by two researchers, incorporating detailed observer field notes, photographs of lessons and collection of artefacts (for example, worksheets, student work samples, lesson plans)
- teacher interviews after the lessons
- teacher questionnaires completed through the duration of the project
- teacher responses to other relevant questions and tasks posed to them (see Clarke & Clarke, 2004, for more detail).

Decisions needed to be made on the kinds of notes that would be taken on the lessons. The ENRP research team made the same decision as Stigler and Baranes (1988) who conducted mathematics classroom observations in three countries and 'decided to trade the greater reliability of an objective coding scheme, for the inherent richness of detailed narrative descriptions of mathematics lessons' (p. 294).

The description of effective teachers of P–2 mathematics, as revealed in the ENRP study, formed the basis for the 25 Characteristics of Effective Mathematics Teaching used in the LAND project. These characteristics (classified by theme and related action) are shown in Table 3.1.

In the following section, we outline the ways in which the findings from the ENRP research on effective teaching of mathematics were used in the LAND project.

Table 3.1: The 25 characteristics of effective mathematics teaching

Theme		Action
Mathematical focus	1	Focus on important mathematical ideas
	2	Make the mathematical focus clear to the children
Purpose and choice of task	3	Structure purposeful tasks that enable different possibilities, strategies and products to emerge
	4	Choose tasks that engage children and maintain involvement
Materials, tools and representations	5	Use a range of materials/representations/contexts for the same concept
Adaptations, connections and links	6	Use teachable moments as they occur
	7	Make connections to mathematical ideas from previous lessons or experiences
Organisational style(s), teaching approaches	8	Engage and focus children's mathematical thinking through an introductory, whole-group activity
	9	Choose from a variety of individual and group structures and teacher roles within the major part of the lesson
Learning community and classroom interaction	10	Use a range of question types to probe and challenge children's thinking and reasoning
	11	Hold back from telling children everything
	12	Encourage children to explain their mathematical thinking/ideas
	13	Encourage children to listen and evaluate others' mathematical thinking/ideas, and help with methods and understanding
	14	Listen attentively to individual children
	15	Build on children's mathematical ideas and strategies
Expectations	16	Have high but realistic mathematical expectations of all children
	17	Promote and value effort, persistence and concentration
Reflection	18	Draw out key mathematical ideas during and/or towards the end of the lesson
	19	After the lesson, reflect on children's responses and learning, together with activities and lesson content
Assessment methods	20	Collect data by observation and/or listening to children, taking notes as appropriate
	21	Use a variety of assessment methods
	22	Modify planning as a result of assessment
Personal attributes of the teacher	23	Believe that mathematics learning can and should be enjoyable
	24	Are confident in their own knowledge of mathematics at the level they are teaching
	25	Show pride and pleasure in individuals' success

Developing and practising effective mathematics teaching

One of the premises of the LAND project was that we were working with school teams who had developed effective practice and thoroughly understood their contexts. As a research team, we had no intention of imposing practice; indeed, this would have been impossible with such a variety of schools and contexts. Instead, we invited participants to determine the features of their mathematics teaching practice that they wished to develop through the project.

In our first workshop, we asked individual participants to select three of the 25 characteristics: one that they felt was a feature of their practice (acknowledging expertise already present); one that they would like to develop; and one that they would like their school to develop. The next stage involved individuals moving to their school teams to select the characteristics they wanted to work on as a school. The responses are shown in Table 3.2.

These selected characteristics were recorded on the project wiki and were used to plan workshop sessions in mathematics teaching practice. It was an advantage to have experienced mathematics educators on the research team as we planned sessions for the next day based on the needs that emerged from participants.

High expectations

A characteristic of interest to teachers working with Indigenous students in remote settings was characteristic 16: 'have high but realistic mathematical expectations of all children'. One teacher working in the Northern Territory wrote, 'If I have high expectations of the students, they start to have higher expectations of themselves and aim to achieve more'. For another school in the Northern Territory, their work on this characteristic led to profound change. It became clear that children were making little progress year to year. On investigation, a plausible hypothesis was that the high turnover of staff with little, if any, opportunity for handover of information meant that new teachers responded to what the children 'appeared' to be able to do. For example, a new teacher, when meeting children in remote and regional school settings, often formed the impression they were able to do much less than they could.

The school team decided on two strategies to tackle the lack of progress. The first was to maintain accurate achievement records with a formal process of handing on to the next teacher. The second had the most profound consequences: the teachers decided to teach the children the curriculum specified in the Northern Territory Curriculum Framework for their year level. No longer were the children trapped in a cycle of being retaught the same (and very elementary material) year after year. By the end of the second year of the project, the school reported data demonstrating dramatic jumps in attainment of the children. This approach has

Table 3.2: LAND school participants' choices of effective mathematics teaching characteristics (*n* = 47)

Theme	Characteristic #	Action	South Australia	Northern Territory	Broome	Perth	Frequency	%
Mathematical focus	1	Focus on important mathematical ideas	2				2	
Purpose and choice of task	3	Structure purposeful tasks that enable different possibilities, strategies and products to emerge	2			2	4	8.51
	4	Choose tasks that engage children and maintain involvement		1	4	3	8*	17.0
Materials, tools and representations	5	Use a range of materials/representations/contexts for the same concept		1	2		3	
Adaptations, connections and links	6	Use teachable moments as they occur				1	1	
Organisational style(s), teaching approaches	8	Engage and focus children's mathematical thinking through an introductory, whole-group activity	1		1		2	
Learning community and classroom interaction	10	Use a range of question types to probe and challenge children's thinking and reasoning	4		1		5	10.6
	12	Encourage children to explain their mathematical thinking/ideas	3		1	1	5	10.6

Table 3.2 (continued)

Theme	Characteristic #	Action	South Australia	Northern Territory	Broome	Perth	Frequency	%
	13	Encourage children to listen and evaluate others' mathematical thinking/ ideas, and help with methods and understanding		1			1	
Expectations	16	Have high but realistic mathematical expectations of all children		4	1		5*	10.6
Reflection	19	After the lesson, reflect on children's responses and learning, together with activities and lesson content				1	1	
Assessment methods	20	Collect data by observation and/ or listening to children, taking notes as appropriate	1	2		1	4	8.51
	22	Modify planning as a result of assessment		3			3	
Personal attributes of the teacher	23	Believe that mathematics learning can and should be enjoyable	1		1		2	
	24	Are confident in their own knowledge of mathematics at the level they are teaching				1	1	

*All from Broome and the Northern Territory and all referred to Indigenous students.

been termed 'Year Level–Appropriate Curriculum'. The central features of the approach are to begin planning with the expectation that learners will engage with the curriculum as specified for their year of schooling. For example, if they are in Year 5, they will be taught the curriculum for Year 5, the underlying philosophy of the *Australian Curriculum: Mathematics* (Australian Curriculum, Assessment and Reporting Authority, n.d.). Accessing year-level curriculum does not mean all students are treated the same. Teachers plan for diverse learners by providing enabling and extending prompts for lessons (Sullivan, Mousley & Zevenbergen, 2006). That is, they determine additional supports to enable learners to engage with the material and extensions to challenge learners to deepen their understanding. Surprisingly, learning year-level curriculum is possible when learners have not accomplished what had been thought to be prerequisite skills and concepts. (For a fuller discussion, see Faragher, 2014.)

Focus on tasks

Another area of effective teaching of mathematics that was of significant interest to principals and teachers in the LAND project had to do with the features of the task. Characteristic 3 – 'Structure purposeful tasks that enable different possibilities, strategies and products to emerge' – and Characteristic 4 – 'Choose tasks that engage children and maintain involvement' – were both seen as very important. A teacher from the Perth cluster explained her choice:

> I found . . . [these characteristics] very valuable as it [the activities] enables all students to participate at their own level and often allows them to learn from each other through partner or group collaboration. Open activities also often provide opportunities for incidental learning.

Closely related to this choice was the focus on classroom interaction (Characteristics 10, 12 and 13). Teacher questioning and encouragement of students to explain their thinking and listen to other students were seen as important means of developing the proficiencies outlined in the Australian Curriculum, particularly, reasoning, problem-solving and understanding.

This focus on encouraging higher levels of classroom interaction and more sophisticated questioning had widespread positive effects. For example, a principal from one of the Kimberley schools observed that teachers, staff, students and parents' attitudes towards mathematics were changing for the better, commenting that there is now 'an exuberance and enjoyment of maths activities throughout the school'. Another principal similarly commented that using a range of questions types to probe children's thinking and encouraging different ways of keeping a journal 'helped children to be more reflective about what, why and how they processed tasks'.

The research team based much of its work on the growth of pedagogical content knowledge around the development of mathematical thinking. Teachers responded with enthusiasm to the ideas presented and began to use them in their practice. Of particular value was the process of explicitly teaching and learning mathematical thinking. We used an approach based on the work of John Mason and colleagues (Mason, Burton & Stacey, 2010). The focus of documenting mathematical thinking while working on rich tasks assists teachers to improve their own problem-solving as well as their ability to teach the strategies to their students. The process of teaching mathematical thinking is explained further in Faragher (2011).

Gather and use evidence – assessment of learning

Assessment of learning has always been a part of the core business of teaching. Over recent years the focus on assessment has been intensified by the Australian Government's agenda of the assessment of numeracy and publication of data through the vehicles of NAPLAN and the My School website (Australian Curriculum, Assessment and Reporting Authority, 2013). These policy developments were seen by LAND project participants as having positive as well as potentially negative effects on assessment and broader curriculum and teaching practice in their schools. While some warned of the dangers of a narrowing of the curriculum and teaching practice, others commented that the intensified focus on assessment and accountability was helping to bringing about school-wide change. For example, one principal noted that the gathering and use of evidence of student learning was 'opening up the professional conversation among staff members and encouraging them to work collaboratively as a village to assist children's learning'. This principal added that such evidence was obtained from a range of sources, including 'anecdotal records, photo, video, assessment grids, test results, both class and standardised'.

The assessment practices of schools in the LAND project generally reflected the patterns highlighted in the research literature (Webb, 1992). For example, some schools were making use of task-based student interviews (such as the early numeracy interview of the ENRP) and most devoted time to the assessment of whole student cohorts at periodic intervals: for example, at the beginning of each year. In this sense, NAPLAN results were seen as adding further information to their existing 'bank of evidence'. Given the increasing amount of data available, it became evident to the LAND leadership school teams that they were not necessarily making the most effective use of the information they had. In short, they felt that they needed to improve in these areas:

- developing expertise in statistical analysis
- making better use of data from the task-based interviews – there was a tendency to regard the interview data as an end in itself rather than seeing the results as the starting point for planning teaching

- ensuring consistency of assessment across the school so that evidence of learning was systematic
- enhancing record keeping – this included formal handover processes to subsequent teachers.

These needs were recognised and dealt with by the research team and the LAND project officers in workshops, via school and classroom visits, and through networking using the LAND wiki.

Recognising needs and responding to interests

In our LAND workshops, the research team presented professional learning opportunities based on the needs expressed by participants. The team travelled with a kit of basic mathematics equipment and key resources suitable for emphasising the elements of effective mathematics teaching. The development of mathematical thinking was an underlying theme. The focus was how this could be taught using 'rich tasks'. Rich tasks are described as those 'that provide high quality, reliable information about what students know and can do' (Clarke & Clarke, 2002). Examples of rich tasks were sourced from the Maths300 website (Education Services Australia, 2010) and the collection developed by Downton et al. (2006). One example of a rich task, 'Hunting for stars' that the researchers demonstrated to LAND project participants is described in the box on page 62.

The Maths300 materials include software to enable testing of conjectures – ideas that seem to be reasonable but have not been tested – and to develop generalisations. Further detail about developing mathematical thinking along these lines can be found in Faragher (2011).

Supporting effective mathematics teaching

Through our work, we found there were at least two conditions needed to provide the environment in which good mathematics teaching could flourish. The first was dedicated time for mathematics allocated in the school timetable. The second condition involved ongoing support and professional learning for teaching staff to develop their expertise in mathematics teaching.

Dedicated mathematics time

Some LAND schools found that they had devoted considerable attention to literacy in recent years and sometimes to the detriment of mathematics. Some of these schools had adopted dedicated time for literacy and made the decision to implement a similar program in mathematics. This was a large commitment for schools and involved shared decisions about the amount of time allocated and when it would occur. There is a common view that mathematics is best taught and learnt in the morning. Fortunately, research has indicated that this is not

---

Hunting for stars – a Maths300 lesson

The rich task, 'Hunting for stars', is designed to investigate number patterns. It involves participants forming a circle and passing a rope to a person with a given number. For example, with 12 people in a circle, a rope was passed to every third person. The pattern formed by the rope when it had returned to the starting point was a square. When the rope passed to the fourth person, the shape formed was a triangle. Some arrangements lead to a star, but which? That is the problem to solve!

This problem-solving activity involves teachers in demonstrating the problem and commencing the process of 'specialising': that is, gathering data with their students. As students' understanding grows, they move to their own exploration. This exploration activity concludes with students presenting and discussing their findings with others.

---

necessarily the case (Muyskens & Ysseldyke, 1998). In a number of the schools, attendance patterns indicated that children frequently missed the morning session of school when mathematics had often been programmed. By moving the dedicated mathematics time to different times during the day, some schools found that they were able to increase the likelihood of students being present for mathematics.

Other schools went further and timetabled mathematics at the same time of day throughout the school and established a policy of 'no interruptions' during this time. People unfamiliar with schools may be surprised at the number of distractions with which teachers have to deal throughout their day. Notices to students, school visitors (a particular feature in the remote Indigenous schools), excursions, health checks and so on all interrupt learning. A policy of 'no interruptions' gives a very clear message about how the school regards the importance of mathematics.

Having established a policy of dedicated time for mathematics, LAND teachers were faced with deciding how to structure this time and support other teachers in their schools. For some, it required acknowledgement that their previous planning for mathematics had been too limited. Different jurisdictions and schools developed and adopted different formats for dedicated mathematics time – in part, as a matter of preference for individual teachers and the school contexts involved. Amid this variation the fundamental requirement was to thoroughly plan a block of time each day for mathematics. An outline of dedicated mathematics time adopted by one of the school clusters is shown in the box on page 63.

The template for dedicated mathematics time shown in the box highlights several important elements. First, the introductory phase of the lesson needs to be connected with what is to come in the lesson and be directly related to the learning outcomes. Some teachers had been in the practice of doing 'warm-up' activities such as number facts or maths games that were not related to the lesson. This approach tended to convey to students that they were having essentially two

---

Dedicated mathematics time – What it might look like?

1. Introduction
A short (2–5 minute) 'attention getter', offering success and an introduction to what is to come.

2. Aims
Tell the students:
What they will be learning? [You will need to base this on your unit plan connecting to syllabus documents.]
Why it is important?
What they will be doing?

3. Body
Teaching of whole class, groups or individuals. Teaching may take the form of direct instruction from the teacher, group work, investigations, problem solving, and/or discussion

Time	Teacher does	Students do

4. Check for understanding
Gather evidence of what the children have learnt.
(State here what you will look for. What are the learning outcomes?)

5. Conclusion
Discussion (or summary) about what was covered in the lesson. If there has been group work, it is absolutely critical that the teacher makes sure the children get what they were supposed to out of the lesson. Research has shown that often children take part in activities but don't get the mathematical point.

Main points of the lesson:

Why it is important:

Ideas for continuing the learning:

---

separate lessons of mathematics each day. In contrast, the model shown in the box requires the lesson introduction to engage the learner in the lesson objective and therefore needs to be directly connected. Some ways in which this might occur include using the introduction to review essential prerequisite knowledge, to motivate the students by showing the connection to interesting contexts or to pose an interesting problem.

Similarly, the conclusion of the lesson needs to relate explicitly to the lesson objectives. Research from the UK (Askew et al., 1997) has shown that children (and sometimes their teachers) might have been engaged in ostensibly mathematics activities but they completely missed the point of the task. The concluding phase is critical to ensure learners have gained the key messages from the work they have undertaken (Stein et al., 2009). For example, from the LAND project, one teacher commented that, in the textbook material she had been using, there was always a concluding phase but in the past she had often run out of time in her lessons and omitted that part. Her work on the LAND project had highlighted for her that this phase was essential and, subsequently, it became a feature of her practice.

Dedicated staff roles: The school numeracy coordinator

The development, practice and sharing of insights and ideas about effective teaching of mathematics requires dedicated support at the school level. Our work with the teachers and principals in the LAND project indicates that having dedicated staff roles in numeracy is an essential feature for ensuring maximum alignment of effectiveness throughout the school.

The position of numeracy coordinator has been a feature of many primary schools in recent years (Cheeseman & Clarke, 2005). In the LAND project, the selection of staff for the team frequently included the numeracy coordinator. In some cases, a member of the team was assigned to the role for the project. These were the common responsibilities undertaken by the school numeracy coordinator for the LAND project:

- *managing resources* – this included auditing school collections, developing a system of classification and organisation, purchasing new materials and monitoring the collection.
- *documentation and keeping records* – in the LAND project, this had the additional duty of gathering, organising and analysing data required for project reporting.
- *planning and delivery of professional learning* – including through professional learning community sessions.
- *liaison and mentoring* – coordinators were regarded as key teachers in their schools and were tasked with supporting other staff in the school. As the LAND project unfolded, the role included extending the work of the team to others in the school as part of the process of developing shared understanding and eventually school charters (see Chapter 9).
- *teaching* – all our LAND coordinators were classroom teachers. Some had reduced teaching loads to account for the additional tasks of the role.
- *course planning* – numeracy coordinators worked with other teachers to develop year-level and whole-school mathematics programs.

Lessons on effective mathematics teaching

Teaching mathematics effectively is the most important school-based influence on students' numeracy development. To teach mathematics well requires practice and support at the local level. The findings from the LAND project indicate that, while some teachers may underestimate their ability and lack confidence in teaching mathematics, each and every teacher displays at least some of the characteristics of effective practice that have been identified in the literature. Through building on these existing strengths, and demonstrating how other characteristics may be developed, the LAND project was able to encourage a more research-based, empowering and collaborative model for enhancing teachers' pedagogical content knowledge in mathematics.

In this chapter, we have provided an overview of the research on teaching mathematics effectively that underpinned the LAND project. In particular, we have described some specific teaching ideas that were covered in the LAND workshops and shared insights about how teachers worked with the 25 Characteristics of Effective Teaching of Mathematics developed from the ENRP research. The findings from the LAND project also highlighted that continued professional learning in mathematics teaching and student numeracy development is best supported at the local level through having dedicated roles (for example, numeracy coordinators) and regularly scheduled time to teach mathematics. Importantly, we also found that these forms of support will not be properly implemented or sustained without the direct involvement and encouragement of the principal and the willingness and capacity of teachers to also exercise leadership in supporting their colleagues at the local level. These themes are explored in the next chapter.

CHAPTER 4

LEADING MATHEMATICS TEACHING

Michael Gaffney, Michael Bezzina and
Chris Branson

Bill and Shirley are primary school principals in low socioeconomic status areas of Australia. Bill's school is on the outskirts of Australian Capital City. It has a high proportion of newly arrived families from non-English-speaking backgrounds as well as a sizeable proportion of single-parent families on welfare support. Shirley's school is in a remote area on the north-western coast of Australia. Most of her school's students are Indigenous and speak at least two languages other than English.

The numeracy results of both schools on the National Assessment Program in Literacy and Numeracy (NAPLAN) tests are comparable with schools in similar circumstances. But both principals are concerned that this is not acceptable – 'being top of your division, when your division is well below the national average, is simply not good enough' was how one of them put it.

As principals, they are aware of their responsibility to ensure that all their students receive the very best opportunities to develop their numeracy knowledge and skills. They also know that a significant number of their teachers are not confident in their own understanding of mathematics. Most did not take mathematics past Year 10. Similarly, both Bill and Shirley are aware of the limited 'teaching repertoire' that their teachers have to help their students understand important mathematical concepts. Added to these challenges is the fact that most years, more than one-third of their teaching staff move to another school (or sometimes out of the profession altogether); this has meant that it is very difficult to 'get any traction' on improving mathematics teaching and numeracy achievement levels in their schools.

What's more, from a personal standpoint, it has been quite a while since either Bill or Shirley participated in any professional development specifically to do with mathematics teaching or student numeracy achievement. It is something that they usually leave to the coordinators or individual teachers. Besides, they have their own particular leadership demands. For example, they are required to attend important principals' meetings on school performance, compliance and accountability at central office; manage urgent staffing, student welfare, parent and budget matters; and liaise with builders and education authority personnel about the Australian Government's Building the Education Revolution program.

All these demands and commitments take time away from what they know deep down was the reason they went into teaching in the first place – to help students learn. They also realise that bringing about lasting improvement in key areas of student achievement like numeracy is going to take more time and effort than they alone can give. They need to bring others into the process, especially teachers who are closest to the core work of teaching and learning in their schools. This means that they need to encourage their staff to exercise more leadership responsibility in numeracy.

When the LAND project came along, Bill and Shirley saw the opportunity to develop a team approach to leading the development of numeracy in their schools. They felt that the time was right to do something about leading mathematics teaching and improving student numeracy levels.

Introduction: It's time for leadership in numeracy!

This story describes the general context of the schools invited into the LAND project, a pilot research project funded by the Australian Government to inform program development focused on raising the numeracy achievement of students living in low socioeconomic status communities. The LAND project schools were in low socioeconomic status areas and, while most were doing reasonably well compared to schools in similar circumstances, the principals were keen to explore how they might go about further improving their students' numeracy levels. Over the past several years, there was a general feeling that much effort had been put into various types of literacy programs and that numeracy had taken somewhat of a back seat.

The LAND project was welcomed as an opportunity to put the spotlight on numeracy. More than that, LAND was different. It required principals to be *directly* involved as participants with their teachers – and because it was designed to build on existing approaches to mathematics teaching and numeracy development rather than as 'a package to follow and fix dodgy teaching practices', LAND enabled school leaders to take a broader perspective. It strengthened the bases upon which principals and the teacher leaders with whom they worked were able to develop their school numeracy strategies. In some cases, new approaches and resources were adopted. In other cases, existing programs were strengthened, revamped or dropped altogether. In all cases, schools progressed toward a more informed, agreed and explicit set of pedagogical principles to guide the teaching of mathematics and numeracy achievement. Each school's journey was different but the common thread was that each involved combinations of leadership by principals and teachers, exercised in collaborative and complementary ways.

The approach to educational leadership taken in the LAND project reflected contemporary research on the connection between leadership and learning, and was grounded in the idea that leaders are recognised by their actions and that educational leadership means making a positive and meaningful difference to the lives and learning of others (Gaffney, 2012). While the greatest 'within school' influence on student achievement is teaching quality (Hattie, 2009; Reeves, 2005), there is a growing body of literature that points to the significance of school leadership in enhancing student learning (Marzano, Waters & McNulty, 2005; Robinson, Hohepa & Lloyd, 2009). This makes the actions of leaders a pivotal element of any process aimed at improving teaching practice and student outcomes. Consequently, this was also a focus for the LAND project. The project provided opportunities for those in school leadership roles to develop their capabilities to lead numeracy development. Importantly, by 'school leadership roles', we are not only referring to those in formal positions of authority like 'the principal', but also to teachers who through their actions make a difference to the lives and learning of others, their professional colleagues as well as their students. The LAND project also sought to investigate the nature of these leadership capabilities and the effect of their associated actions on teacher confidence, teaching practice and on student engagement and achievement in numeracy.

In this chapter, we will provide an overview of the approach to leading mathematics teaching and student numeracy development used in the LAND project. We explain the research base underpinning the leadership of numeracy development, describe the workshop program and other aspects of the research methodology and report the findings relating to the leadership capabilities that contribute to numeracy learning in the school. These findings include developing shared purpose; valuing teaching and professional development; organising curriculum and infrastructure; engaging the community; and thinking strategically and acting practically to build alignment. The chapter concludes with some implications and suggestions for leadership development and practice at school and system level to ensure sustainable improvement in student numeracy achievement.

As you read through this chapter, we hope that you will gain an insight into the nature of leading mathematics teaching and what it takes to lead numeracy development.

Linking leadership and numeracy development: Messages from the research

The last decade has seen increasing interest on researching the relationship between school leadership and student learning outcomes (Bezzina & Burford,

2010; Dempster, Robson & Gaffney, 2011; Leithwood et al., 2004; Marzano, 2003; Pont, Nusche & Moorman, 2008; Robinson, 2007; Robinson et al., 2009). This interest has been accompanied by the development of various forms of school leadership standards frameworks that seek to describe the range of dimensions and actions that are involved in leading schools effectively (Australian Council for Educational Leaders, 2010; Australian Institute for Teaching and School Leadership, 2011b). It is possible to distil a series of themes that emerge from these two fields of endeavour that can be used to describe and research the work of school leaders as they seek to enhance the learning outcomes of the children and young people in their care:

- promoting teacher quality
- setting the direction and shaping the culture
- managing financial and human resources
- developing school community relationships
- acting strategically by using evidence about causes and effects.

While these themes are expressed in different ways by different writers, the common thread and shared understanding from the literature is that the themes somehow interact with each other to influence student learning outcomes. One example of this thinking is the framework developed by the Australian Catholic University Flagship for Creative and Authentic Leadership – or ACUFCAL (2007). The framework is based on the idea of dimensions of leadership capabilities, where the term 'capabilities' refers to qualities that integrate knowledge, skills and attitudes in such a way that they can be used appropriately and effectively in new and changing circumstances (Stephenson, cited in Duignan, 2006, p. 120). Four dimensions of leadership capability were identified through the research:

- *personal* – the capabilities of the leader as a person: their sense of identity and self, their ethical and moral stance, their emotional capacity and their spirituality
- *professional* – the capabilities of the leader as educator: their mastery of their craft and their knowledge of their discipline
- *organisational* – the capabilities of the leader related to working with the school as an organisation, building on shared purpose and creating an environment that is supportive and challenging for their fellow professionals
- *relational* – the capabilities of the leader that deal with interpersonal skills including presence, sensitivity to others, listening and communicative skills (ACUFCAL, 2007).

These dimensions not only correspond to the themes emerging from the literature noted above, but they can also be aligned with the models of school improvement that formed the foundation for the LAND framework, as described in Chapter 2 (see Figure 4.1).

One further insight into the connection between school leadership and student learning outcomes becomes apparent when we examine the correspondence between the Caldwell and Spinks (2008) and Crowther et al. (2002) models of school improvement and the ACUFCAL leadership dimensions. It is the evidence from the research literature that the dimensions of leadership (that is, the personal, organisational, professional and relational), like the elements of school improvement (for example, Caldwell and Spinks' forms of capital, 2008, and the research-based framework of Crowther et al., 2002), interact with one another to influence student achievement.

One common, and somewhat limiting, characteristic of school leadership standards frameworks (for example, ACUFCAL, 2007; Australian Council for Educational Leaders, 2010; Australian Institute for Teaching and School Leadership, 2011a) is that they tend to deconstruct leadership practice without providing a clear and practical insight on how the various 'parts of leadership' can actually work in unison to produce something greater than the sum of those parts. An exhortation to appreciate that 'everything is connected', along with an artistic

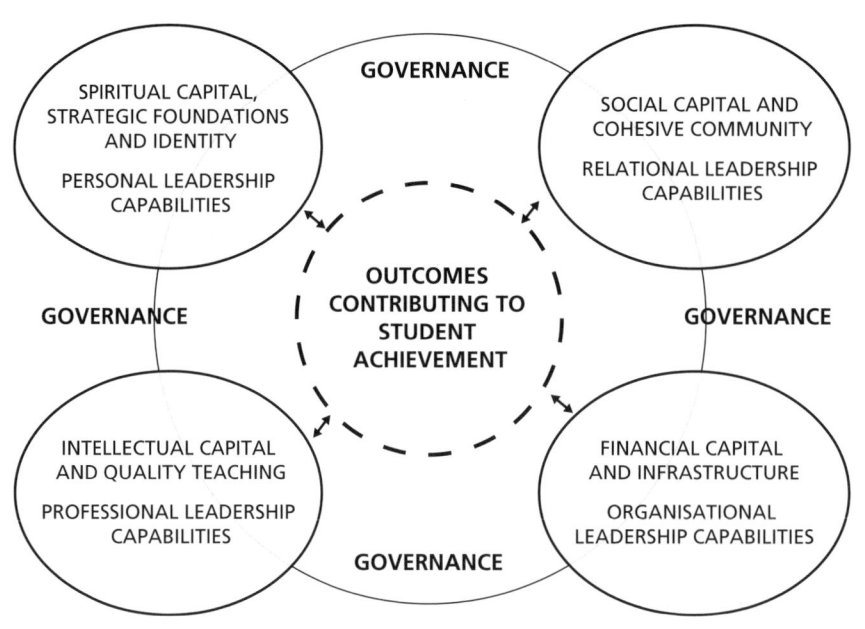

Sources: Australian Catholic University Flagship for Creative and Authentic Leadership (2007); Caldwell & Spinks (2008); Crowther et al. (2002)

Figure 4.1: School improvement and related leadership capabilities

representation of such, is no substitute for explaining exactly *how* the parts might come together.

The question is therefore how to incorporate some form of connecting or integrating leadership capability into the study and practice of leadership for numeracy development. We suggest that the answer can be found in the Caldwell and Spinks (2008) model of school transformation. They defined school transformation as the process of providing quality learning opportunities for all students in all settings. They contended that what is required for transformation is the alignment of four forms of 'capital' – intellectual, spiritual, social and financial – and that this occurs through the process of 'governance' (which can be considered as 'organised decision-making' at the school level). Taking Caldwell and Spinks' ideas, it is possible to suggest a fifth dimension of leadership capability that builds upon the ACUFCAL (2007) and other research into leadership capabilities. This fifth dimension has been described by Gaffney (2012) as 'transformational leadership capability' and refers to thinking strategically and acting practically to build alignment among the elements associated with numeracy development at the school and system level. Combining this thinking with the research themes emerging from the studies of school leadership and student learning outcomes cited above, it is possible to recast and supplement the ACUFCAL (2007) dimensions of leadership capability in the context of numeracy development as follows:

- *personal* – developing shared purpose (for example, enlivening the school's vision for mathematics teaching and learning)
- *professional* – valuing teaching and professional learning (for example, supporting mathematics teaching and the growth of shared understandings and pedagogical principles of numeracy development)
- *organisational* – organising curriculum and infrastructure (for example, managing the organisational support for mathematics teaching and learning)
- *relational* – engaging community (for example, developing a community for improving numeracy development in their schools)
- *transformational* – thinking strategically and acting practically to build alignment (for example, having focused discussions about numeracy outcomes and causes).

Conceptualising the leadership of numeracy development in this way provides ready opportunity for linking the practice and development of educational leadership with the process of numeracy development. For example, the five dimensions of leadership capability can be laid over the LAND framework, as described in Chapter 2 (see Figure 4.2).

The LAND project sought to investigate the validity and applicability of these leadership capabilities to school leaders (principals and teacher leaders) engaged in the work of numeracy development. Seen in this way, the LAND framework

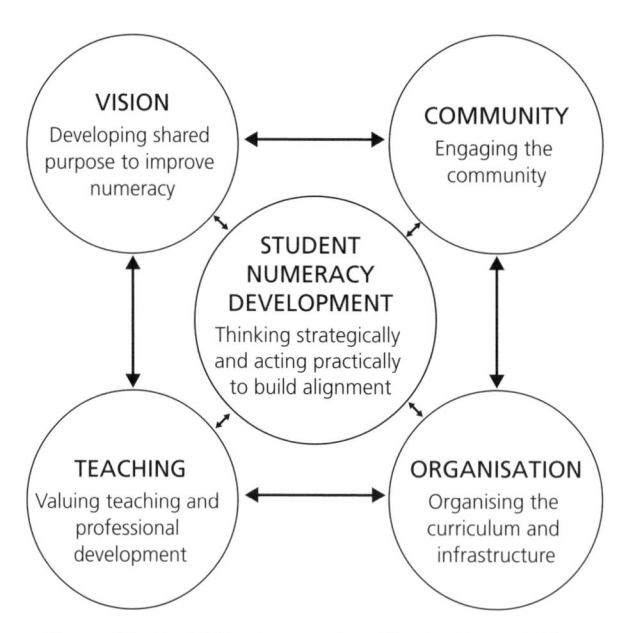

Figure 4.2: The LAND framework and leadership capabilities

provided a basis for examining the nature and effect of their leadership on student numeracy development. In fact, enhancing each of the LAND framework elements (vision, teaching, organisation, community and outcomes) and strengthening the connections between them was the leadership challenge of the LAND project.

Professional learning for leading numeracy development

Professional learning in the LAND project took many forms: from externally facilitated events, conferences and workshops to local school and classroom-based discussions, school visits, peer demonstrations and professional learning community meetings led by principals and teachers. One of the main vehicles for professional learning was a series of workshops. The LAND schools committed to participating in a series of four two- to three-day workshops and associated follow-up work across their two-year period of engagement with the project.

A key element of this commitment was the formation of a LAND school leadership team. Each team consisted of the principal and two or three teachers. In some cases these teaching staff were experienced and held formal positions of responsibility (for example, a numeracy coordinator). In other cases, they were new to the school or the profession, and looked to their involvement in LAND as a means of developing their knowledge and skill in leading numeracy development. The composition of the LAND school leadership teams was based on the premise that sustained improvement in student numeracy achievement at the school level requires a combination of principal and teacher leadership and that each has something important to contribute – teachers from their pedagogical base and day-to-day classroom practice, and principals from their school-wide organisational perspective.

Each workshop was designed and delivered by the ACU LAND project team in collaboration with the LAND project officers and the LAND school leadership teams, and consisted of a combination of input, interactive activity and planning opportunities for each school team. The content and the processes used in the workshop series drew upon the expertise and experience of the ACU team in mathematics education and in educational leadership research; and expertise and experience of the project officers and teacher and principal participants in classroom, school and system numeracy development. This meant that ideas, research, approaches and issues associated with effective mathematics teaching and numeracy achievement were always closely integrated with the theory, research and practice of educational leadership.

This combination of perspectives and insights had several advantages. First, it provided the opportunity for teacher participants to learn about leadership of numeracy development from the principal's perspective: that is, what is involved in leading and managing improvement at the school level. Secondly, it gave principals the opportunity to refresh their thinking about mathematics teaching, put themselves in the shoes of their teachers, and expand their pedagogical content knowledge of mathematics teaching and student numeracy development. Thirdly, the integrated focus of the LAND workshops brought the ACU research team together in unusual ways. It encouraged us to look closely at our discipline (whether this was mathematics education or educational leadership) and at our colleagues' discipline and, as a result, gain a deeper appreciation of the potential and the consequences of approaching the complex problem of how to achieve sustainable systemic development in numeracy from a cross-disciplinary perspective. In essence, the educational leadership component provided the strategic capability to disseminate and embed principles of effective teaching of mathematics and bring about numeracy development within and beyond the classroom, while issues of student numeracy achievement and the teaching focus of the mathematics education component gave substance to the exercise of school leadership. Along with this, the workshop participation of the LAND project officer from each central office was vital for workshop planning, delivery and review, and for providing strategic and practical advice and follow-up support to the LAND school leadership teams and the ACU research team (see Chapter 7 for more detail on the role of LAND project officers).

Let's now look more closely at the educational leadership component in each workshop.

The primary focus of Workshop 1 was leading learning to bring about whole-school numeracy development. Research literature on the connection between educational leadership and school improvement was used as the basis for considering various leadership capabilities and roles of school leaders: for example, as visionaries, as leading teachers and learners, as community developers and as organisers. Emphasis was placed on the role of school leader in promoting and strengthening the alignment between the vision for numeracy, the agreed principles and practice of effective mathematics teaching, the engagement of the school community and school organisational elements (for example, curriculum, staffing, infrastructure and financial resources) to support improved student achievement in numeracy. Workshop 1 also included an introduction to school planning for improving numeracy, as well as a self-reflective instrument that tapped into the personal, professional and peer-related aspects of leadership as a process of influencing student learning. The resources used for these planning and reflection activities were adapted from the Leaders Transforming Learning and Learners Project (LTLL – Bezzina & Burford, 2010) and are presented in Appendix 3. LTLL, conducted by researchers from the Centre for Creative and Authentic Leadership at the Australian Catholic University, investigated ways in which leaders promote learning in values-based school environments (Bezzina, 2008). Because of its focus on values-based leadership action, LTLL provided a useful reference point for the LAND research. Its ideological underpinnings were similar to that of the LAND project with its values-based purpose of improving the numeracy achievement of students living in communities with low socioeconomic status. The planning and reflection activities at the conclusion of Workshop 1 provided the basis for follow-up activity of the LAND school leadership teams in their schools in preparation for Workshop 2 to be held four months later.

The leadership component of the second LAND workshop had a dual focus on the importance of 'knowing yourself' and 'achieving values alignment' among members of the participants' school community when leading others in educational change processes. The workshop included opportunities for developing self-awareness with particular emphasis on notions of self-concept, self-esteem, motives, values, beliefs and ultimately behaviours using the model of self developed by Branson (2009, 2010). A variety of approaches to leading change were discussed, including the technical, social, cultural and political aspects of the phenomenon. These discussions were based on three key ideas:

- leading numeracy development is leading education change
- change happens as people find meaning
- leaders help people find meaning by building capacity.

Building capacity involves leaders in encouraging meaningful involvement of staff, in being flexible and adaptable and in promoting organisational learning and internal accountability (that is, responsibility to oneself, one's students and one's colleagues). The approach that was hence taken to leading numeracy development highlighted the need to build shared understandings among the LAND school leadership team members and their colleague staff members. This involved investigating the values that were held and working through a process whereby shared values could be identified and used as a basis for further action. The process used for identifying these values and achieving values alignment among the LAND school leadership team members was based on the work of Branson (2009, 2010) and is detailed in Appendix 4.

The material considered in Workshop 2 was used to refine the LAND school leadership team plans. These refinements tended to concentrate on how best to lead in relation to the emotional dimension of educational change: that is, helping colleagues to find meaning in their current practices and in the possibilities for developing their thinking and practice in relation to student numeracy achievement.

By the time Workshop 3 was held (some four months after Workshop 2 and eight months after the commencement of the project), the LAND schools were well advanced with their plans and were beginning to consider data about progress. As a consequence, one of the emphases of the third workshop was on gathering, analysing and using evidence. For a number of schools, this included investigating the effects of various forms of intervention that had either preceded or been adopted after the commencement of the LAND project. Accordingly, some workshop time was spent looking at the purpose and nature of different numeracy interventions and issues associated with validity, and the reliability of evidence of their effect.

A closely connected emphasis in Workshop 3 related directly to the proposed transformational leadership capability of thinking strategically and acting practically to build alignment between the LAND framework elements of vision, teaching, organisation and community to develop and to sustain higher levels of student numeracy achievement. This involved the explanation and use of a process known as 'causal mapping', introduced as a means of investigating the nature of cause and effect relating to the 'wicked policy problem' of raising and sustaining student achievement in numeracy. Causal mapping was seen as a way of demonstrating how strategic thinking can be developed and lead to practical action by school leadership teams. The process of causal mapping and the resultant findings on how the LAND school team members viewed the causes and effects related to improving student numeracy achievement are described in Chapter 8.

A third element of Workshop 3 emphasised the significance of the LAND school team members working with the school community, especially parents.

The relational leadership capability of engaging the community was explored through the application of research literature to school case studies of community development and parental involvement. Concepts and understandings relating to community engagement were practically enacted through the organisation and delivery of parent information nights held at LAND project schools as a part of the workshop experience. This topic is covered in detail in Chapter 5.

The final workshop took place some 18 months after the commencement of the LAND workshop series. The focus of this fourth workshop was to provide opportunity for the LAND school teams to share their learning from the LAND project. The workshop took the form of a series of showcase presentations, with time for discussion and feedback from peers, from other LAND school teams, from the LAND project officers and from the ACU research team. Instead of the usual four workshop sites, two pairs of clusters (the Western Australian clusters – Perth and Kimberley – and the South Australian and the Northern Territory clusters) came together to share their experiences. As part of their presentation, each LAND school leadership team was asked to present their draft Charter for the Effective Teaching of Mathematics. This took the form of a statement, written specifically for their school community, that comprised a set of principles of effective teaching together with a rationale for each principle, along the following lines: 'We believe that effective teaching of Mathematics at [name of school] is evidenced by [stated principle] … because … [reason for the principle]'.

The intention of the charters was to serve as a reference point for sustaining effective teaching practices beyond the period of the LAND project. During their presentation, the LAND school teams described how these statements were developed in consultation with their teacher colleagues, and then explained, based on their experiences in the LAND project, how they intended to sustain development of student numeracy achievement at their schools. Each school also formulated recommendations about future directions for systemic numeracy development for consideration by their education authority (see Chapter 10 for further detail).

The content relating to the theory and practice of educational leadership treated in the LAND workshop series is summarised in Table 4.1.

Determining capabilities for leading numeracy development

What capabilities are required for leading numeracy development in schools? What specific actions linked to these capabilities do principals, teacher leaders and school leadership teams take and what effects do these have on the quality of mathematics teaching and the levels of student numeracy achievement in

Table 4.1: Educational leadership theory and practice by LAND workshop

Workshop	Content: theory and practice of educational leadership
1 Leading learning and school-wide improvement in student numeracy	The nature of educational leadership and links to school improvement. The educational leader as visionary, leading teacher and learner, community developer and organiser. The role of educational leader in aligning outcomes, vision, shared principles and practice of effective mathematics teaching, and school organisational elements (curriculum, staffing, infrastructure and financial resources) to support improved student achievement in numeracy. Introduction to school planning for improving numeracy.
2 Knowing self and leading others in educational change processes	The person of the leader and the investigation of the components of 'the self' including self-concept, self-esteem, motives, values, beliefs and behaviours. Developing consensus and shared understandings with others around improving student learning. Perspectives in leading educational change (technical, social, cultural and political). Factors that support effective change including identification and alignment of values within the school community.
3 Working with evidence and engaging the community	The significance of evidence and the collection, analysis and use of data. The nature and impact of numeracy interventions and issues associated with validity and reliability of evidence. The process of causal mapping as a means to examine the nature of cause and effect relating to the 'wicked policy problem' of raising and sustaining student achievement in numeracy. The leadership capability of 'engaging the community' explored through school case studies, and demonstrated through the organisation and delivery of parent information nights held at LAND school sites.
4 Aligning the LAND experience and sustaining valued practice	School leadership team presentations on their LAND project journey noting the achievements and issues encountered in bringing about improvement in student numeracy achievement, and including the Charter for Effective Teaching of Mathematics at [their school]. This charter includes principles of effective teaching and reasons underpinning those principles. LAND school leadership teams indicate how they intend to sustain development of student numeracy achievement at their school and make recommendations to their education authority regarding system numeracy policy and programs.

the school? The research component of the educational leadership strand of the LAND project sought to answer these questions. The focus of the research was to investigate how various leadership capabilities and associated actions of LAND school leadership team members influenced the teaching of mathematics and student numeracy achievement in their schools. A set of five dimensions of leadership capability was identified from the research literature linking school leadership with improved student learning outcomes. These five dimensions (personal, professional, organisational, relational and transformational) were aligned with the LAND framework, as shown in Figure 4.2. They provided the basis for naming and categorising the actions of the LAND school leadership team members.

Researching leadership capabilities and actions associated with leading numeracy development required access to a range of data sources. In order to develop an appropriate set of data, a combination of participant surveys, field-work observation and facilitation strategies were used. The Leadership Capability Development Survey was administered at the conclusion of Workshop 3; the LAND Participant Perception Survey was administered three times during the project period: at the beginning, the midpoint and the end of the workshop series. An online survey tool was used for ease of response and analysis. The LAND Participant Perception Survey covered the following issues:

- the perceived priority of numeracy achievement in class, school and central office
- the extent to which the school was perceived to have a common purpose in numeracy
- the extent to which professional development at school level and central office level was seen as assisting teachers
- perceptions of school leaders (principals and others in positions of authority at school level) and central office support and encouragement
- perceptions of school leaders and the challenge for central office
- the degree to which participants saw themselves as reflective practitioners.

Finally, participants were asked to rate numeracy achievement in their school, and their confidence in their roles as mathematics educators and as leaders of numeracy development. For a variety of reasons, including some instability in LAND school leadership team membership, only nine of the 17 schools completed all three rounds of the survey. In the interest of using data that are robust, only these nine schools are included in the data discussed in this chapter. For the purposes of comparison, data from individual respondents were averaged for each school.

In addition, research team members made observational notes during the workshops and school visits, undertook content analyses of school presentations and facilitated structured discussions with LAND school leadership teams about the significance of each dimension of leadership capability and the types of actions associated with each.

A draft listing of actions categorised under particular leadership dimensions was developed using data collected from the surveys, observational notes and content analyses of school presentations. In the final workshop, after their showcase presentations, LAND school leadership teams were invited to reflect on their experience of the LAND project as a whole and consider the draft listing of leadership actions, using the protocol described in the box.

Determining capabilities and actions for leading numeracy development

The purpose of this exercise is to identify and analyse the significant educational leadership capabilities and actions that contributed to the outcomes achieved in the LAND project.

Reflect on your observations of the school presentations from the point of view of the leadership capabilities and actions that were in evidence:

- Choose one dimension of educational leadership capability (from those listed).
- Identify what actions (from those listed) were evident.
- What other actions (i.e. those not listed) were evident?
- What are the 2–3 most significant actions associated with this area of capability? Why are they significant?

Once you have considered this leadership dimension in detail, please choose another to discuss.

Each LAND school team then gave a report of its discussion in response to the questions on the protocol. The responses to the questions from each team were noted and synthesised, allowing the draft listing to be refined. The research team facilitated discussion, inviting questions and comments from the entire participant group as particular actions were explained, added, deleted, reworded or combined with others until consensus was reached regarding the final listing (see Table 4.2).

The research methodology used in the LAND project to determine the types of capabilities and actions required for leading numeracy development in schools was successful in that it enabled the trailing of a draft listing and the subsequent validation by the LAND school leadership team members on the basis of their experience in the project. The capabilities and actions listed in Table 4.2 represent a tangible and potentially useful outcome of the LAND project. We believe that they can be used by principals, teacher leaders and school leadership teams as a reference point for leading numeracy development in school settings.

Table 4.2: Leadership capabilities and actions for developing numeracy

Leadership capability	Action
Personal – developing shared purpose to improve numeracy	• Setting high personal expectations for numeracy teaching practices and student achievement • Encouraging high expectations in others • Building consensus on goals for numeracy development • Communicating the goals for numeracy development • Being clear and consistent in regard to leadership roles and responsibilities • Developing and exercising teamwork and shared accountability with and among teachers
Professional – valuing teaching and professional development	• Supporting, developing and evaluating teaching quality • Participating with teachers in professional development • Observing classroom teaching and providing specific feedback • Developing knowledge about numeracy learning and teaching • Promoting skills in data analysis and interpretation among teachers • Ensuring that teachers are engaged in worthwhile professional learning
Organisational – organising curriculum and infrastructure	• Ensuring that numeracy achievement goals are embedded in school and classroom routines • Designing school organisational structures to support teachers and learners • Participating in curriculum decision-making • Monitoring numeracy development and the mathematics curriculum for quality, balance and integration • Managing resources by aligning funds with school numeracy priorities • Applying resources to improve the conditions for teaching and learning
Relational – engaging the community	• Understanding and respecting difference among teachers, students and other members of the school community • Displaying interest in student and teacher work and achievements • Involving parents in the school numeracy programs • Encouraging community support to improve numeracy • Networking with other schools and teachers about numeracy and leadership • Seeking advice from researchers, practitioners and other professionals beyond the school about numeracy and leadership
Transformational – thinking strategically and acting practically to build alignment between outcomes, vision, teaching, organisation and community	• Fostering discussion about numeracy outcomes, causes and strategies • Emphasising improved numeracy as the motivation for discussion • Developing shared understanding of outcomes, purposes, teaching quality and professional learning, community characteristics and engagement, curriculum and infrastructure – and how these components align with each other to support numeracy • Implementing strategies to improve student numeracy achievement as the outcome of discussions • Ensuring systematic monitoring of student learning • Evaluating numeracy outcomes and teaching practices on a strong evidence base of qualitative and quantitative data

Source: Gaffney (2012) , p. 32

Building capabilities for leading numeracy development

How effective was the LAND project in building participants' capabilities for leading numeracy development? Evidence gathered through the Leadership Capability Development Survey administered at the conclusion of Workshop 3 indicates that it had a positive effect on the ability of LAND school team members to lead numeracy development. The survey used a 6-point Likert scale, with a score of 1 indicating that it had contributed 'Not at all' and a score of 6 indicating 'A great deal'. The results are presented in Table 4.3.

Table 4.3: Growth in LAND school team capability to lead numeracy development (%)

Through the workshop series, I have developed ...	1 (not at all)	2	3	4	5	6 (a great deal)
my appreciation of myself as a leader – who I am, what motivates me, what I value, what I believe, and how I behave	–	–	–	21	48	31
my appreciation of what it takes to lead change in schools	–	–	–	20	39	41
my confidence in working with others in bringing about numeracy development in my school	–	–	–	35	43	22
my ability to engage others and develop shared understanding about our purposes and processes in numeracy in the school	–	–	–	26	65	9
my skills in using data and evidence	–	–	–	26	52	22

These findings indicate that LAND school team members believe that they developed their sense of themselves as leaders and what it takes to lead change in schools. This includes their confidence and ability to work with others in building shared understanding and approaches to numeracy development. They also believe their skills in using data and evidence were developed to a significant extent. These findings were supported by a number of comments from participants:

> I feel that our little LAND team is going to go places in regard to being able to support and challenge our staff and to support and challenge our students.

> I have taken a great deal of information from most of the workshops. I know that it made me think about myself as a leader and not just looking at how I lead others but how I lead myself – those things about myself that make me do things the way I do.

The challenges in leading numeracy development were also evident, particularly the need for continuing school executive support in building teacher confidence in teaching mathematics; as one LAND school team member noted: 'There is still a reluctance to change among some teachers'.

Related evidence gathered during workshops and school visits supports the view that the LAND project had a positive effect on the development of leadership capability of the LAND school team members. In the following sections, we describe the nature and development of leadership capability across each of the dimensions listed in Table 4.2.

Developing shared purpose to improve numeracy

The development of shared purpose has repeatedly been shown to be a key element in the leadership of change in schools, in the nurturing of shared leadership and in changing teacher practice for enhanced learning (Bezzina, 2007; Bezzina & Burford, 2010; Fullan, 2002). One of the key issues in discussion of purpose is that for it to be shared, it must be explicit and understood (Bezzina, 2007). These features are evident in the actions, listed in Table 4.2, that focus on the importance of building consensus, communicating goals, high expectations, role clarity and consistency, teamwork and shared accountability. These are some sample comments related to these actions made by LAND school team members during the showcase presentations: 'We are making numeracy an important focus and developing passion for addressing students' numeracy learning. We are making positive changes as a result of low scores'; 'Staff have a common sense of the vision'; 'Numeracy is now a high priority'; 'There is a great team, with lots of communication. There is a focus and purpose to improve; and to achieve the right balance across all learning areas'; '[The principal] realised there was need for improvement and acted on it, we looked at it as a shared leadership challenge and a need to change attitudes'; and 'There's a developing stability and commitment of younger staff'.

The growth of leadership capability evident in these comments was generally reflected in the trends noted in responses to the LAND Participant Perception Survey. Initial responses to this survey indicated that schools rated the extent to which they had a shared purpose about numeracy teaching and learning (on a scale from 1 to 6) across a range from 2 to 4.7. Different schools had different mean scores on 'shared purpose'. For those schools with complete data sets, the initial exposure to LAND led to an improved perception of shared purpose from inception to midpoint for six schools, and a lower rating for three, while eight of the nine improved across the life of the project (with one remaining unchanged). School average ratings after the third use of the self-perception instrument ranged from 4 to 6, which might be characterised as 'moderate' to 'strong'. It is conceivable, although not tested in the LAND research, that the dip in ratings at the midpoint of the project was a result of an increased appreciation of, and sensitivity to, the issues of shared purpose – and, hence, a more critical approach to self-rating.

Findings from the school visits also provided some interesting insights, especially in relation to the role of the principal. For example:

- Where the principal was involved and expressed understanding and a vision for numeracy learning, shared purpose developed more readily (Kimberley school cluster).
- Greater stability in LAND school leadership team membership and direct involvement by the principal facilitated more pronounced growth in shared purpose and expectations (Northern Territory, Indigenous, Catholic community cluster).
- Schools where principals genuinely worked with teacher leaders in LAND teams had a clearer sense of direction and teacher leaders had higher efficacy (Adelaide school cluster).

A common thread across all LAND project sites (and especially evident in the Perth school cluster) was that LAND provided a strategic vehicle for enhancing the profile of numeracy and therefore helped all schools develop a shared purpose and understanding with regard to numeracy achievement. The LAND school leadership team members were responsible for this and each developed their capability in this dimension of leading numeracy development in the process.

Valuing teaching and professional development

Teacher professional development has long been regarded as a key element in enhancing teaching and learning (Sparks, 2002). The importance of school leaders, especially principals, in taking a key role in professional development has been established in recent meta-analyses of the research (Robinson et al., 2009). This professional dimension of the leadership capability of school leaders valuing teaching and professional development was described through the actions listed in Table 4.2. It emphasises teacher quality and professional learning through school leaders participating with teachers in professional development, engaging in classroom observation, developing their pedagogical content knowledge and their skills in data analysis and sharing this with their teachers. Evidence of these actions was apparent in the comments of LAND school leadership team members during their showcase presentations: 'The school has concentrated on how maths lessons are delivered'; 'We are focusing on engagement of assistant teachers and the building of capacity of all staff'; 'There has been a deliberate move away from textbooks, and some teachers are unsure of the implications for their teaching'; 'Over recent times, there has been a move to provide more constructive support. This is evidenced by shifts in the role and use of teacher aides'; and 'There is now equality of literacy and numeracy in professional learning community meetings'.

The LAND Participant Perception Survey asked respondents to rate the extent to which school- and system-level professional development was of assistance to them. Initial ratings (on a scale of 1 to 6) of the extent to which school professional development assisted teachers yielded a mean of 4.2 (range from 2.7 to 5.5), while those of the extent to which system professional development was helpful yielded a mean of 4.0 with a range from 3.3 to 5. The sample is too small to make statistical conclusions but it appears that initial perceptions of system-level professional development were lower than those at school level. Seven of the nine schools improved their ratings of system professional development from the start to the midpoint, but five of these fell back slightly between the midpoint and the final rating. Once again, this may have been due to some specific incident in system professional development at that time, or to increasing sophistication of understanding of professional development needs. In any case, seven of the nine schools ended up with an improved perception of system professional development – albeit slight in some cases.

Perceptions of school professional development reflected a decline in ratings of the level of assistance to the midpoint of the project for four of the nine schools, but overall (start to finish) improved perceptions for seven schools – in three cases a mean improvement of 2 or more points on the rating scale. Given the activities related to LAND that were being implemented in each school, there is a high probability that these activities contributed in some way to these perceptions. This assertion is supported by comments cited above from the showcase presentations. It is worthwhile noting that these comments have a very practical emphasis – that is, on what actually happens 'in the thick of classroom teaching'.

This professional dimension of leadership capability has to do with the extent to which school leaders are seen to value teaching. One item on the LAND Participant Perception Survey asked teachers in the LAND school leadership teams to rate the extent to which their leaders (principals and others in positions of authority at school level) support and encourage them. Another item asked about the extent to which their leaders challenge them. These items were drawn from Fullan's (2002) emphasis on pressure and support as means of bringing about change in schools. The ways that school leaders exercise pressure and provide support can be viewed as an indication of how they value teaching and professional development.

Initial school mean ratings of the extent to which school leaders encouraged them ranged from 3.7 to 6 (moderate to high) and final ratings ranged from 5 to 6 (high) reflecting perceptions that schools were starting from quite a strong place, but that the engagement with LAND had moved them in a positive direction. Six of the nine schools showed improved ratings from start to finish, and those that did not showed only very small declines. With respect to the perceptions of challenge by leaders, ratings ranged from 2 to 5.3 (low to high) with final ratings from 4 to 6 (moderate to high). Only four schools noted an improvement in the level of challenge by leaders in the course of the project. It would seem that the leaders in the LAND project schools were more likely to demonstrate the way in which they value teaching through support and encouragement than through challenge, and that the project resulted in less improvement in this regard for challenge than it did for support.

Further insights on the development and exercise of the professional capabilities related to the valuing of teaching and professional development, gleaned from school visits by research team members, were as follows:

- professional learning community meetings were used to develop agreed principles and model practice (Perth school cluster)
- peer classroom observation increased as the project progressed (Perth school cluster)
- LAND school team capability to effect changes in teaching practice across the school was determined more by its direct focus on pedagogy than by work in curriculum planning, assessment and organising resources (Kimberley school cluster)
- LAND teams that deliberately structured time and space to bring teachers together, and *together* advocated a consistent message and priority for numeracy effected more change in teacher attitude and practice (Adelaide school cluster)
- access to a blend of timely external expertise, and internal context knowledge and follow-through capability helped in sustaining the focus on numeracy development (Northern Territory Indigenous Catholic community cluster).

These findings emphasise the value of school leaders providing space and time for collaborative, classroom practice–oriented professional development opportunities, as well as taking a longer term strategic view in terms of how to use external expertise as a means of sustaining momentum. Of further note was the finding that, as the project progressed, the norms of professional learning were modified for the better. In this case, it involved the opening up of teaching practice through classroom observation.

A common characteristic of the LAND school leadership teams was the way that the members (principals and teacher leaders) worked collaboratively and complemented each other in the manner in which they valued teaching and professional development. The important point was that through their team leadership the strategic and practical elements of this capability for leading numeracy development came to the fore.

Organising curriculum and infrastructure

The way that schools are organised has a big effect on what and how teachers teach and what and how students learn. The organisational dimension of leadership capability is focused on how a school's organisational arrangements can be made more conducive for effective teaching and learning. The actions of school leaders that were identified through the LAND project as associated with this dimension related to organising the school curriculum and infrastructure, and included ensuring numeracy achievement goals were embedded in school and classroom routines, designing supportive organisational structures (including timetables), monitoring numeracy programs and managing resources for effect and efficiency, and participating in decisions about curriculum, particularly in the areas of mathematics and numeracy (see Table 4.2). Some of these organisational aspects were evident in the comments of LAND school leadership team members in their showcase presentations: 'There are numeracy teams and scheduled time for numeracy'; 'There is dedicated numeracy time each day (between 45 and 60 minutes)'; 'Timetabling and integration of curriculum with numeracy dedicated time are happening'.

Other insights on school-level actions related to the organisational dimension were noted through school visits. These related to areas such as the appointment of specially designated staff in numeracy (either from Australian Government National Partnership Program supplementary funding or through reorganising existing general recurrent funding), and the auditing and purchasing of mathematics resources. The role of principals in these types of decisions was vital, as is indicated by the following observations by researchers:

- Actions by the principal (especially in relation to structural changes and resourcing decisions) facilitated the development of shared purpose, teaching quality and sense of community (Perth school cluster).
- Decision-making by the principal in consultation with LAND school team members that recognised connections between various government and system priorities and numeracy programs (including National Partnership Program) assisted in aligning efforts and generating efficiencies (Kimberley school cluster).

Similarly the organisational dimension of leadership was apparent in the types of decisions made about staffing. For example:

- Having a dedicated position (as a LAND school leadership team member) responsible for, firstly, curriculum and resource planning, and, secondly, coordinating and validating student assessment is reaping benefits (Northern Territory Indigenous Catholic community cluster).

- Schools with dedicated National Partnership numeracy positions are progressing further in developing school-wide teaching practice (Adelaide school cluster).

The key finding relating to the exercise of leadership in organising the curriculum and infrastructure was that LAND school leadership teams that did it well always linked their decisions about resources and staffing arrangements to their core purpose of improving numeracy and what, therefore, needed to happen to best support their teacher colleagues in this task.

Engaging the community

The relational dimension of leadership capability highlights the view of renowned management theorist Henry Mintzberg (2009) that an effective organisation is a community of human beings not a collection of human resources. This view was foundational in the design of the LAND project. LAND was firmly based on the assumption that sustainable numeracy development requires engagement by the school community, especially the teachers and parents – and ultimately the students – in deciding and supporting the purposes and approaches used for mathematics teaching and learning.

In practical terms, the LAND school leadership team members demonstrated this dimension of leadership capability through understanding and respecting differences among members of their school community, displaying interest in students' and teachers' work and achievements, involving parents in numeracy programs, and in networking and seeking advice from beyond the school (see Table 4.2). These actions were evident in the following comments of LAND school leadership team members during their showcase presentations: 'The whole school is involved in maths'; 'Achievement is celebrated with the school community and there is an enthusiasm from students' improvement in all years'; 'There's a desire from teaching staff for more engagement with the wider school community to improve numeracy outcomes'; 'There's been a change of attitude towards maths from parents, teachers and students'; 'We are having a Maths Day'; and 'We are interested in developing parent and community engagement'. These comments highlight the features of schools where the community has come alive with interest and possibilities for their students' and children's interest in mathematics and their numeracy achievements. More generally, they demonstrate that engaging the community is a vital component of sustainable numeracy development. They reflect the following findings of researchers who visited these schools over the period of the project:

- All schools acknowledged the role of parents as one component of the school community and deeper understanding of parent expectation and greater parent involvement are higher priorities as a result of LAND (Perth school cluster).
- Fostering engagement of assistant teachers, parents and other community members is seen as the next stage in leading aligned numeracy development. Investigation and development of homework practice is a related area of interest (Kimberley school cluster).
- School LAND teams that can deal with both the educational-professional *and* the community-relational leadership dimensions are building stronger community engagement as evidenced by more assistant teacher involvement and realising greater learning gains for students (Northern Territory Indigenous Catholic community cluster).
- There is genuine motivation among LAND school teams to build community – professionally and with parents. At times these school teams require and benefit from external feedback and advice about their achievements to maintain motivation (Adelaide school cluster).

The LAND experience has shown that taking deliberate steps to engage the community, especially parents, can be a powerful support for children's interest and achievement in numeracy. Successful LAND school leadership teams recognised this and considered how best to organise their schools to foster such involvement, from running parent nights to engaging parents and other family members as tutors and assistant teachers (see Chapter 5 for more detail).

Thinking strategically and acting practically to build alignment

The fifth dimension of capability for leading numeracy development involves thinking and taking action to bring the key elements of numeracy development together so that transformation in teaching and learning can take place. This transformational dimension focuses on school leaders fostering discussions about causes and effects of student numeracy achievement, developing shared understandings among members of the school community (and the system as a whole) about what is required for sustainable improvement in numeracy, and evaluating outcomes and intervention strategies on a strong evidence base (see Table 4.2). These types of actions were evident in the following comments made by LAND school leadership team members during their showcase presentations: 'There is a developing coherence in offerings, organisation, and shared vision'; 'The strategy focus each week is a great idea!! Assessment changes have a positive meaning for staff'; 'There are more assessments through the year, and the analysis of student data now has a whole school focus. Whole school timetable changes for numeracy blocks'; and 'There's a shared desire to raise numeracy achievement and audit resources'. These comments demonstrate that connections are being made between what is happening in classrooms and how this is supported strategically within the school. In other words, we are referring to members of the LAND school leadership team developing their transformational leadership capabilities. These developments were noted by researchers in their school visits to various clusters. For example:

- All LAND school teams applied strategic thinking and took action to bring about alignment necessary for whole-school development in numeracy (Perth school cluster).
- The capability of the principal to think strategically and lead discussions on alignment with leadership team members is critical to developing numeracy in their school community (Kimberley school cluster).

An important aspect of the LAND school leadership team dynamic was the ability of team members to work together. Researchers, from their school visits, noted the following findings where there was evidence and blending of principal and teacher leadership:

- Links between priorities were more readily identified and the consequent alignment improves efficiency (Northern Territory Indigenous Catholic community cluster).
- LAND school leadership teams progressed more strategically and with tighter alignment of priorities (Adelaide school cluster).

In contrast, those schools that progressed more slowly either perceived themselves as suffering from 'priority overload' or were 'seeking answers' from elsewhere and, at times, 'anywhere'. The leadership dynamic in these LAND school leadership teams was not as conducive to the development and enactment of strategic thinking and practical action as some other teams.

One of the related issues with the transformational dimension of leadership is the mindsets and actions of leaders at different 'levels' in the system (classroom, school, central office and government) and how these qualities are aligned (Fullan & Barber, 2005). Two particular areas of alignment were explored in the LAND Participant Perception Survey. One related to the extent to which numeracy was seen as a priority at classroom, school and central office level by respondents. The other was concerned with the extent to which support and challenge at school level matched that at central office level.

In relation to the first item regarding the priority given to numeracy, the average ratings given at the start of the project for priority at classroom, school and central office levels were: 5.4, 4.5 and 4.1 respectively. Not surprisingly perhaps, the further from the classroom, the lower the perceived priority. Over the duration of the LAND project, the priority on numeracy attributed at all three levels increased to 5.7 (up 0.3) for the classroom, 5.3 (up 0.8) for the school and 5.0 (up 0.9) for the system. In other words, the priority increased and the gap in priority across the three levels narrowed over the period of the project. From these findings, it may be that LAND – as an example of a central office–sponsored activity affecting the whole of school – created a greater degree of alignment, at least in the minds of those entrusted with the key work of teaching and leading in schools.

Regarding the second issue of perceived support and challenge at school and central office levels, across all schools at the start of the LAND project, the average rating for support and encouragement for school leaders was 4.8, which improved to 5.3 by the end. On the other hand, central office level support was rated at 4.2 and 4.3 respectively. So while there has been a greater alignment across levels for priority, the gap has actually increased with respect to support. In terms of challenge, school leaders moved from an average of 4.4 to 5.0, while the central office challenge moved from 4.0 to 4.5. While both improved, the level of alignment remained fundamentally unchanged.

Summary insights for leading numeracy development

The LAND project had a positive effect on the leadership capabilities of the principals and teachers in the LAND school teams. This is based on the analysis of the qualitative and quantitative LAND school leadership team data. The findings demonstrate that LAND school leadership team members became more discerning in their observations and more confident in their leadership of numeracy development in their school communities. They highlight the diversity of school contexts and LAND school team leadership capability development evident within and across the four clusters of project schools. Several themes emerge from this diversity:

- The capabilities and actions for leading numeracy development drawn from the research literature were validated by the LAND school leadership team participants and can serve as a reference point for further school leadership practice and for further research.
- The leadership role of the principal is crucial. Where principals expressed their vision for numeracy development, made decisions in consultation with other LAND school leadership team members about supporting infrastructure, and had (or were able to develop) the capability to link various priorities and programs at school and system level (their 'transformational' capability),

the work of the LAND school leadership team was greatly facilitated and the school community progressed in numeracy understanding and performance.

- The involvement of teacher leaders as members of LAND school leadership teams helped to blend the pedagogical and organisational elements required to develop shared purpose and principles of practice for numeracy development.
- The engagement of the parent community is an important but sequential priority. LAND school leadership teams saw the value of parent involvement and recognised that this should be encouraged in a timely fashion (after teachers have developed a solid and shared understanding of effective teaching practice, and the principles and priorities upon which to base such parent involvement). The timeline of the LAND project meant that schools were only beginning to make inroads on this dimension toward the end of the project period.
- Participation by schools in projects supported by central office (like LAND) has the potential to build consensus about the priority given to system initiatives; where 'system' refers to 'the whole' including classroom, school and central office. This requires principals and teacher leaders (and those working in central offices) to develop a system mindset that incorporates an appreciation of different perspectives held by people across the system and a desire to build better understanding and alignment in effort. This type of leadership certainly calls upon the transformational dimension of leadership capability.

From the ideas and findings presented in this chapter, we conclude that leading numeracy development at the school community level requires a sustained team effort. It demands the support and involvement of principals and teacher leaders, as well as their desire and capacity to engage teachers and parents in working with their students and children to bring about better learning outcomes. In other words, quality mathematics teaching and higher levels of student achievement in numeracy can only happen when teachers and principals collaborate to ensure their vision and purpose are shared, and their approach to teaching, school–community relationships and organisational arrangements all work together to support student learning.

CHAPTER 5

ENGAGING SCHOOL COMMUNITIES WITH NUMERACY

Doug Clarke, Rhonda Faragher and Michael Gaffney

St Polymath Primary School lies on the outskirts of Capital City. Its community is not particularly well off. In fact, house prices in the surrounding suburbs are among the lowest in the country. The area therefore attracts many younger families and first homebuyers. There are a couple of immigrant hostels nearby, meaning the school has a steady stream of students who are 'newly arrived' and mostly from non-English-speaking countries. Just over 25 per cent of the students are identified as Indigenous. The school community also has a relatively high proportion of students from single-parent families or subject to joint custody Family Court rulings. The school's outer suburban location means that the daily commute for those parents who are working is over an hour each way. The before- and after-school care facilities are in high demand.

The school has been open for six years and has had a strong and consistent enrolment growth over that time. According to the planners in the central office, this is due to the continuing house construction in the surrounding areas and the role that the principal and her staff have played in connecting the school with its community. The principal, Ms Fab, has been there since the beginning and has adopted a policy of employing early career teachers, partly out of choice and partly out of necessity. Her school is not that attractive to experienced teachers living closer to town.

On the other hand, younger teachers jump at the chance to work at St Polymath. It has a reputation as being a really vibrant place to teach. Some teachers have said that simply by being on the staff you can become a better teacher. Everyone places a lot of value on working together and sharing ideas and practices. The principal makes a point of supporting professional learning and development. She builds time and space into the week for teachers to collaboratively plan and observe one another's classes. Every second week, they run Professional Learning Community meetings for an hour after school. Various people take turns in leading these sessions. Very occasionally, they bring in someone from outside. The meetings have a clear focus on outcomes and evidence, what teachers expect their students to learn, and the teaching practices that can help students achieve those outcomes.

Tonight Ms Fab and her staff are running a parent night with the theme 'Helping my child understand maths: Count me in!' The school runs these nights at least twice a year – and they are always well attended, despite the challenge of attracting parents back to the school after dinner.

As Ms Fab was arranging the tables, the digital projector and sound system with several of the teachers, one of the first parents to arrive remarked: 'We are not going to have a test are we?' As the evening progressed, his anxiety, along with that of the other parents, lessened. As he was having supper afterwards, he came over to his child's teacher and said, 'Thanks. This is the first time I've ever been to something like this. I've now got a couple of ideas to help Mike with his maths'.

Introduction

Engaging school communities with numeracy can be considered from a range of perspectives. In this chapter, two of the most prominent are examined. First the concept and practice of professional learning communities of teachers, through drawing on the research literature and the development and functioning of these communities in the LAND project, are considered. Next we examine the role and importance of parents, and illustrate some ways, trialled through the LAND project, in which school staff can engage parents in supporting their child's numeracy development. These perspectives provide the basis for discussing the opportunities and demands associated with engaging school communities in challenging contexts. Here the experiences with LAND schools in low socioeconomic status communities and remote locations in particular are drawn upon.

The chapter concludes by highlighting the multifaceted nature of school community engagement. The message is that sustained school- and system-wide development in student numeracy requires educational leaders at classroom, school and central office levels who have the capacity to promote a collaborative learning culture in which teachers, principals, parents and central office personnel work together in schools and across the system to ensure students have the best possible opportunities to become more numerate.

Developing professional learning communities

The concept of professional learning communities has its origins in the work of Peter Senge (1990) on learning organisations and has become increasingly prominent in the school improvement literature over the last 20 years. When applied to schools, 'professional learning communities' refers to more than just groups or teams of teachers. Rather the literature (DuFour, 2004; Fulton & Britton, 2011;

Garmston & Wellman, 2009; Harris, 2010; InPraxis Group, 2006) emphasises that professional learning communities are groups of teachers who are motivated and guided by principles designed to improve student learning and achieve specific results through promoting a collaborative learning culture. Further, professional learning communities do not happen by chance, as DuFour explained:

> When a school begins to function as a professional learning community teachers become aware of the incongruity between their commitment to ensure learning for all students and their lack of a coordinated strategy to respond when some students do not learn. The staff addresses this discrepancy by designing strategies to ensure that struggling students receive additional time and support. (2004, p. 8)

In their review of the literature for Alberta Education, the InPraxis Group (2006) identified the following six recurring attributes of professional learning communities:

- *supportive and shared leadership capacity* – leadership within the school community is shared
- *shared mission, focus and goals* – a shared sense of the vision and goals of a learning community is constructed by its members, embedded in daily practice and visible to all
- *collective learning and application of learning* – collaborative relationships within the school community are centred on developing informed decision-making and a knowledge base that affects practice positively
- *continuous inquiry and practice* – school and classroom initiatives involve an inquiry-based model and support for processes such as action research, coaching, mentoring, and collaborative and collegial decision-making
- *focus on improvement* – all initiatives are centred on the critical goal of improving student learning and achievement, and evidence-based decision-making is part of school culture
- *supportive condition and environments* – conditions that are necessary for change in school communities to be identified, embraced and acted upon.

The development of professional learning communities was a feature of the LAND project. While not labelled explicitly in some participating schools, at least some attributes of professional learning communities were evident across all the schools in the project. For example, in its report to the Commonwealth Department of Education, Employment and Workplace Relations at the conclusion of the project, the Northern Territory Catholic Education Office explained that LAND had helped to shape school culture through clear articulation of support for numeracy learning. They added that dedicated time at staff meetings was a valuable strategy and, while there had been 'some initial staff reluctance and wariness', this had been gradually overcome through 'ongoing professional learning and collegiate support'. Similar findings were reported by the other partnering education authorities (Western Australian Catholic Education Office and Catholic Education South Australia) in their reports to the department.

The term 'professional learning communities' has been referred to explicitly in Western Australian Catholic Education Office schools, and was already understood and used by members of LAND school leadership teams in that state before their participation in the LAND project. Each school in the Perth and Kimberley clusters had professional learning community meetings in place. The 'leading numeracy development' theme of the LAND project was readily incorporated into this thinking and practice. For example, professional learning community meetings for one of the participating schools, the Xavier Catholic School in Hilbert, Western Australia, during its involvement with LAND covered the following points:

- exploring the 25 characteristics of effective teachers of mathematics (Clarke & Clarke, 2004)
- exploring the current pedagogical content knowledge of staff and their teaching of mathematics
- sharing ideas, activities and professional reading
- developing a common mathematical language among staff, agreed elements of Numeracy Dedicated Time and useful informal assessment practices across different year levels.

The types of priorities and activities described reflect the attributes of collective learning, continuous inquiry and a focus on improvement identified by the InPraxis Group (2006). In a similar vein, the final project report from Banksia Grove Catholic Primary School Western Australia stated:

> Regular consecutive PLCs [professional learning community meetings] focussing on pedagogy and content and analysis of data increased teacher confidence and resulted in
> - aims being clearly displayed
> - 'work/think' pages embedded in most year levels
> - reflection time honoured across most year levels
> - greater usage of concrete materials across all year levels
> - teacher skill recognised and valued
> - greater dialogue and sharing of resources among staff members.

Comments about the value of professional learning communities were made by LAND school team members from many of the participating schools, including those in the Northern Territory and South Australia. For example: 'I can see how the PLC meetings have been crucial in setting up a culture that is reflective and accommodates changes'; 'Using a PLC to make teaching resources is a wonderful idea. Everyone could see what was being made and for what purpose'; and 'It's great how they run their PLCs like they would run a maths lesson. It helps teachers who might not be so confident teaching that way'.

In their showcase presentations at the conclusion of the LAND project, school teams were invited to provide an overview of what their school did during the project, what they achieved, and what challenges they expected in continuing to develop numeracy in their school communities. Table 5.1 summarises the actions taken by two Western Australian schools.

Table 5.1: Sample actions of LAND schools as professional learning communities

St Brigid's Catholic School, South Australia	St. Joseph's Primary School, Waroona, Western Australia
Used NAPLAN data as a base line for student progress	Invested in key teaching staff
Discussed samples of work from three students in each class	Provided regular PLC meetings and in-school professional development
Developed checklists to collate notes about the three students	Audited mathematics resources
Staged process with our LAND team during weeks 3, 6 and 9 professional learning meetings	Implemented dedicated numeracy time
Ensured lesson structures incorporated three stages: introduction; explicit teaching and student enabling; plenary	Collaboratively analysed data
Increased weekly time devoted to numeracy	Held workshops and information sessions with parents
Catalogued and centralised numeracy resources	
Conducted regular assessments of targeted students using standard templates	
Monitored community perceptions of numeracy development	
Publicised work in school newsletters	

In addition, St. Joseph's identified the following achievements:

- 'A definite movement up the bell curve. We now have students in the upper levels and fewer in stanines [categories] 1 and 2'.
- improved teacher understanding of mathematical learning and teaching strategies
- ongoing discussion and improved teaching practice
- activities more suited to students' developmental levels
- noticeable shift in teacher attitudes to mathematics
- small but noticeable positive shift in parent and student attitudes to mathematics.

St. Joseph's also recognised a number of challenges still to be dealt with:

- continue to move students up the bands
- conduct assessment for learning and of learning
- understand and use common contextual mathematics language
- refine the structure of a 'good' mathematics lesson
- enhance planning and teaching of integrated and differentiated units of work in mathematics.

The experience of LAND schools with professional learning communities suggests that the concept has value and promise for sustaining numeracy development. It reflects the characteristics of successful professional learning communities identified by DuFour (2004), which are now discussed in turn.

Ensuring that students learn

The LAND schools leadership teams explored the following questions: what do we want a student to learn? How will we know when each student has learnt it? How will we respond when a student experiences difficulty in learning? Significantly, this last question was not left up to the individual teacher – collaboration in answering this question is a distinguishing characteristic of professional learning community compared with a traditional school staff meeting.

A culture of collaboration

LAND school conversations moved beyond 'What are we expected to teach?' to 'How will we know when each student has learnt?' As Garmston and Wellman (2009) explained:

> Professional communities are born and nurtured in webs of conversation. What we talk about in our schools and how we talk about those things says much about who we are, who we think we are, and who we wish to be both in the moment and in the collective future that we are creating for ourselves as colleagues and for the students we serve.

LAND team members recognised that they could not accomplish individual student, class and school-wide development in numeracy unless they worked together. Their collaboration was systematic and evident in the regular scheduling of professional learning community meetings, encouraging staff to 'make public what has traditionally been private – goals, strategies, materials, pacing, questions, concerns and results' (DuFour, 2004, p. 10).

A common feature of successful professional learning communities in LAND was that staff had time to meet, to focus on questions that generated answers, and to develop norms and protocols to clarify expectations regarding roles, responsibilities and relationships among members. An example of a protocol used in some schools was the 'rule of five whys', where any decision that is made should be scrutinised through asking 'why?' five times.

A focus on results

LAND schools judged their effectiveness on the basis of results. Their goals reflected this. They were outcome-focused on what students were learning, rather than input-focused on what interventions or packaged resources they would adopt. Data were a catalyst for improving practice, and common formative assessments were developed to facilitate collaborative analysis. One consequence was that teachers stopped working in isolation and hoarding ideas, materials and strategies.

While the benefits were forthcoming, the LAND experience highlighted that professional learning communities are hard work. Their success depends on commitment and persistence. They require supportive and shared leadership, including teacher leadership. Schools that moved further along the path of numeracy development had principals who actively enabled teacher leadership. These men and women exhibited many of the qualities of principals identified by Crowther et al. (2002) including communicating purpose and reasons, incorporating teacher aspirations and views, providing challenge and support, making space for initiative and innovation, knowing when to step back, and celebrating and building on achievements. Those schools that were less successful in making gains in student numeracy achievement had principals who either tended to withdraw and 'leave it to the teachers' or take over completely, denying teachers the opportunity to contribute.

A systemic dimension to professional learning communities

Harris (2010) argued that systemic change requires capacity building not only across all schools but also at the local education authority level, and that professional learning communities can serve as vehicles for building capacity through professionals working together to generate new knowledge and practices. She said that, while professional learning communities generate collective commitment, responsibility and accountability, the existing school culture, system culture and outside influences can frustrate efforts to build capacity.

In their report for the National Commission on Teaching and America's Future, Fulton and Britton (2011) advocated that school systems need to develop staffing policies that promote professional learning communities. They recommend that such policies should be designed with these aims:
- to provide structured, stable time and space for teacher teamwork
- to embed professional development through using outcomes of professional learning community work as the basis for decisions regarding further staff development

- to recognise the contributions of professional learning community members
- to create leadership opportunities for teachers.

Importantly, this policy work needs to be focused on results. Building capacity is not an end in itself. It needs to be linked explicitly to results (Levin & Fullan, 2008).

The Ontario Ministry of Education (2009) went a step further in promoting professional learning communities. In their *Leadership framework*, they listed one of the five core leadership capacities as 'promoting collaborative learning cultures'. This capacity is described as 'enabling schools, school communities and districts to work together and learn from each other with a central focus on improved teaching quality and student achievement and well-being'. For example, leaders in promoting collaborative learning cultures:

- 'facilitate a shared understanding and ownership of student achievement and well-being as a central focus for collaboration among staff, federations, associations, the school board and the diverse school community'
- 'improve and build on existing models of professional learning communities'
- 'enable teamwork and collective decision-making among teachers and staff, providing opportunities for teacher-leadership'
- 'engage parents and the broader school community to be part of the learning culture' (Ontario Ministry of Education, 2009, p. 6).

Successful principal and teacher leaders in LAND project schools, and project officers in education authorities, demonstrated these capacities within and beyond school boundaries. A related key feature of engaging school communities with numeracy is examined in the next section.

Involving the parent community

Decades of research into the links between student background characteristics and achievement have confirmed the common-sense view that parents have significant influence over their children's learning at school (Coleman, 1966, 1987; Jensen, 2009). It stands to reason that schools should therefore look for ways of involving parents that will support student learning. From a community viewpoint, parents are an important component of the learning culture of a school. Their interests, expectations, needs and support shape what is valued, what is practised – and what is learnt. The importance of parents was highlighted by the Australian Association of Mathematics Teachers in their *Joint policy statement on maths, families and teachers* with the Family Maths Project of Australia:

> Parental support and encouragement are vital to children's mathematical development and success in school. Parents are their children's first and most

> influential teachers. Many schools are devising programs to help parents provide additional support in teaching mathematics to their children. These programs are not dependent on the background of parents in mathematics, but involve parents in doing mathematics with their children. What parents do with their children counts more than anything else in fostering a positive attitude to and an interest in mathematics. (1985, p. i)

There is a long history of active and constructive parental involvement in children's literacy development. Parents are recognised as key players in children's early literacy development and are often involved directly in school programs. In the case of mathematics, there has not been the same tradition or expectation. Nevertheless, there are a number of strategies for enhancing parental involvement in mathematics learning. These range from fostering home–school communication (for example, through information nights) to encouraging parent involvement in numeracy programs at the school. In the following sections, some of the issues surrounding parental involvement are discussed and practical suggestions made for maximising the contribution that parents make to mathematics learning, with an important emphasis on children's disposition to mathematics.

Some issues in parental participation in mathematics

Parents' personal confidence with mathematics

Most parents can use language in written and oral form to a level that makes them comfortable in assisting their children's language development. In contrast, many parents (whether justified or not) believe that their own level of mathematical understanding is insufficient to play a useful role, even in the early years. Many teachers would recall comments by parents during parent–teacher interviews or corridor conversations to the effect that they were 'never any good at maths', and therefore were unable or unlikely to be of much help to the teacher or their child in mathematics development. On the other hand, some parents, whose confidence with mathematics is high or who possibly use mathematics at a very high level in their working life, can be threatening to a primary teacher for whom mathematics is neither a favourite subject nor one which they feel overly confident in teaching.

The importance of parent attitudes to mathematics

The negative attitudes of some parents to mathematics are possibly of even more concern than a lack of confidence with mathematics. While a lack of confidence can be infectious, a hatred for the subject *expressed to the child* (and hatred is not too strong a term in some cases) has the potential to undermine the attempts of the classroom teacher in the crucial early years. But many parents, as has been the case for many primary teachers in training (Clarke & Clarke, 1996), have overcome their anxiety for the subject, as they realise the many and varied ways in which they do mathematics in everyday life, and as they are engaged by the exciting experiences of their children's learning, in class and at home.

'Maths isn't for girls'

Many attitudes regarding the importance of mathematics for future study and work, and the belief in one's capacity to use mathematics can be established early. The home–school partnership has a part to play in providing positive messages in this respect. The situation still arises where mothers will say to their daughters, 'Don't worry, I was never any good at maths, either'.

Cultural perspectives

Different cultural groups may have different perceptions regarding the relative roles of teachers and parents in children's learning. There are also some specific aspects relating to mathematical conventions that may cause difficulty for children and parents of particular ethnic backgrounds (Thomas, 1986).

According to different conventions across countries, the number 5.982 could be written in three different ways: with the decimal point at 'ground level', halfway up, or as a comma. For example:

> Imagine the confusion of a child recently arrived from a country where English is not the first language, when faced with
> 1. 3.400
>   Does the child interpret the symbol '.' as:
>   Three multiplied by four hundred? Or three thousand four hundred? Or three point four?
> 2. Total the numbers 6, 2, and 4
>   Is the symbol ',' interpreted as a decimal, i.e. 6.2 + 4 = 10.2, or is it recognised as a comma? (Thomas, 1986, p. 4)

When one of the author's family members was living in the United States, one of his daughters came home from school and asked, 'What is a foot?' The teacher had assumed universal understanding of imperial measurements among her Grade 5 class. The same kind of difficulty can arise when a parent (of any background) seeks to explain an algorithm to their child that may be quite different from what has been developed at school.

Changes in content and pedagogy in mathematics

A frequent comment of parents is that 'It's all completely different from when I was at school, and so I couldn't possibly help my children in maths'. Indeed, some significant changes have occurred in both teaching approaches and content in the last 20 years. Two examples are the importance placed on probability and statistics, and the increased use of technology, particularly calculators. But these changes in content in many ways reflect changes in society, a society in which parents are heavily involved. Indeed, the new content may well be quite familiar to parents who are bombarded with data in various media (used both appropriately and inappropriately) and to parents whose own use of technology has greatly increased.

Concurrent changes in pedagogy include the increased use of work in small groups and problem-solving, a greater emphasis on relevance to the child and using mathematics in context, and greater valuing of children's methods and strategies. Most parents agree that the needs to solve problems and to work cooperatively with others are now accepted by the community as important outcomes of schooling, and are pleased to learn that a variety of methods are valued in solving problems at school, unlike the school experience of many of them.

Education is a partnership between the school, the parents and the student being educated. Developing a balance can be a challenge for teachers, especially in the early years. Being clear on what is appropriate for the child's development so that the teacher can provide guidance is likely to be a key feature of a successful partnership. Each of the contributors in the partnership has a different but complementary role. The aim is not to make parents into teachers, but to build an active partnership where each acknowledges the key role of the others, and the child's mathematical development (in both understanding and disposition) is the major focus.

Types of parental involvement

A summary of some different kinds of parental participation in school mathematics programs is given in this section (adapted from unpublished work done by Ian Robinson in Victorian schools). Each level tends to represent a more direct involvement by the parents than the level before. It is not suggested that all of these should be implemented at a given school, but discussion between parents and teachers will determine the appropriate mix for a given community, and even a given child. Parental participation options include:

- *exchanging information* – reports; how parents can help at home through everyday activities; displays of children's work; parent–teacher interviews; questionnaires on parental expectations; distribution of school mathematics policy; maths newsletters; notes to the teacher from parents; parent evenings
- *observing* – visits to classroom; open days; mathematics displays
- *sharing in the work* – supervising small groups; collecting materials; making structured materials; helping with excursions
- *participating in the learning* – attending professional development; family sessions, including activities to assist with homework

- *participating in the planning* – school council; school review; mathematics curriculum committee; individual education planning (particularly for students with disabilities) (Robinson, 1983).

The LAND project experience showed that parents were most interested in how they could assist their child's mathematical development in practical, hands-on ways – especially given the limited time that many had in light of their work and travel commitments. Ideas on how parents might help their children were demonstrated at the parent information evenings, and followed up by class teachers: for example in setting 'homework' activities.

The following sections discuss some further ideas drawn from the LAND experience that also relate to the suggestions from Robinson's (1983) work.

Everyday family activities that support mathematical development

Encouragement of informal development of mathematical concepts through everyday activities is the focus of a number of initiatives, particularly in the early childhood and junior primary context. It is important not to try to force development, but to make activities fun and interesting. If an activity is frustrating and unenjoyable (for example, resulting in tears around the kitchen table), parents are encouraged to 'give it away!' Learning happens most effectively when the learner is ready for it.

Home maths activities

The traditional setting of unfinished exercises or worksheets unrelated to class work to be completed at home is not appropriate at the primary school level. Children need time to play and to relax in the hours between school and bed; such 'homework' seems unnecessary and counterproductive in building understanding and enjoyment of mathematics. This type of homework in the primary years can serve to exacerbate disadvantage. If a parent is unable or unwilling to help with this work, it is sometimes the case that the children least in need of help are those who are assisted by parents, while those in greatest need miss out.

Family and parent evenings

The Family Maths Project of Australia (FAMPA) is an example of a program that is designed to assist parents in their supportive role. It is usually a series of evening programs led by parents and teachers, where parents, teachers and children work together on enjoyable mathematics activities. It is not designed to teach curriculum but to provide a link between the school and home and to have a dialogue about mathematics. It developed out of a project in the USA that focused on improving home and school links in disadvantaged schools (Stenmark, Thompson & Cossey,

1986). Parent evenings conducted during the LAND project are discussed later in this chapter.

Parents assisting in the classroom

Though parents are common classroom participants in school literacy programs in the early years, this is much less common in mathematics. The issues discussed earlier may be factors in this but care must also be taken in the level of direction given by parents to the children. Just as parents listen to children read, parents must also listen to them doing mathematics. In the early years, the imposition of methods on children and the premature introduction of symbols that adults can easily recognise can be detrimental to children's early number development. A number of schools have used parents to supervise a rotation of mathematics tasks within the classroom. There is a range of mathematical topics that can effectively use this structure. It can free up the teacher for more intense work with students in greatest need or in areas requiring specialist help.

A related means of parent assistance is making use of parent helpers during mathematics activity days. This may involve the supervision of games or other hands-on activities.

Parent–teacher interviews and reports

A discussion of parental involvement in mathematics would not be complete without a discussion of more formal assessment-related interactions. These communications are often the only ones that occur in the upper grades. In the early years, it is more likely that the regular contact between parent and teacher provides opportunities to discuss the child's development. The regular interactions relating to reading suggest that many parents are well aware of their child's progress, but is that the case in mathematics? What messages are parents to be given in these more formal contexts? How can these interactions best be used to improve the partnership and ultimately the child's mathematical development?

The expectations of parents need to be balanced with a knowledge of children's needs in their mathematical development. Parents might need to be made aware of the importance of concept development and problem-solving as well as more traditional aspects of skill acquisition. Having children's work available can provide a useful image of development over time, as well as conveying important messages that mathematics is more than arithmetic, and demonstrate the kind of classroom environment that the teacher is seeking to create. This is also a time when the discussion and recording of aspects relating to children's mathematical disposition are important.

There is a range of ways in which parents can participate in a constructive, supportive way in their children's mathematics learning. These have been summarised in a position statement by the Australian Association of Mathematics Teachers (1985):

> Parents can take an active role in their children's mathematics education by:

- Engaging with their children in appropriate family games, puzzles and other activities that use a variety of mathematics skills
- Talking to their children about the use of mathematics in everyday life
- Regularly discussing with children their classroom activities and listening carefully with interest to their explanation of what has been learnt
- Encouraging their children to persist when the work becomes difficult
- Communicating to their children the importance of mathematics at all stages of schooling, through to Year 12
- Participating in parent–teacher activities
- Taking advantages of opportunities to visit mathematics classes.

The types of parental participation in mathematics initiatives will be distinctly different from those used in literacy programs. For example, greater emphasis may need to be placed on initial or preparatory activities such as parent meetings and home tasks that may lead to more classroom-based involvement.

Parent involvement in action: LAND parent information evenings

The design of the LAND project enabled its content and approach to be customised on the basis of participant need and the context of the particular school community or school cluster. One example of this customisation was the identified need and opportunity to organise and present parent information evenings about mathematics. Three parent evenings were conducted during the LAND project. These were held at schools in Adelaide, Darwin and Perth, and were designed and delivered through a collaboration between the hosting school, the project officers from the education authorities involved (Catholic Education South Australia, the Northern Territory Catholic Education Office and the Western Australian Catholic Education Office) and the Australian Catholic University as the university partner.

The purpose of the event was to provide a practical example of how a school might engage parents in the numeracy development of their children. The event was scheduled at a time and place considered most convenient for parents. LAND school team members from other schools in the same cluster also attended as 'participant observers' to gain some insights as to how the event might work at their schools.

The format for the evening involved a combination of formal input from the research team and the local LAND project officer, hands-on activities, and plenary discussion about how parents can help their children's learning in mathematics. The event was promoted to parents using the flyer details shown in the box.

Helping my child to understand maths

An information session for parents about mathematics

The presenters will share with you information about:
- How the teaching of mathematics is changing and why
- Examples of the kinds of activities used in classrooms, which engage children in worthwhile and enjoyable mathematics
- The kinds of everyday, fun activities that you can do with your children to support their maths learning

There will be handouts covering the main ideas and lots of suggestions on how you can support your child's learning at home.

The evening is open to all parents of children from Kinder to Year 6. Please RSVP via email.

Issues covered during the evening related to the importance of mental computation, the use of calculators, use of real-life examples, and the nature of homework. The evenings generally ran from 7.00 to 8.30 pm followed by a light supper and more conversation between parents, the teachers and presenters. The LAND project evaluation report from each of the education authorities to the Commonwealth Department of Education, Employment and Workplace Relations indicated that the evenings achieved a number of positive outcomes:
- increased parental awareness of directions in mathematics education – curriculum, assessment and teaching approaches
- increased parental capacity to assist their child's learning in mathematics
- increased LAND school team members' awareness of the means (resources and modelled delivery approach) of running a parent evening
- increased LAND school team motivation to involve parents in school numeracy planning.

The experience of parent involvement in the LAND project varied across the schools that were involved. While the parents in all school communities were interested in helping their children succeed with mathematics, those in metropolitan areas had different needs, capacities and expectations from those in rural and remote settings. In the following section, some of the more challenging aspects of engaging school communities with numeracy across these different contexts are examined.

Engaging school communities in complex contexts

Student engagement and attendance in Indigenous schools are major challenges, but case examples from LAND schools offer some insights into ways to encourage engagement. The LAND project included schools in a range of contexts. All the teams desired engagement with their school communities, but some schools found this more difficult than others. In this section, the potential barriers to engagement and what schools in the LAND project did to overcome these will be examined.

Cultural backgrounds of the school communities varied widely across the LAND project, and even within clusters. For example, some of the Adelaide schools, though geographically close, had very different parent bodies. One school reported over 40 different first languages spoken in the homes of their students. They found many of the school students were serving as translators for their parents. This has clear disadvantages when schools endeavour to involve parents in activities such as parent nights. One school adopted the approach of translating key documents into a number of community languages.

A traditional method of communicating with parents and carers is through a school newsletter. LAND schools did not always see this mechanism as useful. One principal noted wryly that if she wanted to bury any information, she would put it in the newsletter.

The principal of a Perth school raised a further challenge. In her school, she was aware of a number of parents who recalled bad experiences from their own school days and as a result were quite intimidated by schools and avoided engagement if they could. This principal, in common with all the LAND principals, was at pains to point out that she was very aware these parents cared deeply about the education of their children; they just needed a non-threatening way to learn how to engage with the school as parents.

Teachers in most cases have enjoyed their time as students in schools. For many it comes as quite a surprise to learn of the depth of distress some parents feel in entering school grounds. Cultural differences and differences in life experiences between teachers and parents lead to complex contexts for engaging school communities. For teachers working in remote Indigenous communities, the cultural differences are frequently pronounced. It takes time for teachers to understand the communities in which they are working, often for a short time. For example, in one community, an enthusiastic teacher decided to put a display of photographs of school activities on the noticeboard at the local shop. To her dismay, after a few days, most of the photographs had been taken away. Initially, she was very annoyed and resolved not to bother with the effort to make a display in future. Conversation with staff about this episode during one of the LAND visits by the research team enabled her to see this in a different light. It was an example of the interest the community had in their children. They loved to see photos of the work the students were doing. As a result, it was decided that photographs with a story written about the activity and the progress of the student would be sent home on a regular basis, forming part of the school's reporting program.

Many residents of remote communities have access to a wide range of information and communication technology. DVD players are commonplace and one school decided to make use of the format to take school to the homes, rather than bringing parents into the school, at least initially. They made slide shows of student work and activities they were undertaking. Ideas for parents to help at home were also included. These were then burnt onto DVDs and sent home with the children. Another community had access to a community television station that allowed the school to broadcast information. Internet access was also surprisingly common in the remote communities, although subject to problems of dropping connections and power outages. One mother of a child with a disability was asked by a member of the LAND research team about where she found information to help her child. 'The internet!' came the reply that could have been given by a parent in metropolitan Adelaide. The teachers of this mother's child had felt the mother was not engaged or interested in what was happening at school. They were unaware that she was accessing support externally. Opportunities for partnership between parent and school were not being realised, meaning duplication of effort.

Even though some school communities can pose particular challenges for engagement, the ways in which principals, school executive and teachers view the roles and contributions of parents to their child's numeracy development can give strong impetus to look for innovative solutions. In most cases, parents (and grandparents) care a great deal about the education of their children, and with support and guidance are usually grateful for the opportunity to work in partnerships with schools and especially their child's teacher.

'It takes a school community to raise a numerate child'

In his recent closing address to the Learning without Frontiers conference on the theme of leading a learning revolution, Sir Ken Robinson (2013) advocated several features that need to govern the actions of teachers in the midst of contemporary global changes in education. One was that teaching, as the 'heart of education', needs to shift from being a solitary endeavour to a collaborative enterprise. Another was that education needs to be customised to the communities where it is taking place. And finally, that by working locally and sharing their insights and expertise within and beyond their school boundaries, teachers can shape the direction of the revolutionary changes to schooling that are already underway. The findings of the LAND project on engaging school communities bear out all of these themes.

The concept and practice of professional learning communities in the LAND project is a powerful example of what can be achieved by teachers working together to improve student numeracy outcomes. But teachers cannot do this by themselves. Parents also play a valuable role in supporting their child's development in numeracy through engaging with teachers in feasible and practical ways. The nature and extent of this engagement varies from child to child, class to class, and school to school. It therefore needs to be customised, as Robinson (2013) argued, to the school communities involved. A practical illustration of this was the ways in which the LAND project parent nights were organised and attended in different schools.

The message is that engaging school communities with numeracy is a multifaceted undertaking. It involves having a clear and consistent focus on student outcomes (in terms of student attendance, cognitive and affective engagement, and results on learning assessments) as well as the means to develop these outcomes. This can be done in a number of ways:

- building staff collaboration and a sense of efficacy in teaching mathematics
- developing parental awareness, involvement and support for their child's numeracy development
- fostering community discussions about students' numeracy achievements
- involving the community in defining purposes and setting directions for numeracy development.

Taken together, the ways that professional learning communities are directed toward student outcomes, foster teacher collaboration and parent engagement, and adapt to different school contexts represent powerful bases for numeracy development. They give credence to a variation of the old adage that 'it takes a village to raise a child'. The work of the LAND project shows that 'it takes a school community to raise a numerate child'.

SECTION 3
ALIGNING EFFORTS, ENCOURAGING COHERENCE

CHAPTER 6

NETWORKING NUMERACY DEVELOPMENT

Rhonda Faragher, Megan Poore and Michael Gaffney

Jen and Carl were a little wary at first. Although experienced primary school teachers, they tended to use digital technology sparingly in their teaching. While their familiarity with various digital technologies was increasing (they both had smart phones!), their classroom use of these technologies was fairly conservative: it was basically limited to using PowerPoint for presentations, posting digital photos and encouraging student use of Word and Excel. They certainly were not confident with using social media either in their teaching or in professional development and so were a little apprehensive when it was suggested by the research team that developing a wiki might be a good idea to help them share their learning with colleagues in other schools and school systems.

Their school, like 16 others around Australia, was participating in the LAND research project. Jen and Carl were members of the LAND school leadership team at their school and were responsible, along with their principal, for leading the project at the local level. They were keen to work with the university team members as well as the project officer from their local central office on developing a whole-school approach to numeracy. So, when the opportunity came along to be involved in the national project, they thought, 'Why not?'

As they sat at their computers at the beginning of the first workshop, the instructor asked, 'Who knows what a wiki is?' A hush came over the group, and eyes darted around the room.

Twelve months later, Jen and Carl were invited by the Australian Government to Canberra to present a seminar about what their school was doing to improve students' numeracy levels. The seminar provided an opportunity to network with colleagues who were working on similar projects in other parts of the country. During their presentation, Jen and Carl made mention of how the wiki had helped them share ideas, ask questions and celebrate achievements. Over morning tea, one of the seminar participants came up and asked, 'How do I join your wiki?' …

Introduction: Transforming schooling and professional development through networking

Raising student achievement presents both possibilities and challenges for today's schools. In examining these, at least two major themes that inform the current thinking on student success can be distilled. The first theme is highlighted by the call for higher levels of achievement in 'the basics' – meaning, literacy and numeracy – so that students have a better chance for a fulfilling, productive life and so that they can make a significant contribution to the social and economic wellbeing of their community and to Australian society as a whole. The second theme expresses the notion that schooling needs to educate 'for the 21st century' – that is, to extend the basics to incorporate emphases on creativity, problem-solving, teamwork, imagination and innovation (Robinson, 2011). At the same time, digital technologies are becoming more and more ubiquitous in life outside schools, and students and their parents have increasing expectations of schools to incorporate these emerging tools in regular teaching and learning practices.

These themes underscore the need for schools to play a new learning game (Barber, 1997), one that satisfies demands for the basics but also creates possibilities for embracing a future of change. In essence, schooling is being 'transformed'. Transformation in this sense means giving attention to raising the bar and decreasing the gap in student achievement, as well as providing opportunities for students to develop 21st-century capabilities while continuing to ensure that their engagement with others is – and continues to be – life giving. In other words, the role of principals and teachers is to find and implement contemporary ways of blending the economic and social purposes of education with the moral imperative of educating each and every student so that they can have life and have it to the full (John 10:10).

To play this new learning game, principals and teachers need to be informed about these major themes and be competent in their choice and use of digital technologies. Part of playing the game is having an understanding of, and being comfortable with, the game's key tenets. One of these tenets is the concept of the networked school community and its significance for improving teaching and learning through drawing upon people and resources from both within and beyond the school walls in new, flexible and worthwhile ways. For the purposes of this chapter, a networked school community is one in which teachers and principals work together with students, parents, local community members, professional colleagues and school partners, sponsors and advocates from their local region and across the country and the world to provide successful learning opportunities for all their students (Gaffney, 2010).

In this chapter the concept of the networked school community is applied to the educational challenge of improving the numeracy achievement of students in disadvantaged circumstances. Networking numeracy improvement is examined through investigating the development and use of a wiki. The wiki is focused on because it supplies an example of social media that was used to support the sharing of professional practice within and among schools, the school system and university partners in the LAND project. The purpose and the design of this piece of digital technology (referred to simply as the 'LAND wiki') is outlined, as is the way in which both principals and teachers participating in the LAND project were trained in using it. Some of the benefits of – as well as some of the issues associated with – using wikis as tools for sharing professional practice about numeracy development are described. Second, we describe how findings from the LAND project were disseminated more broadly, especially through the support of the Australian Government. The chapter concludes with some recommendations about how social media can be used to support the networking aspects of professional learning and development so that the lessons learnt find their way into more classrooms, as well as more program and policy discussions, with the aim of bringing about sustained improvement in student numeracy achievement.

A networking tool: The purpose and design of the LAND wiki

The 17 schools taking part in the LAND project were far-flung, to say the least. From the outset, it became clear that the project needed some form of web presence if information was to be circulated effectively among project participants. But, more than this, some way of bringing together geographically dispersed groups was needed so that they could share their learning and collaborate on resource building. The wiki medium which allows members to collaborate on building and editing their own web spaces – has an emphasis on knowledge construction and distribution; establishing a wiki thus seemed an effective way of meeting the technical, online requirements while at the same time encouraging the co-construction of web pages among LAND project participants. The main purpose behind the LAND wiki therefore was to create a safe, members-only space where participants could meet online to share resources and gather information via wiki pages, and to swap experiences and chat with colleagues via the wiki's discussion forum.

In addition, the researchers also wanted to provide a professional development opportunity for staff who had little experience of using social media either in the classroom or for building a community of practice. At the start of the project, wikis were relatively new, and the LAND project being part of a series of pilot projects provided an opportunity to explore and trial new technologies and practices and to investigate the benefits and pitfalls that new social media might present to teachers. Teachers could thus gain experience with this technology and researchers could see what aspects were helpful, what were difficult and what were not useful at all.

Importantly, the research team needed an easy-to-create site that they could run themselves, avoiding the need for university administrative support that required centralised, controlled access to a university computer system through the creation of university accounts with logins and passwords. Furthermore, projects with short-term funding and regular reporting requirements need to become established quickly – and the LAND project was under this pressure.

Learning to use a wiki

The LAND project team set up a free wiki and created a structure (based around the various school clusters) that would allow each school in each cluster to post and share materials, and, most importantly, develop their school plans for action. Training in how to use and contribute to the wiki was then rolled out.

An introduction to the wiki was delivered to each cluster in the first face-to-face workshop held for each group. Initially, school computer labs were used to ensure sufficient access to the internet; later, wireless networks were used, although network speeds often presented problems. Participants were first introduced to wikis in general (Wikipedia providing the most familiar example), and then the LAND wiki itself. For some, setting up personal profiles proved challenging; however, this challenge was used to encourage peer-learning among participants. This, in turn, had the subsequent effect of bringing people together to feel a part of the network more broadly. The first glimpse of the promise of the wiki to join teachers across the clusters came in just the second workshop in the introductory series when a teacher from the Northern Territory cluster noticed with surprise and delight that one of the teachers from Adelaide was an old friend of hers with whom she had lost touch.

One of the main workshop challenges, though, came through managing the balance between those participants who were experienced and confident in using social media for both personal and professional purposes, and those who felt a degree of apprehension around the wiki; apprehension both in terms of their own skill level and their sense of comfort at being online and exposed to potential online risks. Thus, the training also dealt with matters of educating participants about how to manage risk in web-based environments such as how to keep safe online and what happens to your data once it goes on the internet. Understanding risk was also essential to the project management team, and a risk management plan was developed around potential breaches of privacy and security, exposure to advertising, service reliability, copyright, data control, backups and similar points of risk.

Although the team had great aspirations for the wiki, and although most participants expressed a keenness to contribute to it, several factors conspired against building the vibrant online community that had been hoped for. These included access and bandwidth problems, lack of foundational technical skills on the part of participants, coupled with time-poor teachers, some of whom were also reluctant users. A few of these teachers were not 'natural' users of any web-based platforms and avoided the use of the wiki except in the workshop sessions, where they experienced frustration with such things as forgetting their personally chosen usernames and passwords.

In retrospect, the project team would have benefited from more explicitly considering Jonathan Davies' (2004) three key factors in wiki collaboration: understanding of social and technical elements; building trust in the wiki; and recognising the personal value of 'wiki-ing'.

Davies stated that, first, there must be understanding of both the social and technical elements of wikis, and in particular how wikis support collaboration and 'distributed ownership' (2004, p. 65). In dealing with this factor in the LAND wiki training, the researchers explained to participants that wikis are good tools for supporting online collaboration and knowledge construction; described the key technical characteristics of wikis (those related to editing, discussion forums, and revision functions); and gave participants the opportunity to work on their own wiki pages. But many participants were starting with little knowledge of the use of social media, making it difficult for them to conceptualise how the wiki might support their work for the LAND project. Coupled with limited time (two hours) for training, it was difficult to bring a few participants up to speed with the potential of the wiki as a collaborative, professionally useful tool.

Davies also pointed out that trust is essential if a wiki is to be successful: 'This includes trust in the technology, in the wiki contents, in the wiki community and belief that the concept can and will work' (2004, p. 65). Although most participants, it can be said, had trust in their colleagues, trust in the idea that the technology could support their professional goals was harder to come by. The researchers were heartened to see this trust in the value of the wiki grow over the life of the project. It was perhaps unrealistic to hope all participants would trust a new process from the outset, but the approach of supporting participants over a sustained period of time proved effective.

Finally, Davies argues that using the wiki must be valuable on a personal level (2004, p. 66) and users need incentives and encouragement to inspire them to make ongoing contributions to the wiki. In the case of the LAND project, the wiki became a valuable repository of project material, and some participants shared resources with other clusters. This could have been encouraged further. Even so, at the conclusion of the project, a number of participants specifically requested the wiki remain open so that they could continue to build their networks with teachers across the project and thus share resources.

From this, it can be noted that the introduction of social media in professional settings requires a good deal of time both for professional development activities and for ongoing support. In the early stages of building a wiki community the support primarily needs to come in the form of increasing the technical skills of wiki members. Once a base level of competency has been reached, support needs to switch focus to motivating, encouraging and inspiring wiki users to make continuing contributions to the site – contributions that are both professionally and personally valuable. To this end, being clear about the purpose and design of any work-based wiki project is essential.

Issues in the use of the wiki

The use of the LAND wiki evolved over the life of the project and both benefits and challenges were encountered as this technique for collaboration and communication was explored.

The wiki was invaluable for the posting of school plans, which could be accessed by new participants when the members of a LAND school team changed due to staff turnover. This allowed personnel entering the project to read and contribute to what the school was working towards. Others used their plans to look back over what they had planned to achieve and to check their progress. Initially, project officers needed to provide considerable leadership and encouragement to teams to post their plans, particularly after the first meeting. This is not least because – and perhaps surprisingly to some – teachers frequently lack confidence in putting their work on public display; indeed, they can be very critical of their own practice. In the LAND project, the project officers encouraged teams to develop their plans for action and then to post them on the wiki, and this 'living document' format soon became distinctly motivating. Moreover, once the plans were posted, the wiki proved a very useful medium through which the research team could determine what schools were working towards. This proved very helpful in the team's preparation for school visits.

With the LAND wiki, the project manager – a member of the research team – took on the role of regularly posting information, sending messages through the wiki and commenting on discussions. As LAND participants were all busy working in other roles in addition to the project work, this moderation role was essential to ensure that wiki members received regular email alerts to keep them involved. These reminders to communicate via the wiki kept participants aware of the project and their commitment to required action.

Views of participants on the use of the wiki

At the conclusion of the LAND project, participants were surveyed about their experiences of, and attitudes towards, using wikis as a means of communication. They were asked the following questions:

- How often did you access the wiki?

- What were the main activities you used the wiki for?
- What were the main aspects that reduced your engagement with the wiki, if any?
- What is your opinion of the use of wikis in general for communication?
- If you experienced technical difficulties and if these were able to be resolved would this change your level of engagement with the wiki?
- What should be done with the wiki at the completion of the project?
- Other comments?

At the end of the project, participants were largely happy and comfortable with the use of the wiki. There were some persistent issues to do with access such as school firewalls blocking the site, which forced teachers to access the site from home. There were also issues for some, such as personal confidence, that remained after two years. The responses for the different clusters were separated and this was helpful in isolating possible factors affecting the participants' issues. The data support the need for adequate time to introduce participants to the wiki. For example, early in the project, in the first workshop of the introductory series, held in Adelaide, it became clear that insufficient time had been allowed to orient participants to the wiki. In the three subsequent introduction workshops, the research team attempted to add more time for this activity, although this was not possible in Darwin due to the need to allow travel time for participants. Participants in both the Broome and Perth clusters reported more frequent use of the wiki. The greater acceptance of the wiki can possibly be explained by the greater time allowed for induction to the platform in the first workshop for those clusters.

Technical difficulties were a constant concern throughout the project. In some jurisdictions, participants were unable to access the wiki from their school sites due to the presence of firewalls. Some problems were due to inexperience with technology (one participant noted *she* was 'the technical problem'!). Other factors such as outdated browser versions, slow download speeds and unfamiliarity due to infrequent use of the wiki were cited as inhibitors. Even so, teachers in the remote schools were prepared to persist, due to the perceived value of the wiki.

Some of the advantages cited were the opportunity to access resources after workshops, to see what others were doing, to make contact with participants in different schools and clusters, and to keep in touch with the project. A participant who came late to the LAND project found it a particularly helpful mechanism to jump into what others were doing.

A clear divide between younger and older participants was evident, with the younger teachers generally very comfortable with the platform. Some expressed disappointment that others did not engage as much as they would have liked and which they said limited the use they could make of the wiki. One of our principals commented, 'Great for digital natives – harder for old folks'.

There were also benefits noted by project officers. In particular, they valued being able to access school information to prepare for school visits and were also able to see where potential difficulties with implementing their school plans might lie. This advantage also applied to the university research team who were also able to use the wiki to prepare for workshops by reviewing school action plans and noting progress.

Networking across the project for numeracy improvement

Ensuring lasting educational innovation requires the involvement of many people who come from a variety of backgrounds, and who include students, teachers, parents, school and system administrators, and government policy-makers. The LAND project emphasised and researched the importance of alignment of purpose across all sectors, which necessitated strong communication and networking among and between these groups.

The LAND project thus involved the direct collaboration and coordination of dozens of people working towards a common goal: the improvement in numeracy outcomes for learners in schools with low socioeconomic status across 17 sites. Ongoing communication in the online space occurred through the wiki, which, as already outlined, served many purposes including as a repository of resources, a record of commitment, action and progress, and a means of keeping in touch with participants between workshops and school visits. But other forms of communication were also needed, as discussed below.

Mechanisms for networking

The wiki was not the sole mechanism of communication and networking. The project manager, a member of the research team, maintained regular email and phone contact with the project officers, who, in turn, were continually involved with their school teams. Most project officers were undertaking their LAND work as an extension to work as consultants to schools. Our most successful project officers encouraged and motivated their school teams through personal visits, phone calls and email contact. These project officers were aware of the special difficulties that school teams were dealing with and accordingly could provide resources and targeted support as required. They were also part of the network of consultants within their systems and so were able to tap beyond their usual sphere of involvement into resources and ideas from participants and take ideas from one school to another.

School visits: Seeing LAND in action

School visits were an essential part of the LAND project and aimed at embedding the professional development of the workshops in the day-to-day work of the school teams. Continuing professional learning, the learning of practising professionals (Webster-Wright, 2009, p. 705), is at the heart of significant pedagogical improvement. The LAND process was built on a view of continuing professional learning not as something 'done' to people but a process that continues throughout the career of a professional. Continuing professional learning is likely to involve professional development where teachers attend workshops or meetings related to their practice. These activities may be selected by teachers, such as conferences, or required by their employer. Research suggests that the effectiveness of the professional development depends on the way teachers integrate it with their practice, the process of continuing professional learning. 'Shifts in mathematics pedagogy require time and ongoing support in the form of authentic and collaborative professional learning opportunities that are supported and classroom embedded' (Bruce et al., 2010, p. 1607).

The research team was aware of the fact that members could not work alongside teachers as much as they would have liked. Several thousand kilometres between the schools and the researchers was a major factor in this area, as was the lack of time – none of the researchers worked full-time on this project. But researchers (accompanied by project officers) did make at least one school visit between each workshop. Project officers made additional visits.

School visits, although limited, provided an important opportunity for the research team to see the work of the LAND project in action. Visits took a variety of approaches: in some places, team members were invited to observe lessons; in others, they jointly planned and taught lessons. The research team took part in professional learning communities, staff meetings and planning sessions. Occasionally, school visits were used to provide mentoring where difficulties had arisen or where there was a lack of progress. One visit to a school in the Northern Territory cluster involved inducting an entirely new team into the project, as only the principal remained in the second year of the project. Significantly, one of the most important results of the visits was the opportunity to identify some of the outstanding practice that was developing – it is not always easy for teachers and school leaders to be aware of aspects of their practice that are remarkable and that merit sharing with others.

Gathering findings: Judging impact

An additional benefit of networking across the project was the opportunity to share results and judge the impact of interventions. One of the most powerful indicators of the success of a strategy aimed at developing effective teaching is the effect that strategy has on the learning of students. Teachers in the project were encouraged to document the progress of their students as the LAND project unfolded. This progress took a number of forms, including accomplishment with mathematics, changed attitudes to work and improved ability to communicate mathematically. One school in the Adelaide cluster focused on developing mathematical thinking and reported improvements in students' willingness and ability to ask mathematical questions.

Innovations in one school were able to be adopted by other schools when successes were shared and a number of cases were observed where successful ideas and strategies gained wider impact among partner schools. For example, a number of schools resolved to make better use of mathematics resources, a resolution that took the form of having schools audit their collections and then disseminate their approaches to the organisation and cataloguing of resources.

From the outset, the LAND research team worked with school teams as professional partners. It was the team's firm tenet that teachers understood their own contexts best and therefore researchers relied on them to adapt approaches suggested in the professional development workshops to ensure they worked well for their students. In sharing results and approaches, this process was honoured and enriched. Teachers shared and refined strategies across the network of schools.

Networking the news about numeracy improvement

For any funded research project, promulgation of findings is important, not least because it increases the effectiveness of the initial funding investment. In the LAND project, opportunities were supplied for participants to report their findings both on a regular basis throughout the project and at its conclusion. These opportunities took a number of forms:

- within schools, specifically between LAND participants and other teachers. These included presentations at staff meetings as well as lesson or topic discussions in Professional Learning Communities (see Chapter 7).
- through communication to parents and others in the school community (see Chapter 5)
- via the wiki
- by discussions with project officers and other school visitors
- through presentations at LAND workshops, including the final showcase
- by presentations and reports to external parties.

Such reporting was essential to the reconciliation of funding against the project's intended and actual outcomes and demonstrated quite clearly the success of the project in general.

Sharing results within the project

Participants were encouraged to report their progress towards goals they had set themselves through the LAND project. As was discussed in Chapter 3, schools identified their choice from the list of 25 characteristics of effective mathematics teaching (Clarke & Clarke, 2004), and agreed to focus their attention on the development of these goals. In the busy work of schools, it can be easy to forget goals that were set during professional development workshops. Maintaining a commitment to action that can transform professional development into professional learning can be difficult – but it is assisted by regular opportunities to report results. Schools undertook to do this with each other within their LAND school teams, as well as with other staff in the school. Importantly, project officers encouraged participants to work towards their goals by following up with school teams to ask after their progress. These informal, often verbal, reports were essential. They were supplemented by written reports that were forwarded each semester and by formal presentations of progress that were given at LAND workshops.

The two-year Leading Aligned Numeracy Development professional learning project culminated in a final showcase. In this important phase, pairs of cluster groups joined together: Adelaide with the Northern Territory, and Perth with the Kimberley cluster. School teams gave a final presentation highlighting what they had selected for their focus during the LAND project and reviewing of their achievement over the two years. As would be expected, schools varied in the progress they had made. Reasons for the variation can be attributed to factors discussed throughout this book, and particularly in the alignment of leadership.

Sharing results beyond the project

In taking part in a national pilot, participants and partners in the LAND project have had both the opportunity and responsibility to share information about the project with their professional colleagues and with members of the wider educational community. Schools in the LAND project have highlighted their progress relating to the improvement of student numeracy outcomes in a range of ways. In particular, LAND school teams demonstrated their willingness and capacity to share their school's journey, in the following forums:

- *the Ministerial Council on Education, Early Childhood Development and Youth Affairs National Biennial Forum* – participation in this forum took two forms. A vodcast, compiling the Western Australian Cross-Sectoral Education Systems' literacy and numeracy pilot projects, was showcased at the forum. The vodcast was accompanied by a supporting briefing paper. The co-director of the LAND project, Professor Michael Gaffney from the Australian Catholic University, gave an address on the 'Education System–University Partnerships'.

- *Teach, Learn, Share: The National Literacy and Numeracy Evidence Base* – developed by the Commonwealth Department of Education, Employment and Workplace Relations personnel from project reports contributed by education systems and researchers
- *Commonwealth Department of Education, Employment and Workplace Relations Literacy and Numeracy Pilots Forum* – the LAND project was highlighted at this forum with representation from both the Kimberley and Perth schools. The regional representatives presented their schools' journeys within the project, elaborating on activities that had been undertaken to date.
- *the Literacy and Numeracy Pilots Forum* – this forum provided the opportunity for participants across the three education sectors in Western Australia to engage with research undertaken in the literacy and numeracy pilot schools within Catholic Education, the Education Department, and the Association of Independent Schools of Western Australia. One Perth LAND school presented a table discussion of its research into improving numeracy outcomes for their students.
- *presentation at the Australian Association of Mathematics Teachers conference* – project participants (school teams, project officers and researchers) attended the conference in Alice Springs in 2011 and presented their work to fellow teachers.
- *presentation at the Mathematics Education Research Group of Australasia conference* – the researchers, in collaboration with other LAND participants, presented their work in a research forum.
- *Education Authority Conference Catholic Education of Western Australia Keys to Learning Primary Curriculum Conference* – workshop presentations by each of the Perth LAND teams highlighted their journeys within the LAND project. The presentations included discussion of the processes and practices each school had engaged in to improve numeracy outcomes for their students.
- *parent evenings* – an information session entitled 'Helping my child to understand maths? Count me in!' was held for parents and was presented in partnership between the Australian Catholic University and the Catholic Education Office of Western Australia. In addition to the parents from one of the LAND schools, all LAND teams from the Perth schools were invited to attend. (For further discussion of parent evenings, see Chapter 5.)

A necessary part of acquitting grant funds is the preparation of formal reports to funding bodies. Reports allow others to learn from findings, gain insights for project duplication and follow recommendations for improvement, enhancing the sustainability of the work. Essential though reporting is, onerous documentation and frequent changes to formats and data requirements hinder the effectiveness of projects. This was found to be a dilemma with the reporting for LAND, where reporting was required from those in schools and educational authorities as well as the researchers. Report templates changed frequently and required the collection of considerable data, often in formats that were not easily obtained. This was particularly difficult for research projects such as this one that were not implementing a discrete intervention package. Reporting requirements need to be balanced with the time taken away from undertaking research and, indeed, teaching and learning.

In addition to reporting within and at the conclusion of a project, sustainability of project outcomes can be assisted by networking activity beyond the life of the funded project. It is not uncommon for new projects to be commenced before the full effect of current projects has been ascertained. Not only does this reduce the value achieved from the original funding, it can lead to a lack of accountability. Researchers observed an attitude held by some school leaders along the lines of 'It doesn't matter that we haven't made progress because the next shiny, new project is just around the corner and that surely will fix everything'. Projects need to have clear recommendations. Findings need to inform future policy and practice. In order for both of these things to happen, projects must run their course and have time to promulgate their results. Sustained effects are rarely measured and yet this is vital to determine which innovations have become embedded in practice and which have led to ongoing improvements in student learning.

Lessons about networking numeracy improvement

Our experience with networking numeracy improvement through the LAND project provides some useful lessons for those leading schools and school systems. The networking dimension of the LAND project had two related components. The first was the development and use of a wiki as a tool for sharing practice, seeking advice and celebrating achievements. The second was the role played by systems and governments in disseminating and using the findings from the numeracy development projects that they had funded and supported. Eight key ideas for networking numeracy improvement, including the promulgation of findings, were developed through the LAND project that together summarise the discussion of this chapter:

- plan to include digital technologies in useful ways
- provide induction and training, and engage users in the design of the technology
- allow time for familiarisation with new technology and set achievable goals
- people are essential for effective networking: make use of online moderators and ensure communication is part of designated positions
- organise for the findings to be disseminated during and at the conclusion of projects

- limit intrusions of time-consuming external accountabilities and compliances
- assess value by examining the effect projects have on teaching practice and student engagement and achievement
- expect the findings to inform future policy and practice: fund, develop and conduct audits after the project has been completed.

Networking numeracy improvement is a multifaceted undertaking and needs to consider dimensions related to school community, system authority and government. Our experience indicates that much can be gained by approaching the challenge of achieving sustainable system-wide improvement in student numeracy achievement if a networking perspective is adopted. The concept of a networked school community is fundamental to this approach and highlights the fact that schools cannot do it by themselves. Close communication links within the school community, especially with parents, and between school communities and central offices and government departments, universities and others are needed to achieve sustained numeracy improvement.

CHAPTER 7

SUPPORTING NUMERACY DEVELOPMENT
Rhonda Faragher, Julie Southwell and Michael Gaffney

Over the last few years, the NAPLAN results in numeracy at Teamwork Primary and St Solo had been average rather than outstanding – at least compared with other schools in similar socioeconomic circumstances. Still, there was a feeling among the principals and teaching staff at both schools that numeracy levels could be better. So when the opportunity arose for them to be part of a new government-funded program to improve numeracy outcomes, both schools expressed an interest in being involved.

Teamwork Primary and St Solo belong to different school systems, and their respective education authorities took different approaches in using this latest government program to support numeracy development. They had a choice of two program options. While both involved support from central office consultants and university researchers, the central office for Teamwork Primary decided to implement the program option based on the formation and work of principal–teacher leader teams. This was because this option not only aligned with their general systemic principle that principals and teachers can, and indeed should, exercise leadership and responsibility for improving student outcomes in different but complementary ways, but also that principals and teachers have existing knowledge and understandings about teaching, school leadership and how children learn – and that these qualities should be recognised and developed in bringing about numeracy development.

The central office for St Solo, on the other hand, decided to go with the program option that involved working with principals only – at least in this initial phase of the initiative. This option fitted with the view of several central office senior executive staff that most principals had lost touch with current understandings and practice in numeracy, and therefore needed a 'booster shot' of professional development to bring them up to speed.

Over the next 18 months or so, the central office consultants and school-based personnel from both school systems worked with university researchers, attended workshops associated with their particular program option, and conducted follow-up fieldwork in their schools. The central office consultants regularly visited the schools to provide support and monitor progress.

Those who worked with Teamwork Primary were enthusiastic and knowledgeable. They had firm ideas about effective practice, but were also good listeners. They were able to ask probing questions and provide guidance (and direction when appropriate). They were respected and well accepted by staff.

On the other hand those consultants who worked with St Solo tended to either 'go with the flow' or be overly directive – depending on the priorities set by the central office of their educational authority. Consequently, the staff at St Solo did not particularly value their consultants. Still, they did appreciate the role that these consultants played in liaising with the university researchers, and in administering the program budget and related government reporting and compliance requirements.

After two years, the numeracy outcomes at Teamwork Primary were beginning to improve. The teachers had developed a set of principles about effective teaching of mathematics to guide their practice and influence the shape of their school's organisational arrangements. Teamwork Primary had recently had a change of principal as well as some turnover of staff, but both teacher leaders from Teamwork Primary's numeracy program were still on staff. They were busy explaining to the incoming principal the program principles and how they were developed and being used.

Meanwhile, over at St Solo, a new principal had also just been appointed. She was looking forward to 'doing something about numeracy' at her school. The NAPLAN scores had been flatlining over recent years and she was interested in the latest initiative of the central office. The central office for St Solo had just had two of its consultants trained in delivering a series of modules, designed by different university academics based on their research, about what principals needed to know and be able to do to improve numeracy outcomes in their schools. The central office staff really felt that, this time, principals would get the message and be able to drive the types of improvement that schools across the system needed to demonstrate to government. The new principal at St Solo was due to attend the first of five one-day workshops with other principals at the central office conference centre the following week.

Introduction

Numeracy development is a team effort. What the scenarios demonstrate is that 'Numeracy development needs to be a team effort'. Any development based around the efforts of one person can be fickle, depending on changing staff and circumstances. The scenarios described above demonstrate this. Developing shared understandings of effective teaching practice in mathematics and achieving sustained improvement in student outcomes in numeracy are complex challenges that cannot be met by principals or teachers alone. Neither can they be achieved by policy edicts or one-size-fits-all training packages. Rather, they require informed, flexible and coordinated support from within as well as beyond the school.

In this chapter the pivotal role that people external to a school can play in supporting numeracy development is examined. We focus on the work of central office consultants, government officers, and university researchers engaged with school principals and teacher leaders in the LAND project. In particular, the various forms of support provided to members of the LAND school leadership teams at each school is examined, as well as the demands placed on these teams by LAND project officers from education authority central offices, by government officers from the Commonwealth Department of Education, Employment and Workplace Relations, and by the LAND research team.

Effective support of numeracy development in schools and school systems involves the interplay of three fundamental concepts: partnership, alignment and integration. The concept of 'partnership' highlights that those in schools, central offices, government and universities have complementary expertise and roles to play – and that what one does influences, and is influenced by, what another does. Second, 'alignment' of the intentions and actions of these various players is needed so that the whole (in terms of sustained system-wide numeracy development) is greater than the sum of the individual priorities and efforts of those in different parts of the system. Third, sustained systemic numeracy development is only possible when there is effective 'integration' of professional development opportunities provided by government, central office and university partners with the continuing professional learning needs, and professional aspirations and practices of principals and teachers – in combination and in collaboration.

LAND: A partnership for supporting numeracy development

The LAND project was a partnership between schools, education authority central offices, the Commonwealth Department of Education, Employment and Workplace Relations and a university research team, designed to pilot new approaches for achieving systemic development in numeracy. It brought together teachers, principals, central office personnel, government officers and researchers in a collective enterprise to find out and support what works in raising student achievement in numeracy in low socioeconomic school communities. Put simply, it was a partnership formed for a specific purpose.

Partnerships are important because they highlight a major recurring issue with school reform: that is, that top-down or bottom-up approaches alone do not work. Rather, what is required is the right combination of both. Improvement can only be sustained when policy-makers, school system administrators, school-based practitioners and university researchers are brought together, supported and, where necessary, challenged by evidence of what is working and what is not. In fact partnerships of the type formed in the LAND project are vehicles for expressing the wisdom that exists within and across all levels of school systems. They rely on cooperation and the shared desire of those involved to tackle problems of mutual interest. In the LAND project, the problem was how to effect sustainable systemic improvement in student numeracy achievement.

The LAND project drew together two important factors found to influence student achievement in numeracy: the development and delivery of high-quality mathematics teaching, and the exercise of educational leadership at classroom, school, central office and government department level. The design of the LAND project was based on Australian and international research that improving student numeracy requires attention to existing practice and professional learning in mathematics teaching and educational leadership, and that this should happen *in combination* (where mathematics teaching informs educational leadership and vice versa) and *in collaboration* with the educators involved.

The participating education authorities were the Northern Territory Catholic Education Office, Catholic Education South Australia and the Western Australia Catholic Education Office. Staff from each of these education authorities, the principals and teachers from participating schools, the officers from the Department of Education, Employment and Workplace Relations, and the research team each had their particular areas of expertise, roles and responsibilities. They also brought to the LAND project partnership particular expectations, accountabilities and constraints. From these bases, the partnership was formed. While the ways that the project partners worked together evolved over the period of the project, the experience indicated that it was possible to distil certain features of an effective partnership:

- a clear, significant, shared and achievable purpose
- mutual respect for each other's expertise, role, responsibilities, expectations, and work accountabilities and constraints
- teamwork and clear delineation of roles
- capability to think strategically and act practically
- acknowledgement and celebration of contributions to achieving the purpose, involving the sharing of problems and solutions
- flexibility and a sense of humour!

The LAND project displayed most of these features – most of the time. The project partners shared the purpose of finding ways to develop and sustain higher levels of student numeracy achievement. The dual discipline focus and multi-level design of the LAND project – incorporating people with interest and expertise in mathematics and educational leadership, and from different places and parts of the Australian school education system – meant that there was great diversity among the project participants. This diversity incorporated schools in low socioeconomic status communities in metropolitan, regional and remote areas across the country; Catholic education authorities in Western Australia, South Australia and the Northern Territory; the Australian Catholic University; and the Australian Government. It needed to be managed sensitively. The school community contexts in which teachers and principals were working needed to be carefully appreciated by their central office, government and university partners so that the line between supporting and challenging practices was clearly and respectfully negotiated based on the evidence and the expertise of those involved. Of course, running through the project was the sense of teamwork and the distinctive value and role that each person brought to it. The challenge was to continually work at linking big-picture strategy with what was happening and what needed to happen on the ground. And, at times, all participants needed to not take themselves too seriously!

Another distinctive and valuable feature of the LAND partnership was the governance and contractual arrangements. This involved the establishment of three similar contracts between the Australian Government and the Northern Territory Catholic Education Office, Catholic Education South Australia and Western Australia Catholic Education Office respectively. A national advisory group, including representatives from each of the three education authorities, the research team and the Department of Education, Employment and Workplace Relations, was formed to liaise on matters of program implementation and evaluation. This formal grouping facilitated other forms of communication among the researchers, and officers at central office and government levels across the jurisdictional contexts. In fact, the LAND project partnership exhibited features of a professional network where those involved at school and central office levels had opportunity to work with colleagues in other school clusters including those in metropolitan Perth and Adelaide, and in regional and remote areas of the Kimberley and the Northern Territory. This was a rare opportunity for school personnel to work across jurisdictions and with colleagues in very different contexts. The university researchers played an important linking and brokering role in facilitating this network, including establishing and maintaining the LAND wiki as a vehicle for digital communication (see Chapter 6).

While the LAND partnership generally worked well, it was also subject to particular constraints. These mostly had to do with tight timelines (especially the lack of time to assess longer term effects of project work), and with competing priorities at all levels in the system – including student, teacher and parent demands at the school level, demands of related programs (and unrelated programs!) at central office level, and the accountability requirements of government officers to regularly monitor (and therefore for those in schools, central offices and the university research team to provide progressive reports about) project outcomes at government level.

Despite these constraints, the LAND project partnership for supporting numeracy development worked well but differently in each context. Some of these differences relate to the extra time and cost of communication and engagement with remote schools. Others can be explained by the particular talents and motivations of the teachers, principals, central office staff and university researchers involved. In summary, the LAND project partnership brought people together and it got them involved and talking about numeracy – as one LAND school leadership team member explained:

> LAND has meant that lots of people are talking – here [at the workshop], in their schools, across schools, with consultants from central office, with parents, and in the community. And I think once the conversations start, they can't be stopped.

Aligned numeracy development: Principles underpinning support

One of the challenging features of systemic reform in education is not only the number of different stakeholders but also the various needs, roles, expectations, accountabilities and expertise that each contributes. Put another way, while everyone may be seeking the same end – improved student numeracy achievement – the particular actions that each person takes can sometimes work against rather than support this objective. For the greatest effect, the intentions and the actions of all the stakeholders need to be aligned. With this in mind, this section outlines a series of principles developed from the LAND project to assist those involved in supporting schools in numeracy development.

Numeracy development happens with and through people

The first principle is that people are central to numeracy development. It simply cannot happen without them! In the LAND framework (see Figure 2.5), people are the ones making the connections, guiding the arrows. Teachers, numeracy coordinators, principals and other school executive, central office staff and consultants each have a role and responsibility for improving mathematics teaching and student achievement in numeracy. It is therefore important to consider how each person understands the elements of the framework and how the people impinge on each other – through their actions, and those of their colleagues. Each person's understandings and the actions they take (or don't take) are important to achieving success. As a consequence, the focus of numeracy development strategies needs to be on working with and through people to develop and realise shared goals.

Professional development needs to be integrated with professional learning

The second principle is that professional development needs to be integrated with professional learning. 'Professional development' usually refers to formal programs that take place away from one's normal work situation, whereas 'professional learning' is used to describe a process of continuing professional growth that occurs through regular, day-to-day work practices as well as in more formalised education and training settings. Both are needed to improve practice. For example, LAND workshops were held periodically through the project. On their own, they would be regarded as professional development. Through explicit processes such as the professional learning communities (described in Chapter 5), school teams incorporated the material from the workshops into their personal practice and hence transformed professional development into professional learning.

In her review of the literature, Webster-Wright highlighted the link between professional development and professional learning:

> From an increasing amount of empirical research, a consensus has developed within the educational research community that effective professional development is based on a notion of professional learning as continuing, active, social, and related to practice. (2009, p. 703)

The LAND project reflected this view of professional learning in the characteristics of what was offered and how it was offered:

- *continuing* – the project involved the same schools over two years and in most cases the same LAND school leadership team members
- *active* – the LAND school leadership teams chose what they wanted to focus on and what would be of most benefit to their students and school communities
- *social* – members of the LAND school leadership teams worked with each other, with other LAND school leadership teams, with the research team, and most importantly with the LAND project officer in their school cluster
- *related to practice* – the material considered in the professional development workshop sessions was directly connected to the participants' school programs and priorities, and in some cases driven by it.

With reference to this last point, Webster-Wright (2009) has claimed that the connection between formal professional development sessions and the professional learning that continues in the workplace is acknowledged but poorly understood. In the LAND project, this problem was tackled and the links between the learning from the workshop sessions and the ongoing professional learning in schools were explored. As a result, the researchers were able to note the challenges for schools, support them through these and develop processes for sustainability. Some of the challenges included the inherent busy-ness of schools. School teams returning to their workplace after three days of workshops were often consumed by responding to issues that had arisen in their absence. Processes for sustainability were critical with the high turnover of staff in all participant schools, not just the remote ones. Two strategies were particularly effective. The wiki served as a record of planned action and accomplishment that could be easily accessed by new team members and other staff in schools. The second strategy was the development of LAND school charters, where teams gave an explicit description of aligned numeracy development in their context. These strategies are explained more fully in other chapters of this book.

Context is important – so be flexible and adjust!

The third principle underpinning support for numeracy development is the need to appreciate the importance of context and to adjust the nature of numeracy development accordingly. While the effect of context on professional learning is widely acknowledged in theory, the practice of professional development too often separates the learner from the context in which learning occurs or fails to specifically examine features of that context (Webster-Wright, 2009).

Context surrounds and influences how teachers make decisions about teaching mathematics. In their study of primary schools, Millett and Bibby (2004) offered a description of the 'situation' or immediate school environment in which these decisions are made. The situation includes the teachers themselves, their students and their professional colleagues, as well as the external professionals, policy-makers, the public and those in private enterprise (for example, commercial publishers). Millett and Bibby (2004) proposed a model of change that included the notion of a 'zone of enactment' as the space in which individual teachers make sense of the proposed reform. One's zone of enactment is an essentially social construct, and involves the teacher's interactions with those exerting influence on them. Teachers' capacity and will to change, their beliefs about themselves (for example, their confidence and how they see themselves as professionals), their views about the situation, their opinions and involvement with various forms of professional development, and their personal relationships can all influence their decisions on how they teach. In essence, a teacher's situation acts as a filter for external influences, such as those that come from central offices, government, university academics and private consultants. The work of Millett and Bibby (2004) focused on the question of what factors made a significant difference that enabled teachers to work effectively with change in their zones of enactment. The LAND research was concerned with similar questions.

Schools in the LAND project were characterised by their disparity of context. For example, one was a metropolitan school with a parent body that spoke over

40 different languages, another a remote Indigenous community school where all in the community spoke the one Indigenous language, with little English spoken outside the school; another a school on the edge of a capital city with all its community speaking only English. The common feature across these schools was the low socioeconomic status of their surrounding communities. The variety of contexts was a source of growth for the development of the project. It was not for outsiders (such as university researchers) to claim to understand the contexts in which the LAND school leadership teams were working nor was it feasible for them to consider a model of 'let us tell you how to fix things up'. Instead, LAND from the outset was a collaborative enterprise built on a sense of professional respect and partnership between all involved. The school teams chose the focus of their numeracy development within the perimeters set by central office and the Australian Government. The research team responded to those focus areas in the ways that they developed and delivered the series of workshops, and the LAND project officers supported the LAND school leadership teams as they enacted their plans in their local school contexts. The LAND project evaluation highlighted that this approach was highly valued by schools, as evidenced by the following exchange:

> INTERVIEWER: Has the LAND project given you enough flexibility so that you can just adjust it to your context?

> LAND SCHOOL LEADERSHIP TEAM MEMBER: Yes I think it has. It has also provided a collaborative framework, so I can't just go back and waffle on about anything that I feel like, a pet subject of mine or whatever else. There are three of us here [at the workshop]. I think that set up is good. We have to agree to a plan. We then have to sell that plan and get agreement with the rest of the people [back at school] or it just won't work. The basic premises of LAND really mean that, you know, don't be the 'show pony' because we need more than one. All of us will have to be the 'show pony' not just one of us – that's built into the LAND approach.

Professional learning is a continuing process done by people, not to people

Continuing professional learning, the learning of practising professionals (Webster-Wright, 2009), is at the heart of significant pedagogical improvement. The LAND process was designed on the principle that continuing professional learning is not something 'done' to people but rather a process that continues throughout the career of a professional. Continuing professional learning is likely to involve professional development where teachers attend workshops or meetings related to their practice. These activities may be selected by teachers or required by their employer or decided on some other basis. Research suggests that the effectiveness of the professional development depends on the way teachers integrate their experience of professional development with their practice over time (Bruce et al., 2010).

The critical step is therefore to enable professional development opportunities to become part of a process of continuing professional learning. The findings of the LAND project support the argument of Bruce et al.: 'We conceptualize teacher professional learning as embedded in the classroom context and constructed through experience and practice in sustained iterative cycles of goal setting/planning, practicing, and reflecting' (2010, p. 1599). The LAND project workshops involved teachers in considering ideas from research to set goals for implementation in their school context. Active planning processes were evidenced by the publication of planning documents on the LAND project wiki. These plans were implemented in schools with the support of the LAND project officers. The research findings align with those of Bruce et al. (2010).

During the LAND project, the role that LAND school leadership teams could play in supporting staff to develop their professional practice was demonstrated. From helping the teacher who was struggling in his classroom, to encouraging the teacher who found her stride by affirmation from the Characteristics of Effective Mathematics Teaching (see Chapter 3) that she was working towards something that mattered and would make a difference, and to helping the beginning teacher who wished to establish herself, these school-based teams played a vital part in bringing about better teaching and learning in classrooms. But teachers and principals cannot continue to exercise this type of leadership without the right type of support. The principles described provide some insight into what happened in the LAND project. Further observations, based on the work of the LAND project officers, are described in the next section.

LAND project officers: Building connections to support numeracy development

The most immediate and consistent forms of support available to members of the LAND school leadership teams were the LAND project officers. These were staff members employed and based in the central offices of the participating education authorities. They came from an organisational area associated with school support in numeracy or school development or both. Most already had a well-established relationship with the schools participating in the LAND project.

The role of the project officer was crucial, playing a key liaison role between the schools, their central office, the university as the research partner, and the

Department of Education, Employment and Workplace Relations as the funding agency. Their responsibilities were to support LAND school leadership teams, monitor their progress, collaborate in the design and refinement of the project with researchers, link LAND project activity with education system priorities and programs, and manage project administrative, accountability and compliance requirements. They provided on-the-ground support to schools, building connections between vision, teaching, organisation, community and outcomes elements of the LAND framework at the school level. The project officers, through their mobility across classrooms and schools, were also the people best placed to be the conduit to encourage alignment between what happens within and between the classroom, school and the central office levels of their school systems.

The project officers' role involved the provision of a range of support and advice to school and central office colleagues. It could be given various titles including 'consultant', 'critical friend' and 'expert adviser'. Whatever the job title, their work in the LAND project convinced the researchers of the importance of their role in supporting their colleagues and their system to integrate and align numeracy development in schools and across the school system.

Supporting integration of professional development with professional learning

Project officers supported members of the LAND school leadership teams in integrating the ideas, concepts and skills covered in the workshops with their day-to-day school leadership and teaching practices. They helped them make the connection between professional development and professional learning. For example, by knowing the strengths and limitations of school teams, one of the project officers was able to provide specific advice about issues arising from plans being developed. Project officers were part of all workshops and were able to assist school teams to follow up actions after workshops on planning for embedding practices at the classroom level. School project teams were supported by the project officers in the preparation of on-site and in-class professional learning opportunities to be facilitated by the teachers of the leadership teams. The project officer was a critical part of ensuring the professional development of the workshops became part of professional learning and embedded in practice. University research projects rarely have the funding, or the researchers the time, to undertake extensive follow-up work in schools. In the LAND context, this was particularly the case due to the locations of the schools. The project officers could be where the researchers could not. Even so, project officers are not based in schools and, they too must therefore ensure their time in schools is strategic. The LAND project officers combined their work in schools with encouraging teams to engage with the wiki to maintain momentum with the project between visits and workshops.

> INTERVIEWER: How have you interacted with the LAND project officer? What have they done in relation to your school and the project?

> LAND SCHOOL LEADERSHIP TEAM MEMBER: She visits the school and then we'll have a school professional development session where we might work together to do some activities or presentations. At other times she is on the end of the phone if we need it. The LAND project officer also does most of the organising. This sounds simple but airflights, accommodation . . . all of that stuff is important. That's what she's doing. We wouldn't be able to live without her quite frankly. She visits other schools, helps us to get together a couple of times a year and visit each other's schools occasionally. The project officers . . . are out there so they then can feed back important things that are happening in other schools, which may or may not work for us . . . so that's important feedback to keep the whole conversation going.

Supporting alignment through understanding context

The LAND project officers were appointed from within each educational system. Project officers have a unique and multifaceted role. The role requires movement between classrooms, schools and central office and ideally requires a deep understanding and experience of each context. The project officers were the connecting link between the school, educational system, university and government. In addition, reporting requirements necessitated working with public servants in government departments.

The project officers' close connection with school teams proved to be vital. The project officers were on-site in schools, working with the LAND leadership teams before and after the workshops. Project officers who, as facilitators of discussion, were able to encourage and motivate as well as challenge proved most effective in leading sustained change. Where project officers were given additional roles by their system, such as administering other projects, conflicts occurred with what they were working on. For example, it was very difficult to be contributing to school staffing decisions while at the same time supporting numeracy teams.

Many of the LAND schools were managing a number of projects. Education systems were faced with determining which of many options arising from the education reform agenda they would support and implement in their schools. We found our project officers were frequently in a position to make informed recommendations to senior officers at the system level. They were also aware of system priorities and how the LAND project supported the strategic direction of the system. This became a very valuable aspect of implementing and aligning system-wide and school priorities.

The LAND project officers demonstrated these qualities:

- an understanding of both the big picture and the small details: knowledge of context and the way students and teachers are working, the needs of the school and an understanding of the system initiatives already in place
- strategic thinking to provide targeted support in connecting the classroom, school and system initiatives with the project
- facilitation skills to support the school teams to collaborate, to build leadership capacity for all team members, and to strengthen each team's ability to undertake an enquiry process to effect change
- an ability to articulate the project's vision and progress for improving numeracy outcomes to a wide audience from school staff to parent bodies and system and government departments
- a willingness and ability to hold difficult conversations with leadership teams to ensure compliance in meeting the externally set benchmarks.

These qualities were used by the LAND project officers as they were involved in tasks from providing support in professional learning to making administrative arrangements for program delivery, as well as fulfilling compliance and accountability requirements for their respective education systems. In other words, they performed an important liaison role with two other partners in the LAND project: the education authorities and the Australian Government responsible for the oversight and funding of the initiative.

Oversight and funding of numeracy development

The roles of education authorities and the Australian Government in the LAND project were, respectively, to oversee and to fund program activity. Each of the participating education authorities signed a separate contract with the government, and then subcontracted the research team to deliver significant elements of the project, including the workshop design and delivery, school visits and research to inform the writing of the progressive and final project reports. The salaries for the LAND project officers were paid from federal government funding.

While the administration of the LAND project followed many of the usual procedures of accounting and reporting on project activity, the nature of the project as a pilot initiative to inform future practice at school system and government level meant that opportunities were sometimes sought to include other personnel, from education authority central offices as well as those in the Department of Education, Employment and Workplace Relations, directly in LAND project activity. This was particularly the case in the discussions around the causes and effects of numeracy improvement, and how factors operating at classroom, school, central office and government level interact. (A detailed discussion of this work is provided in Chapter 8.)

A related feature of the futures orientation of the LAND project was its purpose in informing the design of the Smarter Schools National Partnerships (Commonwealth Department of Education, Employment and Workplace Relations, 2011), a targeted program of the Australian Government in cooperation with the states and territories to improve student achievement in literacy and numeracy across Australia. As a research project, its purpose was to trial and to report on ways to support numeracy development across a school system, with a particular emphasis on the context of school communities with low socioeconomic status. Contrary to the initial intention of the Australian Government for the literacy and numeracy pilots (of which the LAND project was one) to be completed and reported on before the national partnerships began, this did not occur. Instead the federal government decided to press ahead with negotiating its agreements with the states and territories while the project pilots were still underway. Unfortunately this had the effect of limiting the degree to which the findings from LAND and the other pilots could be considered – at least in the short term.

Despite this, the findings reported in this book can be used by the Australian Government, government and non-government schools and school systems to inform policy and program development in numeracy over the longer term. In particular the findings support the view that Australian school systems, by and large, should engage in more locally grown, bottom-up and networked approaches to improving student achievement, echoing the findings of Mourshed et al. (2010). Secondly, the LAND project experience provides an example of how system leadership can involve educators from across the system – not just the senior executives in central office. Thirdly, it provides an insight into the administrative complexity of systemic development in numeracy. All things considered, the administrative load (in terms of reporting to government, for example) was significant but manageable.

The urgency to move into funding the partnerships before completion of the pilot studies is indicative of a common occurrence in education: the overabundance of new initiatives. When a problem is noted (for example, too many students not meeting minimum numeracy achievement targets in schools with low socioeconomic status), many potential solutions are proposed, with the effect of new projects being implemented before other initiatives are completed and their effectiveness evaluated. This has at least three problems: full advantage of the value of the investment is not realised; it is not clear whether the initiative was effective as evaluation is confounded by other activities that have begun; and, significantly, schools and systems can be overwhelmed by the requirement to implement a number of projects at the same time.

Implementation of this type of educational policy means the full advantage and the value of each targeted initiative are potentially never realised. There also exists the major disadvantage of the increasingly overwhelming burden on schools and systems as they strive to simultaneously implement and meet compliance requirements across a number of initiatives or projects that may not align or consider their context.

Researching and supporting numeracy development

The LAND project proposal was developed by researchers from the Australian Catholic University in cooperation with the Catholic education authorities of South Australia, Western Australia and the Northern Territory. The role of the research team was to gather and analyse data, draw conclusions and disseminate the findings of the project. This book is a tangible expression of that role.

To work properly, support and advice from project partners needs to be reciprocated. Universities are effective partners when they act as catalysts for revealing and developing the wisdom of educators at classroom, school, central office and government levels of education systems. Those in education systems are effective partners when they are open to the perspectives of others within and external to the system, and work to develop a sense of shared purpose, contribute their expertise and act collaboratively in the basis of evidence and professional insight. Universities can assist educators in school systems to develop a systemic perspective by researching the connections between what happens in classrooms, schools, central offices and government bureaucracies. Those in school systems can assist universities through providing the issues and the context for investigation as well as their experience and expertise from working in such school systems. In this way university–school system partnerships go beyond the usual delivery of professional development or the review of specific programs or policies. When they work well, they add value by providing feedback about the system itself, while also serving as vehicles for universities to assess, maintain and enhance their relevance. The following exchange picks up some of the character of university–school system partnership in the LAND project:

> INTERVIEWER: It has been interesting for me as a newcomer to just see how many people from the ACU [Australian Catholic University] are working on the LAND project. You can have up to four people coming in rather than just one person. Has that worked well for you? What do you think of having a whole bunch of different people coming in and doing different things?

> LAND SCHOOL LEADERSHIP TEAM MEMBER: Personally it's worked well for me because they're a terrific group of people, each bringing something different.

> And if we are talking about, you know, being in the one place and allowing diversity, that's a very clear demonstration about how that can work, very, very easily and very, very well. I think having a mathematics specialist sort of role, then a leadership in mathematics role I think is that kind of set up and I haven't heard of anybody who has been critical of that. Imagine how dull it could have been if there was only one person. If you get on with that person, that's great, but if you don't you are in serious trouble.

Alongside their research role, the research team provided the stimulus for action through facilitating professional development opportunities. These were undertaken through a series of workshops over the two years of the project. The workshops were planned with an underpinning philosophy that valued the expertise of participants and acknowledged their understanding of their school. The research team did not come with a ready-to-roll-out package. This was clearly appreciated by the following participant, a school leadership team member.

> In my experience over a very long period of time, you would have had to drag me to a professional development session. Then when I got there you would have to gag me from making rather insulting comments. Because essentially they were useless, reasonably unprofessional in my view, not really contributing to any significant change happening either in my school or any other school that would have been involved . . . And I think I wasn't the only one. I just generally think they weren't meeting teachers' needs. What I see about this LAND project is something totally different. [It has] a completely new and different focus. So I sometimes get up in the morning and think, 'Oh I hope I'm going to another LAND meeting' because they are very stimulating and exciting. And what's exciting to me is what LAND is doing to something for a subject very close to my heart – mathematics. It has brought teachers and principals together and we are talking about mathematics and numeracy development. I haven't seen that happen in a long time.

The workshop series began with an orientation workshop that introduced participants to the project and provided professional development in the areas of mathematics education and educational leadership. The three-day workshop plan evolved according to the needs of participants. On the first day, each school gave a presentation about their context. They were acquainted with recent and relevant research and invited to make decisions about which of the characteristics of effective teaching of mathematics they intended to develop through the project (see Chapter 3 for more detail).

Another aspect of the orientation workshop was the focus on the development of teams and the establishment of collaborative networks that would set up the project for the two years to come. These networks were welcomed by workshop participants: for example, in the words of one school leadership team member:

> I don't think I'm alone in saying that LAND is organised in getting teachers talking together not only at this meeting, but our obligations back in our school have been to make sure that we bring the rest of our teaching staff, and I include teaching assistants, on to what I would like to call 'the same page'. This doesn't mean the same place, but on the same page that allows for some creativity and flexibility.

These two aspects – targeted and customised workshop content and the development of relationships among LAND project personnel – were instrumental in assisting the move from workshop professional development to continuing professional learning: that is, putting the workshop ideas, understandings and activities into school and classroom practice. This can be seen in the commitment to ongoing development of their pedagogical content knowledge and the collegiality expressed by those in the LAND project schools:

> LAND has been very significant in having teachers to take onboard their responsibility for developing their knowledge of mathematics teaching. And I think that's happened, no matter who you are, or what you think you can do, I think everybody's conscious of that and now doing it on a regular basis.

> We are a very diverse group of people [in LAND]. Whether we be from ACU or schools or central offices, you would think we'd been related for 20 years, don't see each other for months on end – and then when we get together, it's as if we were talking yesterday. So there is such a commonality of purpose and effort that has been invested in getting us together and staying together, I don't think that can go. Probably most of us will still be in touch in five years' time – and still talking about mathematics. You can't stop the conversation.

The value of university researchers extending their role beyond that of observing practice to working with practitioners to broaden and deepen each other's professional knowledge and skills was highlighted through the LAND project. The involvement of the research team with principals and teacher leaders from the LAND school leadership teams, and with project officers from each of the central offices, in designing and delivering a series of workshops, conducting school visits and facilitating networking across the project greatly assisted in integrating professional development activity with continuing professional learning, as well as creating a sense of professional community based on common interest and mutual respect. Particular abilities were identified in the university researchers that brought about these outcomes:

- developing and managing the research
- collaborating with colleagues in other project roles
- establishing and maintaining professional networks and teams
- responding to the professional learning needs of participants
- acting as a critical friend
- recognising the need to respect the professional knowledge and expertise of other personnel: for example, in school teams, system leaders, public servants.

Lessons for supporting numeracy development

There are a number of lessons that have been learnt about supporting numeracy development from the LAND project:

- Numeracy development is a team effort that involves working with and through people with different professional qualities across the various parts of school systems.
- Educational leadership at the local school level is vital, and needs to involve principals and teacher leaders working together.
- Those appointed to lead numeracy development need to be able to share leadership, think strategically and act practically.
- Numeracy development at the school level is most effective and sustainable when it is supported by a combination of internal central office expertise (for example, LAND project officers) and external research and development capabilities (for example, university researchers) working collaboratively with school numeracy teams to support embedding practices within and across classrooms. Opportunity is needed to practise, refine and allow changed practice to become part of a teacher's repertoire.
- Education authorities and governments, as the agencies responsible for funding and overseeing numeracy development, need to engage with schools in practical ways – and be prepared to change their approach in light of the context in which schools are operating.
- The number of initiatives adopted needs to be carefully considered and managed. Systems with an overarching goal or strategic direction are in a position to make decisions about which initiatives to support and which can be shaped to contribute to their overall focus.
- Effective, sustainable numeracy development involves deliberate actions to ensure that professional development becomes part of continuing professional learning and has an effect on learning outcomes of students.

Building shared understandings of effective practice in mathematics teaching and the leadership of numeracy development in a school and across a school system, and putting those understandings into practice, is difficult work. It requires *partnership* among those involved at school, central office, government and university level; *alignment* in their intentions and actions; and commitment to *integration* of new with existing understandings and practices. Insights for supporting such development have been the focus of this chapter.

CHAPTER 8

CONNECTING SCHOOL AND SYSTEM PERSPECTIVES IN NUMERACY DEVELOPMENT

Craig Ashhurst and Michael Gaffney

'Another day, another program' – that was the reaction of some central office staff at the local education authority to the latest Australian Government announcement of targeted funding to improve literacy and numeracy. These staff had heard it all before and, while they had always been committed to raising the achievement levels of all students in their jurisdiction – and grateful for the funding – they were becoming tired of the incessant rhetoric of politicians for schools to 'raise the bar' and' bridge the gap'. They felt continually pounded by governments and oppositions who spoke about the need for Australian schools to be 'up there' with schools in Finland, Singapore, South Korea and Shanghai so that Australia could better compete on the global economic playing field. At the same time, they got the persistent message from political leaders that schools were also instruments of social reform – that schools provide the means for students from families who were doing it tough to rise from their disadvantaged backgrounds and have a better quality of life, as well as contribute to the broader social and economic fabric of the wider society.

In 2012, at the National Press Club, prime minister Julia Gillard said Australians needed to face up to the truths that information from My School (Australian Curriculum, Assessment and Reporting Authority, 2013) and international tests were revealing. She announced:

> The first truth is we have to aim higher for every child in every school. Four of the top five schooling systems in the world are in our region and we aren't in that coveted top five. To take one telling example, the average 15-year-old maths student in Australia is two years behind a 15-year-old in Shanghai.
>
> The second truth is we particularly need to improve the education of our poorer children. By Year Three, 89 per cent of children from the poorest quarter of Australian

homes are reading below average. (Commonwealth Department of the Prime Minister and Cabinet, 2012)

Translating this rhetoric into results requires lots of planning and coordinated action across the various levels of education systems – from governments to education authority central offices to schools. After the prime minister's address, the government bureaucrats continued to refine their program proposals based on her vision for their minister to take to Cabinet. At the same time, the central office staff at the local education authority thought, 'Fair enough, we agree with her vision but what's going to be different this time? Can we expect any changes in the government's program development and funding arrangements? In any case education reform is all about getting schools to do things differently, isn't it?'

Meanwhile back in the schools, teachers and principals were too busy with the practicalities of school and classroom life to pay much attention to 'the big picture'. They were focused on the demands of the new mathematics scope and sequence documents and the forthcoming numeracy assessments. They had some pretty clear ideas about how to improve numeracy at their school and wondered if, this time, their perspectives and experiences might have some influence on what was coming from above.

Introduction

Everyone has experience with numeracy. Students engage with it to varying degrees in their lives inside and outside school. Parents hope their children do well on numeracy assessments. Teachers help their students apply the principles of mathematics to everyday life: that is, to become more numerate. Principals try to create conditions that are conducive to numeracy development across the school, while those in central offices and governments who administer numeracy programs see numeracy achievement as a measure of school and program performance.

Similarly, how people see numeracy development and the 'problem' of low levels of numeracy achievement of students in school communities with low socioeconomic status varies from person to person, depending on their background and where they are in 'the system'.

In this chapter, a process is described and a framework proposed for tackling the problem of numeracy achievement in low socioeconomic status school communities that takes into account the different perspectives that different people in different places have about the problem. The concepts of 'systemic alignment' – relating to how different parts of an education system work together – and 'wicked problems' – referring to policy issues that are especially complex, difficult to solve and involve a range of stakeholders with often contrasting and sometimes entrenched views – are explored. From this background the case is made that raising numeracy achievement in schools with low socioeconomic status is a wicked problem. The process of 'causal mapping' that was used in the LAND project to elicit the views of teacher leaders, principals, central office personnel and government officers about what it takes to improve numeracy levels of students in disadvantaged circumstances is then described. The Niche Wicked Problem Framework developed by Niche Thinking (cited in Ashhurst, 2012) is explained as a way of conceptually depicting wicked problems and a tool for discussion in tackling them. The chapter concludes with some implications for education system leaders on ways to understand and connect the perspectives of those working in schools, central offices and governments so that their aspirations, efforts and expertise, and the policies and programs they design and implement, are better aligned and more likely to lead to sustainable improvement in student numeracy achievement.

Systemic alignment and numeracy development

Significant sustainable numeracy development in school systems is a team effort. It can only come about through the combined efforts of those in schools, central offices and governments to *align* their thinking and practice, so that there is a sense of shared purpose across the system and tangible, dynamic connections between what happens between each part of it (that is, classroom, school, central office and government department).

A distinctive feature of the LAND project, as its title Leading Aligned Numeracy Development suggests, was a focus on alignment. To align something means 'to arrange or place in a line' (*The New International Webster's Dictionary and Thesaurus*, 2000). When applied to a system, 'alignment' refers to

> The correct position or positioning of different components with respect to each other or something else, so that they perform properly i.e. to achieve integration. (Encarta Dictionary: English – UK)

Integration is a term closely associated with alignment. It is defined as

> A combination of parts or objects that work together well, the process of coordinating separate elements into a balanced whole or producing compatible behaviour. (Encarta Dictionary: English – UK)

Alignment and integration are clearly desirable features of schools and education systems engaged in the process of numeracy development. Certainly an important task of educational administrators is to ensure that the 'components' perform properly and are well coordinated with other elements of the system. But worthwhile, lasting numeracy development requires more than this. It calls for educational leaders who can build alignment by working with people, and appreciating and respecting their knowledge, skills and perspectives.

In this sense, systemic alignment can be thought of as comprising two dimensions: 'bureaucratic alignment', associated with the functioning and coordination of organisational structures and processes; and 'professional alignment', concerned with the development and exercise of shared understandings and complementary knowledge and skill of the people involved. The degrees and forms of 'systemic alignment' can thus be represented as shown in Figure 8.1.

Systems that demonstrate a high level of bureaucratic alignment have clear lines of authority and accountabilities. Roles and responsibilities are well coordinated and are assigned to those with the appropriate expertise. In contrast, systems with a low level of bureaucratic alignment are characterised by a lack of clarity and accountability of roles and responsibilities. Such systems usually result in people doing their own thing and having little regard for those in authority.

A high level of professional alignment exists where people have a shared understanding about the meaning of their work and how it relates to and affects that of their colleagues. It is also evident in the opportunity and expectation of people to keep their professional knowledge and skill up to date, and to learn to deal with changing circumstances. On the other hand, a low level of professional alignment is evidenced by a lack of shared understanding and low priority being placed on developing new knowledge, skills and applications to deal with organisational problems.

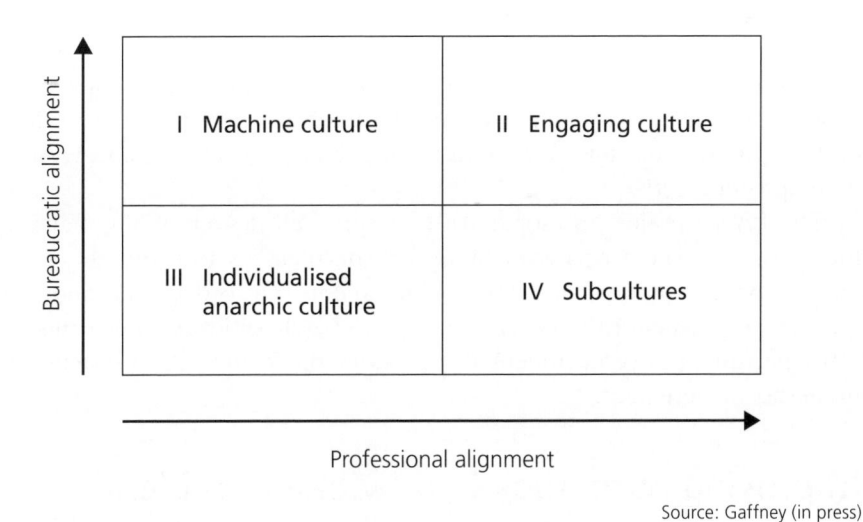

Source: Gaffney (in press)

Figure 8.1: Dimensions of systemic alignment and organisational culture

The combination of these two dimensions results in four types of organisational culture. These are described by Gaffney (in press) as follows:

- *machine culture* (Type I) develops where the tasks that people perform are tightly coordinated and there is little shared understanding or capacity for change
- *engaging culture* (Type II) exists where high levels of coordination and clarity about roles, responsibilities and accountabilities coexist with shared understandings and the capacity to recognise and develop people's attitudes, knowledge and skills to deal with new circumstances
- *individualised anarchic culture* (Type III) arises where there is little coordination and little shared understanding
- *subcultures* (Type IV) emerge where there is a lack of role clarity or respect for authority or both, but there are strong professional norms among certain groups about 'the way things are done around here'.

From an organisational viewpoint, an 'engaging culture' demonstrates systemic alignment in its most effective form. There is shared understanding about the desired ends and means, the components of the system run smoothly, professional capability is recognised and nurtured, and organisational members are aware of changing circumstances, and supported in dealing with them appropriately. In fact, school systems with these qualities are those where the whole is truly greater than the sum of the parts.

Systemic alignment evidenced by an engaging culture enables effective numeracy development and sustainable improvement in student achievement. This type of system culture encourages shared thinking and understandings about numeracy through system leaders developing and applying expertise in useful ways, and ensuring that the actions of individuals and groups in the system are well coordinated, adequately supported and mutually accountable: that is, they work on bringing the top-down and bottom-up perspectives of system-wide numeracy development together.

The LAND project investigated the nature and degree of alignment among the features deemed necessary by project participants to bring about systemic improvement in student numeracy achievement. It afforded the opportunity to identify and compare the *perspectives* of LAND school leadership teams, central office personnel and government officers about the features that influence student numeracy achievement.

Improving numeracy is a 'wicked problem'

Educators deal with a range of issues every day. Some can be easily resolved because there is agreement on the facts and there is a tried and tested way forward. These types of problems have been labelled 'tame'(Rittel & Webber, 1973); they can be defined, understood and solved. A typical example in schools might be adopting a 'wet-day timetable' when it rains. On the other hand, many issues in schools and in education more broadly defy such straightforward resolution. Moreover, these issues tend to be the ones in areas of most significance. Some examples have to do with the assessment and reporting of student achievement, the quality and evaluation of teaching practice, the content of the curriculum, and school funding. These issues are difficult to deal with because of the range of stakeholder views about the nature of the 'problem', the factors causing it, the means of tackling it, and the criteria used to judge whether it has been successfully dealt with.

For these reasons, such problems have been given the label 'wicked', not in the sense of being evil, but due to their nature of being especially complex, difficult to understand and resistant to resolution (Rittel & Webber, 1973). The term 'wicked' was given new currency when the Australian Public Service Commission published the document *Tackling wicked problems: A public policy perspective*, in which the term 'wicked' was described as referring to

> Very complex problems . . . that go beyond the capacity of any one organisation to understand and respond to, and there is often disagreement about the causes of the problems and the best way to tackle them. (2007, p. 1)

Others have commented in a similar vein:

> Contemporary policy problems no longer have clear causes but rather a whole host of loosely connected and interrelated factors [where] each policy issue depends on the complex interplay of a wide range of factors and variables. (Ney, 2009, p. 5)

Given these increasingly challenging circumstances, the question for policy-makers is how to deal with these so-called 'wicked' problems. The Australian Public Service Commission offered some advice – and a warning:

> Wicked problems require innovative, comprehensive solutions that can be modified in the light of experience and on-the-ground feedback. All of the above can pose challenges to traditional approaches to policy making and programme implementation. (2007, p. 1)

It follows that tackling these types of problems successfully requires a different mindset. In essence, this means that those involved in and affected by the problem – the stakeholders – need to work together to reach a shared understanding of the problem and the means of tackling it, and then get started – all the while being prepared to change course as events unfold. Yet, the very nature of wicked problems makes it difficult for everyone to come to grips with their scope, the differing views about their causes and what should be done. The consequence is that these problems are often treated superficially or expediently, resulting in 'solutions' that simply do not work. The Australian Public Service Commission (2007) cited Indigenous disadvantage as an example of a wicked problem: that is, as a policy problem that appears intractable despite the policy action undertaken over several decades.

In light of this background, the researchers in the LAND project contend that improving numeracy levels of students in schools with low socioeconomic status is also an example of a wicked problem. As such, tackling the problem of improving numeracy requires holistic rather than partial or linear thinking; working across agency boundaries, effective engagement of stakeholders in understanding the problem and in identifying possible solutions; changing the mindsets and behaviour of policy-makers; and tolerating uncertainty and the need for a long-term focus (Australian Public Service Commission, 2007, p. 36). The causal mapping process and the Niche Wicked Problem Framework explained in the following sections reflect these requirements. These were the tools used in the LAND project for tackling the problem of how to improve student numeracy achievement.

Mapping the causes of numeracy improvement

What are the causes of the problem? According to whom? And, what patterns (if any) exist between the nature and the priority of causes that different people (that is, key stakeholders) identify? These are questions that lie at the heart of approaches for tackling wicked problems – and numeracy achievement in particular.

Causal mapping is a visual representation tool used to create a representation of the causes of a problem or issue (Langfield-Smith, 1992; Novak & Cañas, 2008; Scavarda et al., 2004). A causal map is made up of two elements: statements of cause; and arrows showing the direction of the cause or influence. Causal mapping was used in the LAND project as a means of identifying the causes of numeracy improvement as seen through the eyes of some of the key stakeholders.

Three groups of stakeholders were involved in casual mapping in the LAND project:

- the LAND school leadership teams comprising the principal and two or three teacher leaders from each of the 17 schools involved in the study: 8 teams were from schools in the two metropolitan clusters (Adelaide and Perth) and 9 teams were from schools in two regional and remote clusters (Northern Territory and the Kimberley).
- program consultants from central offices responsible for each LAND school cluster

- officers from the Commonwealth Department of Education Employment and Workplace Relations responsible for the Smarter Schools National Partnerships, including the National Literacy and Numeracy Pilot program that funded the LAND research.

The process of causal mapping was used to gather information about the perspectives of these groups of educators and compare them. They were asked to nominate and examine the causes of improved numeracy, and explore with the research team some ways of improving numeracy in school communities with low socioeconomic status. They were asked the following question: 'What in your experience are the significant causes of improvement in student achievement in numeracy?' Individual causal maps were drawn, and then used to develop summary maps that represented the thinking of each participant group. An example of a causal map from a LAND school leadership team is shown in Figure 8.2.

The process of causal mapping provided an opportunity for dialogue and a means by which those who have a 'stake' in the problem were able to build a shared understanding of its complexity, that is, what the various causes and effects are and how they interact. The logic is that by building such a picture, the next steps in dealing with the problem become clearer.

In light of the view of the Australian Public Service Commission (2007) that successful tackling of wicked problems relies on the development of different mindsets and understandings, Ashhurst (2012) investigated the extent to which the causal mapping process improved participants' understanding of the wickedness of the problem of improving student numeracy achievement. His study examined changes in understanding using four areas described by Akkerman and Bakker (2011):

- *identification* – Is there evidence of an increase in awareness of participants' own and others' frames of meaning about the problem?
- *coordination* – Is there evidence of the process facilitating conversation (Kraut, Gergle & Fussell, 2002), and tacit understandings being made explicit (Eden & Ackerman, 1992)?
- *reflection* – Is there evidence of increases in participants' 'cognitive diversity' or understanding of alternative ideas and associations (Tegarden, Tegarden & Sheetz, 2007), and increased appreciation of the complexity of the issues (Vo, Poole & Courtney, 2005)?
- *transformation* – Is there evidence of a recognition of a shared 'problem space' between participants, the process encouraging an analysis of critical relationships, and the development of 'hybrid' concepts or ideas?

Taken together, the evidence gathered across these areas not only provided an indication of the extent of alignment in participants' perspectives about the

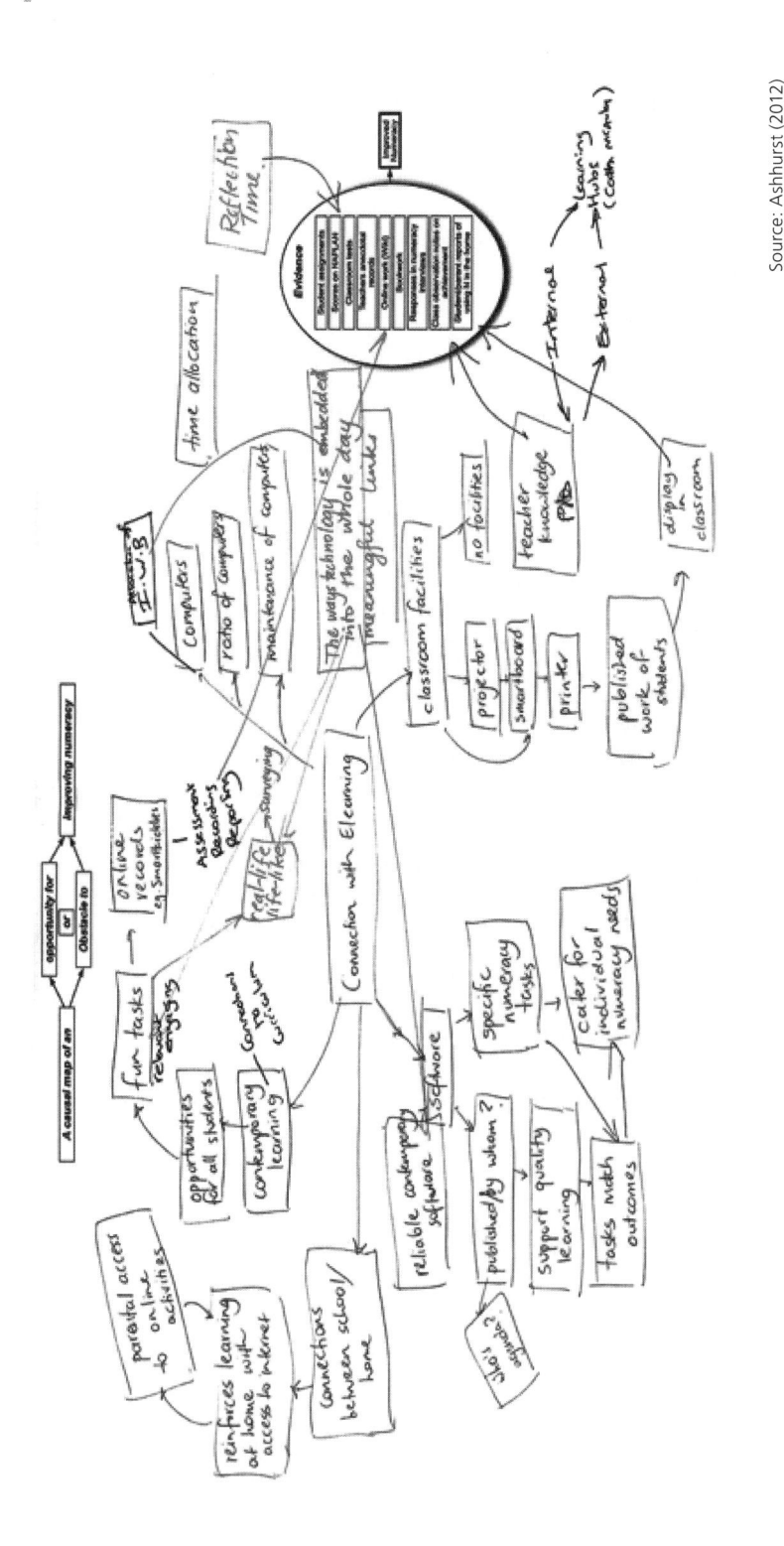

Figure 8.2: A sample causal map of factors contributing to improvement in student achievement in numeracy

Source: Ashhurst (2012)

problem of improving numeracy achievement, but also signalled the development of their 'transformational' leadership capability: their capacity and willingness to think strategically and act practically to build alignment between vision, teaching, organisation and community to bring about numeracy development (see Chapter 4). (Details relating to workshop processes and stages of analysis in the LAND causal mapping study by Ashhurst, 2012, are provided in Appendix 5.)

Making sense of diversity and complexity – the wicked problem framework

The contention that improving numeracy achievement of students in school communities with low socioeconomic status was a 'wicked' problem was supported by the fact that the stakeholder participants in the causal mapping activities conducted during the LAND workshop series came up with almost 700 different causes affecting students' numeracy improvement! Moreover, Ashhurst's (2012) research found that each stakeholder group (school, central office and government staff) perceived and defined the elements of the problem from their own perspective. The types of causes that they identified reflected their role in the system and their specific areas of interest and expertise. These often contrasted with those of other stakeholder groups. For example, most LAND school leadership team members selected causes related to the local community and context as most important for improving numeracy, whereas the majority of central office personnel focused on the need for attention to systemic factors such as high-quality school leadership and teaching practices. Government officers, on the other hand, highlighted the value of good policy and program design and evaluation. In fact, staff from the Department of Education, Employment and Workplace Relations was the only group to list causes under a heading of 'government'. Where awareness of government appeared on school and central office maps at all, it tended to be in relation to the funding of numeracy projects.

Other significant themes related to the ways that different stakeholder groups engaged with the process of causal mapping were observed:

- Strategic thinking, causal focus and use of language vary between stakeholder groups.
- The process of causal mapping increases awareness of wickedness and deepens understanding.
- The LAND framework has general applicability for categorising causes of numeracy improvement.
- Causal mapping has value as a collaborative tool for fostering systemic understandings about numeracy.

Strategic thinking, causal focus and use of language vary between stakeholder groups

The findings demonstrate a number of patterns of causal emphasis. Each stakeholder group indicated a range of causes, but clearly discernable emphases emerged that set each group apart from the others. Figure 8.3 represents this assessment of emphasis as a radar graph. The emphases of LAND school leadership teams, central office staff and Department of Education, Employment and Workplace Relations officers (government) are shown. The completed radar graph was created by joining the rankings on each spectrum. Points for each group were plotted on the following four series of subjective spectra:

- short term to long term
- specific to 'big picture'
- concrete to theoretical
- classroom level to federal government level.

The plotting of emphasis shown in Figure 8.3 shows little overlap between the three stakeholder groups. LAND school leadership teams and government officers have a clear gap between them, being on the opposite sides of the centre point of

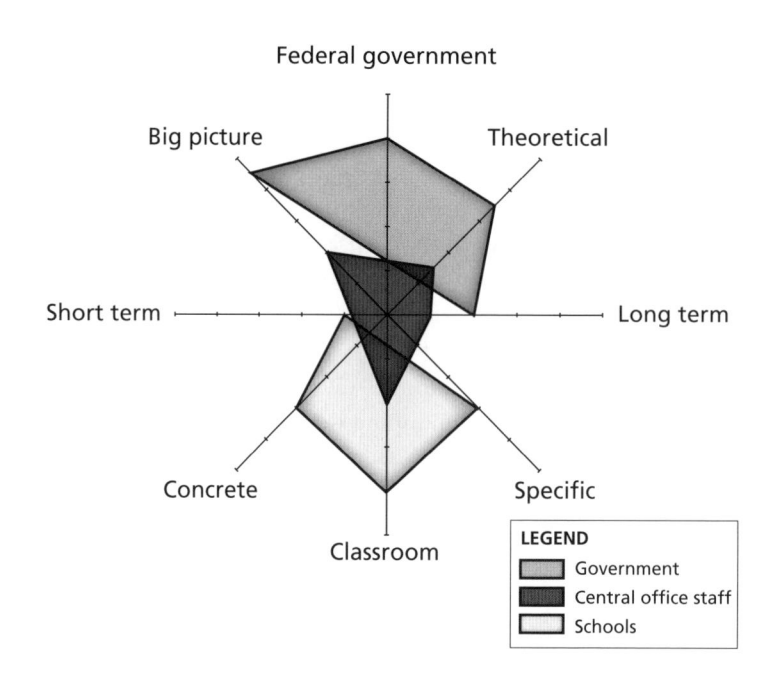

Figure 8.3: Stakeholder group responses plotted on four spectra of causal emphasis characteristics

each spectrum. Central office staff have the middle ground, overlapping in part with both of the other groups. This visual representation is not surprising when the specific work contexts of each group are considered but it does show that, regarding emphasis, there is little alignment in causes between the groups on any of these spectra.

The causes listed by schools were mostly specific, set at the classroom or school level, and concrete. Causes also ranged from short to long term but most were focused on the short to medium term. LAND school leadership teams referred to the need for 'young and enthusiastic teachers' or 'stable and mature staff' and tended to include fewer causal links relating to how this feature might be supported and what influences it has on other causes of numeracy improvement.

In contrast, government officials tended to express causes in more strategic and big-picture terms. This was also the only group to place the federal government as central to the 'system' and many of the causes that they listed were quite abstract or theoretical in nature. For example, they referred to the concept of 'teacher quality' and drew a number of causal links to related concepts affecting and affected by teacher quality, such as 'leadership', 'standards' and 'professional development'.

As shown by their position in Figure 8.3, central office staff act as a bridge between the government and the schools in the education system. The descriptions of the various central office staff groups in this chapter support this contention.

The process of causal mapping increases awareness of wickedness and deepens understanding

The number of causes identified and the links between them increased as the causal mapping process continued. All stakeholder groups found that the opportunity for a structured facilitated discussion around the causes and effects related to improving numeracy widened and deepened their view of the complexity of the issue and helped to make their previously tacit understandings more explicit.

The LAND framework has general applicability for categorising causes of numeracy improvement

The LAND framework (see Chapter 2) proved to be a useful tool for categorising the general types of causes identified by various groups. This was evident in its usefulness for initially grouping the suggested causes from each group of participants. Beyond this general categorisation (that is, by vision, organisation, community and teaching), there was almost no overlap in how different groups of participants understood and connected causes and effects. Their thinking tended to be context specific. In fact, even where participant groups used similar terms, the workshop discussions indicated that different groups meant different things when it came to improving student achievement. For example, see the comments on the system loop on page 159.

Causal mapping has value as a collaborative tool for fostering systemic understandings about numeracy

For most participant groups, the LAND project was viewed as a valuable, though unfortunately too rare, opportunity to discuss causes and effects associated with improving numeracy. Participants appreciated the chance to develop shared understandings of key concepts and terms related to numeracy improvement, and increase their awareness of how those working at other levels in the system saw and understood numeracy achievement, teaching practice, program implementation, policy development and evaluation.

Applying the wicked problem framework

In addition to the sheer number of causes identified and the diversity of perspectives among stakeholders, the causal mapping process highlighted another salient characteristic of wicked problems – the futility of listing causes of wicked problems. Trying to list each cause of numeracy improvement (and then determine means to deal with that cause) not only results in disagreements about causal importance and priority of action, but also artificially compartmentalises the problem into manageable but disconnected components. Apart from the difficulty trying to keep all these causes in one's head, these approaches tend to result in people trying to 'tame' wicked problems. In other words, they treat them as simple or one-dimensional problems, ignoring their complexity and the views of other stakeholders, and apply a solution that fits their view of the problem or just one part of it; it results in different people in different parts of the system seeing the problem only in their terms. They then focus on treating it – as best they can, given their particular patch of responsibilities and resources. Of course, in the end, the wicked problem remains, and is likely to arise again as a policy issue in the next political and policy cycle, albeit with a revised rhetoric or catchphrase. Overall, not much changes. So what can be done to break this cycle?

One promising approach was examined in the LAND project. This involved the application of the wicked problem framework (Ashhurst, 2012) to the problem of improving numeracy. Based on his years of consultancy experience, Ashhurst designed a visual tool that incorporated the key elements of wicked problems drawn from the policy literature. The framework has six dimensions grouped in three loops (as shown in Figure 8.4), and was trialled in the LAND project as a resource for informing policy and program design and delivery for improving numeracy achievement of students in school communities with low socioeconomic

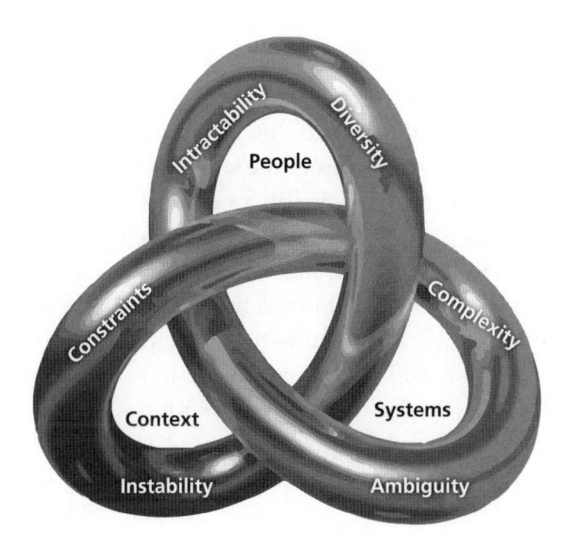

Source: Ashhurst (2012)

Figure 8.4: The Niche Wicked Problem Framework

status (Ashhurst, 2012). The outcomes of the LAND project trial validated the use of the wicked problem framework in these ways:

- as a means of diagnosing and tackling wicked problems
- as a way of capturing the range of thinking on wicked problems without using highly technical lists of characteristics
- as a tool for discussion with stakeholders.

The shape of the model is a trefoil knot, sometimes called the Gordian knot, representing the connected nature of wicked problems. Each of the three 'loops' merges into the next, and the knot as a whole has no start or finish. This is to highlight that each of the areas is seamlessly linked to the others, demonstrating that, while wicked problems can be better managed, they are never actually 'solved'. The following sections provide an overview of each loop and dimension of the framework, and how each of these were evident in the LAND project.

The 'people' loop: Diversity and intractability

People are central to what makes problems 'wicked'. This loop is about differences between stakeholders and includes the two dimensions of diversity and intractability. Both these dimensions can be seen as relating to individuals but can also be applied to organisations, such as schools, school systems and governments. The dimensions of diversity and intractability are critical for establishing that a problem can be considered 'wicked'. Even though the participants in the LAND project were all from the education sector, the findings demonstrated great diversity in response to the question: 'What in your experience are the significant causes of improvement in student achievement in numeracy?'

The differences in the perspectives of the stakeholders seemed to be due to the specific contexts in which the participants were working. At the school level the most important causes appear to be based on those specific issues that the school executive and teachers were currently facing. One example is that 'attendance' was listed as a significant cause by the remote schools but not the metropolitan ones.

School, central office and government participants also differed in their perspective of the problem and in the paradigm they used to make sense of it. A paradigm is a way of looking at and interacting with the world, a set of underlying structures of beliefs, perception and appreciation. Different people understood different parts of the problem and looked at the whole from that particular angle. Their perspectives were often competing or incompatible. Some focused on teachers and pedagogy, some on local community issues, and others on improving organisational systems. These differences affect how 'facts' and causes in a problem are identified and used. Consequently, this means that approaches to improving numeracy achievement need to take into account the following factors:

- Each stakeholder may select different facts as relevant.
- Facts will be interpreted differently depending on the paradigms (or world views) held by different stakeholders.
- The different value sets (associated with different paradigms) mean different sets of priorities may emerge based on the same set of facts.

All these differences affect how stakeholders define the problem, the outcomes they want, what interventions are possible and what consequences will be acceptable. This was evident in the LAND project, with different causes seen as more important while whole sets of issues were ignored. For example, one of the most surprising results was the limited reference to student issues in the results from some school clusters, while the central office and government participants listed a large number of causes relating to students. 'Effective strong leadership' provides another example; all of the central office staff and government officials listed this cause, but no one in the school clusters did.

The world view or paradigm of individuals and groups may differ both in focus and strength. For some, their ideology is fixed and intractable, while for others change and compromise are a normal part of life. This was evident in the LAND project where some issues were non-debatable and discussion was dismissed by phrases such as 'that's just the way it is, we can't do anything about it'. This was demonstrated in the final workshops, where differences between the remote and urban school groups on their attitudes to the constraints they encountered became apparent.

The 'systems' loop: Complexity and ambiguity

The systems loop highlights the intricacy and 'messiness' of school community, education authority and government dynamics underpinning efforts to improve numeracy. In the Niche Wicked Problem Framework, the term 'systems' refers to the various organisations, agencies, authorities, departments, policies, processes, and products in which educators and policy-makers are engaged. The dimensions of complexity and ambiguity are central to understanding how this 'systems' loop works.

Complexity and ambiguity were evident in the LAND project. Participants came from one of the three places in 'the system' (the school, central office or government). Each group of participants viewed its part of the system differently and it is somewhat ironic that the most complex and ambiguous term used by each group was the word 'system' itself. Government officers identified a whole group of causes, under the heading 'system', relating to the actions of government but excluded any mention of schools, teachers and the community. In contrast, school-based participants did not mention government directly but used 'system' to mean their school processes, or their central office, or 'the school system' of which they were a part. All very ambiguous!

When all responses from participants had been analysed there were almost 700 different causes identified, demonstrating a significant degree of complexity based on sheer volume. Once stakeholders began to link these causes, the complexity at least doubled. In the final workshop, participants were asked to link a specific subset of causes with lines and arrows, including descriptions on the links to show how one cause related to another. They were also asked to show where someone should start to interpret their map. This activity provided opportunity to make comparisons between groups because the nodes or intersecting points on the map were limited, fixed and the same for every group. The results showed little similarity, with variability shown on every possible point of difference. Complexity was evident from the vast number of causes and ways that the researchers found that participants linked these causes. This should be a sobering reminder to those who believe that they have the package to improve numeracy achievement of students in communities with low socioeconomic status.

Ambiguity, as the second dimension in this loop, can amplify the complexity of the problem. This is because multiple meanings were found to exist among participants for interpreting terms, labels and consequences of action. For example, there was ambiguity about the word 'leadership'. For some participants, leadership was positional, restricted to those in authority. For others, leadership was expressed through the actions and effects of people regardless of where they sat in an organisational chart. These meanings were largely tacit, and only brought to the surface and made explicit through dialogue at the workshops. During the LAND workshops, significant time was therefore required for participants to develop some shared understanding of the meaning of this and other terms they were using.

The 'context' loop: Instability and constraints

The 'context' loop includes the dimensions of instability and constraints. These dimensions are primarily concerned with the environment within which the problem occurs. The literature uses instability and constraints to contrast wicked problems with tame ones (Horn & Weber, 2007). Instability was evident in the LAND project in a range of ways: from the changing enrolment patterns of students to the turnover of staff at school and central office levels, and the changes in government policy and program officers during the two-year research period. The continual churn of students, teachers, principals, central office and government staff meant that the context lacked stability. As a consequence, time and other resources needed to be allocated to enable newcomers to be brought up to speed. Instability, as experienced in the LAND project, was clearly evident as a wicked problem characteristic.

A related contextual dimension was the constraints under which those at school, central office and government level were working to improve student numeracy achievement. At times, participants noted multiple, interconnected constraints leading some, at times, to express frustration and feelings of powerlessness. Constraints identified in the LAND research arose from a combination of financial, political, ideological and cultural factors. Two particular examples stood out. One was that 'time' was listed as a prominent constraint by most participants. Wicked problems, by their nature, require a lot of time to tackle. Schools are busy and frenetic places and this makes it very difficult for teachers and principals to spend the time required to tackle complex problems. Second, participants felt constrained by the political pressure to demonstrate school improvement on national literacy and numeracy tests. This, they reported, narrowed their focus for improving numeracy achievement and restricted their consideration of other significant causes, and potentially more promising and sustainable improvement strategies.

Once each of the loops, with its accompanying dimensions, has been considered, there is a strong case that improving numeracy is indeed a wicked problem. Further, the LAND research conducted by Ashhurst (2012) highlighted the potential value of the wicked problem framework as a means for educators and policy-makers to discuss the nature and the tackling of wicked problems. But there is one more twist in the story ...

The loops are connected!

The people, context and systems loops are connected in various ways. Increasing diversity among stakeholders increases the complexity of the problem. The more people involved, the more complex the problem can appear. This can lead to greater ambiguity and increased intractability of stakeholder positions as each group attempts to justify its position in the face of competition from others. This was evident in the different priorities that participants gave to specific causes. Some individuals, for example, would focus on a single factor and show why theirs was important. Workshop dialogue activities were useful in overcoming this issue, because they enabled people to see and appreciate the multiplicity of causes rather than just the ones they initially valued.

Another aspect of the 'connected loops' is that problems are harder to tackle if the context is unpredictable and changing. Constraints reduce the options for tackling the problem and are exacerbated by the ambiguity of the issues involved. For example, during the LAND project the high turnover of staff was identified as a major issue for some schools, but trying to fix this particular problem by making adjustments to the 'system' was considered almost impossible because, in the intractable opinion of at least some participants, the context meant that 'teachers just don't stay long in these schools'.

Finally, diversity in the 'people' loop can influence the nature of the issues related to the context loop. For example, different people view different constraints differently. Further, trying to get some shared understanding between stakeholders is made more difficult if the problem keeps changing or the factors involved are unpredictable. Poor student attendance was an example of a constraint identified in the LAND project. For the remote schools in the Northern Territory, this was an obvious and explicit cause of poor numeracy achievement, made more complex by unpredictable community circumstances. For example, one school reported that ongoing problems of riots in the local community disrupted attendance across the whole school for days at a time (Gaffney, in press). For other participants in different contexts, student attendance was just one more factor that needed to be taken into account.

Tackling numeracy improvement through connecting perspectives

Connecting school and system perspectives in numeracy development is about building stronger alignment in the thoughts and actions of those working in school systems. It is a vital foundation for sustainable improvement in student numeracy achievement and requires attention to certain features. The features were identified by LAND project participants through the process of causal mapping and involved a combination of professional and bureaucratic characteristics (see Figure 8.1). These features are also closely linked to the elements of the LAND framework (see Chapter 2) and include shared purpose, common understandings about effective teaching and how it is developed, complementary and efficient organisational arrangements, and a sense of a 'systemic' community: the idea that we are all in this together.

Causal mapping is an essentially collaborative process involving the insights and expertise of a range of stakeholders. In the LAND project, it provided a means whereby those working in schools, in central offices of education authorities and in government were able to identify, clarify and analyse the causes and effects of numeracy improvement. On the basis of its use in LAND, causal mapping constitutes a promising tool for describing the degree of alignment in the perspectives of people working in different roles in different parts of school systems. Gaining a fuller appreciation of the 'wickedness' of the problem and the ways in which colleagues and others in the system understand it provides a more informed basis for deciding what needs to be in place for sustainable system-wide numeracy development. In this way, causal mapping can be a valuable first step in creating greater alignment and stronger connections between what happens in schools and other parts of the system.

Similarly the Niche Wicked Problem Framework, through encouraging a multidimensional view that includes attention to people, systems and context, provides a way of describing wicked problems that can guide the ways in which they are tackled. The LAND project research highlighted that improving numeracy achievement of students in school communities with low socioeconomic status is certainly a wicked problem! It needs to be treated differently from 'tame problems' in order to be tackled successfully. Approaches to systemic improvement in student numeracy achievement therefore need to consider the diversity as well as the intractability of people's views; the complexity and ambiguity of factors that operate at various levels of educational and government systems to influence numeracy achievement; and the instability and inherent constraints of the context in which policies are developed, implemented and evaluated.

SECTION 4
DEFINING PRINCIPLES, SUSTAINING NUMERACY DEVELOPMENT

CHAPTER 9

ARTICULATING PURPOSES AND PRACTICES IN NUMERACY DEVELOPMENT

Rhonda Faragher, Michael Gaffney and Matt Skoss

Once there were two primary schools, St Overwhelmed and St Selective, on the outskirts of Capital City. St Overwhelmed was suffering from 'information overload'. It was drowning in data, all sorts of data, data about student background characteristics (their language, religious, Indigenous and ethnic background; their parents' occupations and education levels), data about student achievement (from standardised tests, norm/ criterion referenced tests, teacher observations and records from student interviews), data about student attendance, enrolment trends, dropout rates, data about staff qualifications, experience, turnover and absenteeism, data about teacher satisfaction, efficacy and participation in professional development as well as data about parent and community attitudes and expectations. In fact, the school had so much data that the principal employed a clerical assistant at casual rates from the school's discretionary staffing funds just to sort through all the information before it went up on the My School website.

St Selective collected and had access to much the same data but it was a very different place. The principal, the teachers and at times the school council were drawing 'evidence' from the data to inform their decisions about all sorts of things, including teaching practices, staffing allocations, investment in teaching resources and other infrastructure, involvement and engagement of parents, and adjustments to the school's organisational structure and timetable. What guided their thinking in these areas was a clear and explicit idea and commitment (some might call it a vision) about what effective teaching and learning were, and how to support them and ensure that they happened in every classroom in the school.

One sunny morning a couple of weeks into the school term, Julie and Christelle from the local education authority central office went on their regular visit to both schools. On arrival, they had the obligatory cup of coffee with the principal. At St Overwhelmed, the principal vacillated between chatting generally about how things were going (especially the new building and renovations that had been funded through the Australian

Government Building the Education Revolution program) and complaining about the level of paperwork and 'other compliance stuff' that was distracting him and his staff from 'the real work of teaching the kids'. At St Selective, the principal spoke directly with them about her school community's priorities, especially the ways teachers were collaborating in trialling different teaching practices and investigating better use of time, space and digital technologies. She also raised particular issues about government- and system-targeted program funding and how it might be 'tweaked' to best effect.

Both schools put on a special morning tea, after which Julie and Christelle were taken on a whistlestop tour of the classrooms with the principal, appreciating the welcomes given on cue by the students and noting the general vibe in the teaching and learning that were taking place. They made mental notes to follow up with particular teachers and update the principal, coordinators and school executive about recent system developments in light of what they had seen.

On returning from their school visits, as they sat down at their adjoining desks at central office, they looked at one another and asked: Why are these schools so different? How did they get to be that way? What's more, how might St Overwhelmed be more like St Selective? And they mused some more, then decided to take some action.

Introduction

Schools are busy places, and they are getting busier because of the demands to be more up-front and transparent about their students' results and the reasons for them (Gillard, 2012). This busy-ness means that sometimes the core purpose and work of the school can be lost. The demands on schools from governments, education authorities, parents and from their own students and teachers mean that schools need to be able to clearly articulate the purposes and practices they employ to achieve their desired ends.

Different schools handle these demands differently. Effective schools have an open classroom atmosphere; teachers readily invite colleagues to observe and provide feedback on classroom practice; such schools gather and use evidence in their decision-making; and as a consequence they develop and continually refine their shared understandings about what constitutes effective teaching at their school.

In this chapter, recent developments in ways of looking at classroom practices in numeracy are explored through drawing parallels between the process of classroom observation and an archaeological dig (Zevenbergen & Flavel, 2007). This provides insights into what to look for when assessing effective teaching of mathematics and students' numeracy development. From this basis, processes and issues associated with gathering and using evidence of numeracy development at school level and their implications for system policies and programs are explored. The use of evidence is a vital ingredient in principals and teachers coming to a shared understanding about the nature of effective teaching. In the next part of the chapter, the process used by the LAND school leadership teams and their school communities to develop charters for effective teaching of mathematics at their school is described and some examples are included. The chapter concludes with some implications for principals, teacher leaders and system officers relating to the importance of articulating purposes and practices in numeracy development as a basis for realising it in improved student numeracy achievement.

The 'archaeological dig' – looking in classrooms

Turning professional development into professional learning (Webster-Wright, 2009) involves incorporating content from workshops into the established practice of a teacher. In the LAND project the aim was to achieve this through a variety of means:

- explicit pledges of commitment to action made by school teams at workshops
- recording of commitments on the wiki (see Chapter 6 for more detail)
- presentations at workshops on school progress
- regular contact (including school visits) with LAND project officers
- school visits by the research team.

For the research team, school visits were a highly enjoyable and professionally rewarding experience. Researchers were aware of the dilemma of observing classrooms, sometimes without children in them, and drawing conclusions about what was being seen. Following the work of Zevenbergen and Flavel (2007), the team recognised the value of seeing the classroom as an 'archaeological dig'. The analogy is that archaeologists make inferences about the lives of people who may have lived centuries ago based on the artefacts that have been left behind and their relationship to location and other objects and buildings. Similarly, an observer can make inferences about the learning and teaching that have occurred in a classroom based on artefacts such as work samples, teachers' planning records, arrangement of classroom furniture, timetable arrangements and so forth.

Consider some of the photographic evidence collected by the researchers, shown in Figure 9.1.

The first photograph shows students' work on the wall of one classroom in a school in the Kimberley region. Although attendance in remote Indigenous schools is frequently a serious problem, it was not for this teacher's class. The children were active participants in the lessons. What the photograph shows is a collection of work all over the walls, including at the children's eye level. The work is in the hand of the children and, around the whole classroom, covers a variety of topics. Table 9.1 suggests what observers such as principals and school mathematics coordinators might look for as evidence of effective mathematics teaching practice (see Chapter 3 for a discussion about the nature of effective mathematics teaching practice).

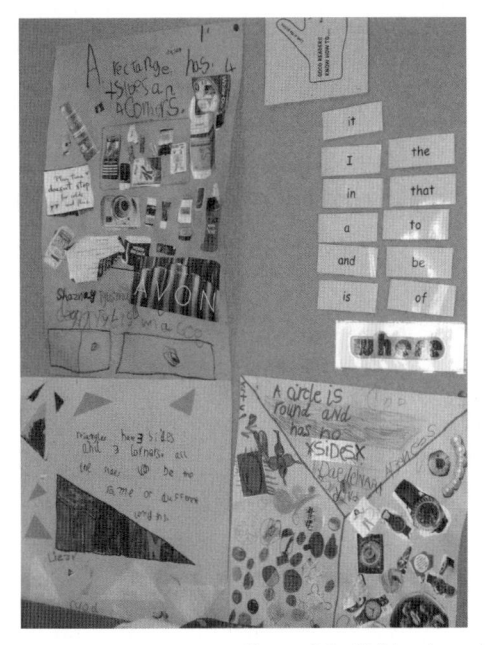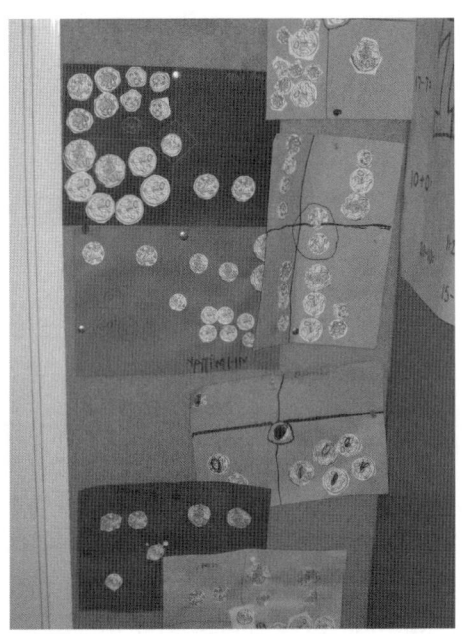

Figure 9.1: Children's work on display in a classroom

Table 9.1: Evidence of mathematics teaching practice

Evidence of effective practice	Signs of potentially ineffective practice
• Variety of solution paths to rich tasks displayed • Work in progress is on display; for example, problems that are ongoing • Majority of work displayed is the children's original work • Work is displayed at easy viewing height for children • Work corresponds to current and recent class topics, and displays are changed regularly • Mathematics from across the discipline (not just Number) is evident • Work from all learners is displayed (not just the neat work, or that of the high achievers) • Resources are organised and easily accessible • Calculators are available and used for more than checking answers.	• Visual displays mostly restricted to posters about rules, including mathematics rules and procedures such as number facts, rules for finding perimeters and areas of shapes, for example. • Work displayed is mostly prepared by the teacher or from commercial sources and displayed high up on walls. • Predominance of worksheets or textbook activities. • Little evidence of mathematical thinking through rich tasks and problem-solving activities. • Resources, including calculators, are not visible or readily available.

There can also be benefits to learners in the classroom of having retrievable products of learning in view, and many of the LAND workshop presentations, particularly those by Matt Skoss (one of the LAND researchers and also a teacher), were focused on ensuring a lasting record remained of the lesson. This could be in the form of posters or photographs or short video clips. Retrievable products allow students to re-enter the experience each time they observe the artefact, effectively aiding the important processes of consolidation and practice. For example, Skoss noticed the box for the shower cap in his hotel room had an interesting shape: a rombus-shaped prism (Figure 9.2). He developed a task for the workshop participants to draw the net of the shape. The task is shown in the box below. The photograph serves to jog the memory for all who were part of the activity. It reminds participants of the mathematics as well as the experience of doing the task. A subsequent summary of findings could also be used to remind learners of key points. This could be done as a wall chart, a videoed presentation to the class or a paragraph reflection in a learning journal. Skoss also advocated the use of a strategies chart for problem-solving that develops as learners attempt each new problem-solving task (Siemon et al., 2011, p. 74).

The task:

The box in the picture is made from cardboard. Draw a pattern for the box so that if you were to cut the pattern out of cardboard, you would be able to fold it up to make the box shown. You will need to show which sides need to be glued and where there will be a flap to keep the box closed.

Is there more than one solution?

Are some designs more effective than others (e.g. use less cardboard or glue)?

Equipment:
- Two-dimensional shapes
- Mini whiteboards (the size of an A4 sheet of paper) for trying designs
- Paper and scissors

Figure 9.2: A box with an interesting shape

Gathering data and using evidence for numeracy development

Looking in classrooms can generate enormous amounts of data. Classroom observations of teaching practices, how students are learning, the set-up of the teaching and learning spaces, and the availability and use of curriculum resources can tell us a lot about the effectiveness of the teaching and learning that are taking place. But to make use of the data, observers need to know what they are looking for, and why. In other words, the purpose and the substance of observations need to be clear. Having this type of clarity enables the data to be used as evidence to make decisions.

Data are the basis for evidence. Evidence is data used for a purpose. In the case of numeracy development, data can be used to make decisions or draw conclusions about students' progress, students' attitudes to numeracy, the effect of teaching, learning and assessment practices, teachers' beliefs and assumptions about students' potential in numeracy, their preparedness to teach mathematics, the effectiveness of numeracy interventions, and the levels of interest and involvement of parents in their children's progress in numeracy. These types of evidence and associated questions are presented in Table 9.2.

The areas of interest and questions listed in Table 9.2 may be applied to a range of purposes. These include improving learning, assessing performance, monitoring progress and demonstrating compliance. In each case, the type of stakeholders and the criteria they employ can vary. This means that teachers, principals and system officers need to be alert to the needs and expectations of their audience(s) and those who provide the resources, and present the evidence accordingly.

Data can come from all sorts of places. To avoid being swamped with information, it is vital that educators take care to fit the data to the purpose, to the audience and to the type of evidence required. Individual teachers, for example, may collect a range of data:

- teacher records of student progress (including pre-testing)
- writing samples
- anecdotal records
- conversations with colleagues
- Individual Education Plan information
- interview folders
- parent interview sessions
- student task-based assessment interview data
- portfolios.

Schools and education systems may similarly collect data from a wide range of sources:
- grade distribution tables
- school counsellor data
- previous years' reports
- school policy documents and reports
- school review processes
- surveys – parents, students
- class profiles

- behaviour information
- referral information
- NAPLAN results
- specialist test data
- attendance information.

While these lists highlight the level at which the data is collected, effective use of such data requires clear and careful communication and analysis among teachers,

Table 9.2: Analysing numeracy development data – types of evidence and questions

Areas of interest for which evidence was collected	Questions: What is your numeracy data telling you about . . .
Student progress in numeracy	• numeracy progress of ◊ individual students ◊ class groupings of students ◊ students from Indigenous and/or English as a second language or dialect backgrounds ◊ students whose attendance has been high compared with those whose attendance has been low ◊ students who have been involved in a particular instructional approach or intervention • trends in numeracy progress across groups of students (e.g. boys, girls, Indigenous students, students with disabilities, students from disadvantaged backgrounds)
Students' attitudes to mathematics	• attitudes towards numeracy of ◊ the student population as a whole ◊ particular groups of students
Teaching, learning and assessment practices in mathematics and numeracy across the curriculum	• the effect of specific teaching, learning and assessment practices on particular groups of students
Teacher beliefs and assumptions about student potential in mathematics	• beliefs and assumptions held by teachers regarding students' potential in numeracy
Teacher preparedness to teach mathematics	• teachers' understanding of how to teach particular areas of mathematics, i.e. their pedagogical content knowledge in mathematics • teachers' confidence in their ability to teach mathematics
Numeracy interventions	• the effectiveness of particular instructional approaches with different groups of students
Parents' interest and involvement in their child's progress in numeracy	• the level and effect of parents' interest and involvement in their child's progress in numeracy

Source: Adapted from Dawson, Faragher & Gaffney (2012)

school executive and principals (in individual schools) and those responsible for system-level planning and accountability (located in the central offices of education authorities).

In collecting evidence, it is important to look for patterns and trends in the data. From time to time, exceptional events occur that may disrupt these trends. It is therefore also important to consider the context: what is distinctive or peculiar about the school situation, and what else is happening in the school and school system that might influence the data. Similarly, if patterns of data occur with different samples, an underlying cause may be suspected. For example, if a school were to notice that boys achieved much higher scores on a NAPLAN test one year, the difference might be due to a cohort anomaly. If the same imbalance occurred at the same year level, for NAPLAN data year after year, the school would need to look for an explanation in teaching and learning practices.

'Focused discussion' was the term used in the LAND project for conversations associated with analysing data. Similar terms include 'discipline dialogue' used in the Principals as Literacy Leaders project (Dempster et al., 2012), and 'focused conversation' used in the IDEAS process (Andrews et al., 2004). The process of focused discussion involves asking a series of questions, each for a particular purpose:

- Why are we having this discussion? (State or determine our purpose.)
- What are we discussing? (Identify the topic or issue.)
- What are the data telling us? (Present the facts.)
- Why is it so? (Propose the reasons.)
- What, if anything, should we do about it? (Decide on follow-up action.)

Given the complexity of causes and effects surrounding sustained school-wide improvement of student numeracy achievement (see Chapter 8), it needs to be appreciated that the answers to these questions may not be definitive but rather may lead to more searching questions about the nature of teaching and learning practices at the school, and throughout the system. This underscores the importance of a related feature of evidence-based decision-making: that data gathering and analysis processes work best when they involve others (from inside and sometimes outside the school community) and bring their expertise and insights to bear. This helps to overcome the problems of reaching conclusions and finding 'solutions' too quickly or failing to appreciate or ignoring the value of outlying data. It also deepens the talent pool, especially where the data analysis requires a degree of technical expertise: for example, in situations where there is a need to decide whether the results are statistically significant or merely due to random fluctuations.

Working through these processes with others not only generates a sense of shared understanding, responsibility, accountability and even credit for a job well done, it also provides the chance for others to exercise leadership. Recent research (Pettit, 2010) on school-level leadership in analysis and use of data from standardised testing shows that schools where principals work alongside their teachers in deciding on the purposes, identifying the issues, presenting the facts, proposing the reasons and deciding what to do are far better placed for using data constructively. Through engaging in focused discussions and follow-up action, principals and teachers are able to display leadership in improving teaching and learning practices and in demonstrating accountability – internally to each other and externally to those requiring compliance and quality assurance.

The Pettit (2010) research highlights that the gathering and analysis of data is not merely a technical process. Rather, it draws upon the personal and professional views of those involved and how these influence others and the organisation of ideas, and consequently can turn information into meaningful action (Senge, 1990). The implication for principals and teachers working with numeracy development data is to build a culture of inquiry in their schools where evidence is developed from data and used in decision-making, where different voices are valued, and where knowledge is shared and built as people find new meanings and discover new possibilities. These are some of the ways that evidence may be used for whole-school numeracy development.

- assessing the nature and quality of mathematics teaching and learning
- making comparisons within and across classes and schools
- informing moderation processes where work samples are shared and discussed
- developing systematic recording of assessment results
- building a culture of inquiry, where different voices and opinions are valued – and 'blame' is not apportioned.

Charters for Effective Teaching of Mathematics

One significant tangible outcome of the processes of data gathering and analysis in each LAND school was a written 'Charter for Effective Teaching of Mathematics'. Each charter represented a synthesis of the collective thinking, trialling, review and reflection of the LAND school leadership teams and their colleagues relating to mathematics teaching in their school. Schools followed different pathways to developing their charters. Some used regularly scheduled professional learning community meetings. Others held periodic review and reflection meetings in which teachers demonstrated examples of teaching episodes, and then discussed how and why those episodes were successful (or not). From there, members of the LAND school leadership teams would work with their colleagues to distil the underlying principles or characteristics of effective teaching practice in mathematics. These tended to be linked to features identified in the literature (Clarke & Clarke, 2004) but they also extended and grounded these features in ways that applied to their local contexts.

Some schools integrated their charters with existing school documents relating to school vision and mission or their statements about 'agreed practices'. Others did not, though most expressed the need and desire to re-examine their existing documents and check their alignment with the charters resulting from their work on the LAND project. In the showcase presentations held at the end of the LAND project, each LAND school team presented its Charter for Effective Teaching of Mathematics. In many cases, the charters were described as a work in progress that was being developed in consultation with teacher colleagues and other members of their school's community, including parents and students. This was not unexpected given the tight project time frame. In fact, it was welcomed as an example of the continuing conversations that were taking place in schools about numeracy development.

Examples of charters from schools in the LAND project are included. The value is not so much in the charters themselves as the process staff undertook to develop them. They are integrally related to the context and the working styles of the LAND teams. The charters have been published as presented and the differences between them are evident. Charters need to be 'living' documents. They allow new staff to quickly assimilate into the school culture – particularly important in schools with a high staff turnover. Having been developed by each school, the charters can be modified over time as professional learning leads to changes in emphases.

Immaculate Heart of Mary School

We believe that effective teaching of Mathematics at IHM is evident when:
- Students are challenged to develop their mathematical thinking because of the variety of teaching methodologies we use (i.e. explicit, exploratory, reflective)
- Students' understanding of mathematical concepts is strengthened because we provide manipulative materials and hands-on interactive experiences
- Students build on their mathematical understandings and skills because we use a variety of assessment methods to inform and modify our planning
- Students are encouraged to approach mathematics with a positive disposition because we model enthusiasm towards mathematical learning
- Students are actively engaged in their learning because teachers provide learning opportunities that are relevant and meaningful to students' worlds and life experiences
- Students apply their skills, knowledge and dispositions into different areas
- Students understand and use mathematical language to communicate their mathematical learning
- Teachers set clear, intentional objectives and learning outcomes
- Teachers use assessment to support learning
- Teachers consistently reinforce mathematical strategies by exposing students to specific teaching practices i.e. *I do, we do, you do.*

Murrupurtiyanuwu Catholic School

We believe that effective teaching of Mathematics at Murrupurtiyanuwu Catholic School is evidenced by:

- teacher confidence, participation and support because they can see the students benefit and feel supported
- student confidence, participation and engagement because both Quicksmart and Count Me In Too are tailored to success by providing level appropriate high interest activities.
- the SENA test results and movement in Northern Territory Curriculum Framework (NTCF) levels because we have a whole school approach with commitment from all staff
- the SENA test results and movement in NTCF levels because we have improved teacher practice through professional development
- the SENA test results and movement in NTCF levels because we have a standard program and set of tests. We are analysing results then staff are planning and teaching to the needs of the student/s. We are targeting numeracy intervention.
- the positive response from the community because they see instances and snapshots of our classroom work.

St Brigid's Catholic School

We believe that effective teaching of Mathematics at St Brigid's Catholic School is evidenced by:

1. EXPLICIT TEACHING which enables increased student knowledge and skills
2. OPEN ENDED TASKS which enable students to access multiple entry points
3. STUDENT ENGAGEMENT which enables increased interest and eagerness to participate
4. ALIGNMENT ON CORE LESSON STRUCTURE which enables students to tune in, apply knowledge and reflect on learning
5. PARTNERSHIPS BETWEEN HOME & SCHOOL which enable all stakeholders to take responsibility for numeracy improvement
6. KNOWLEDGABLE STAFF which enables them to plan, implement and reflect
7. USE OF A RANGE OF RESOURCES which enables students to participate in rich deep tasks
8. USE OF MENTAL STRATEGIES which enable students to develop automaticity.

St. Joseph's School Waroona

These principles underpin mathematics teaching and learning at our school:

1. Children work from simple to complex, concrete to abstract, through **the use of hands-on manipulatives**.
2. Children are immersed in **the language of Numeracy** and solve **mathematical problems** daily.
3. We encourage children **to seek patterns** in Numeracy to make their learning easier and richer.

Whitefriars Catholic School

We believe that effective teaching of Mathematics at Whitefriars is evidenced by:

- **Journaling** because this allows students to gain a deeper understanding of their Mathematical thinking.
- **Mental Computation strategies** because these provide students with strategies to solve number problems.
- **Pre/Post Assessment** because it enables teachers to build on students' prior knowledge, provides evidence of student progress and helps in future planning.
- **Dedicated teaching time** because it encourages explicit teaching, reflective practice and higher levels of student engagement.
- **Whole school focus topic** because teachers can have a dedicated time to plan as a whole school. It encourages professional dialogue and sharing of ideas.
- **Organised resources** so that staff are aware of what resources are available and where resources can be easily accessed.
- **Involving parents** because this provides parents opportunities to gain a better understanding of how children learn maths and how they can support their children at home.
- **Class visits** because it provides teachers with ideas on ways to approach and organise their Maths lessons.

Xavier Catholic School Hilbert

At Xavier Catholic School we believe that …

- **Building teacher capacity** will motivate our teachers to become excited and enthused in their approach to teaching mathematics and encourage them to create positive learning experiences, by improving their skills and creating a Numeracy rich environment. Ultimately, developing an infrastructure of support within our school.
- **Shared leadership** is essential for exercising a meaningful and positive influence on numeracy development as a whole across the classroom and school and so we will recognize that all teachers have a leadership contribution to make and therefore develop the capabilities of teachers to exercise their leadership skills.
- **Celebrating the learning** is an effective way to improve whole school mathematical success and so we will demonstrate in various ways pride and pleasure in individual, classroom and whole school success.
- **Parents are partners** in the education of their children and so we will provide many opportunities for parents to be informed about how they can best support the numeracy development of their children.

At Xavier Catholic School we believe children …

- Should have a strong **I.C.T focus** within the mathematical curriculum and so we will provide well planned, engaging, creative learning tasks incorporating a range of I.C.T activities designed to support and extend mathematical understanding.
- Need the opportunity to **reflect** and evaluate their learning and so we will provide regular, structured discussion times during the Numeracy Dedicated lesson for students to reflect on their performance, ask and answer questions and reinforce their understanding, while planning the next step in their learning.

- Who are indentified as being **at risk** in the Early Years, when learning mathematics, are given the opportunity to take part in an Early Intervention Program in order to achieve future success.
- Need an opportunity to engage in **explicit numeracy learning** and so we will dedicate four hours (minimum) weekly to explicit numeracy teaching.
- Develop and use **mathematical language** and so we will use mathematical terms expecting and encouraging the correct use of them within and across classrooms.

Implications from the charters

The examples of school charters developed at the conclusion of the LAND project indicate some important common features:

- Development is shared by staff.
- Statements of belief are founded on research evidence and substantiated by practice.
- Statements are few in number and readily understood by teachers, including those who were not present at the development. This allows new staff members to be able to understand and continue the development of a shared vision for numeracy development.
- The charters are regularly revised to ensure currency and ownership by new staff.
- Charters are visually attractive and include the school crest, indicating official status. Charters can be proudly displayed on school websites, in prospectuses and on noticeboards.

Conclusion

Articulating purposes and practices in numeracy development is essential for providing direction and sustaining efforts to improve teaching practices and student learning outcomes. Unless the purposes are clear, and the practices are explained, trialled and evaluated, efforts to improve mathematics teaching remain sporadic and have little lasting effect on student numeracy achievement.

In this chapter, ways in which the practice and effect of mathematics teaching can be investigated, made more explicit and more thoroughly embedded in schools have been discussed. The approach of the 'archaeological dig' shone a spotlight on the effectiveness of gathering data from classroom observation, even when lessons were not underway. This approach to looking in classrooms highlighted the importance of developing expertise in the gathering and analysis of data so that it can be used as evidence in decision-making related to numeracy development at school and system levels. In this sense, the process of focused discussion is a key tool, first using data to produce evidence and then using the evidence as a basis for action.

The LAND project took the use of data one step further. The research team worked with LAND school leadership team members in the examination, trial and analysis of mathematics teaching practices in order to build their capacity to identify and develop distinctive approaches to developing numeracy in their school communities. The tangible products of this work were the Charters for Effective Teaching of Mathematics. The charters not only had a summative purpose in describing what had been 'produced' by the LAND project, they also were used by schools as reference points for evaluating existing and proposed numeracy programs. In some cases, they were also used in the selection of teaching staff: candidates were invited to explain how they might bring a particular characteristic of the school's charter to life in their teaching.

There are several implications for teachers, principals, and system officers arising from this chapter:

- Observers can make valid inferences about mathematics teaching and learning practices.
- Gathering data is an essential part of evidence-based practice. Ensuring sufficient, valid and reliable data are collected is fundamental to the generation of useful evidence, which, in turn, can be used to plan appropriate and effective interventions.
- School charters are an effective way of promoting sustainability of reforms. New staff members can be inducted into the agreed common practice of the school, without the risk of the approach being forgotten or ignored.

These implications present a challenging and practical agenda for those in schools and education authority central offices. This agenda is a pressing one because being able to articulate purposes and practices in numeracy development is foundational to achieving lasting improvement in students' numeracy achievement.

CHAPTER 10

EMBEDDING NUMERACY DEVELOPMENT
Michael Gaffney, Rhonda Faragher and Doug Clarke

After all, every child has a right to be numerate.

Introduction

This book began by describing the numeracy challenge for those working in schools and school systems. This challenge is to ensure that every child reaches a level of numeracy that enables them to lead a fulfilling and productive life. Each of the chapters to this point has focused on different aspects of meeting this challenge, including the characteristics of effective mathematics teaching and the nature of the educational leadership required, the importance of building a sense of community with colleagues (through professional learning communities) and with parents, the value of networking and partnerships, the need to connect school and system perspectives, and the significance of clearly articulating purposes and practices in numeracy development.

In this chapter, these ideas are built upon and some insights are shared on how to embed and sustain a strategic and practical approach to numeracy development at school and school-system level. Firstly, the design features of the LAND project are recapped and its key outcomes summarised. The experience with the LAND project has enabled the identification of some general principles that need to underpin thinking and action associated with numeracy development. These principles are explained along with an associated approach for planning and monitoring numeracy development. The chapter concludes by offering some advice and encouragement to educational leaders in schools, central offices, government departments and universities to maintain their focus on numeracy development. This involves continuing to develop their understanding and knowledge of effective mathematics teaching and their capability for leading numeracy development – and to undertake this with a system mindset that sees the whole as well as the parts. In this way, they will be better able to imagine and realise greater alignment between their thoughts and actions and those of their colleagues involved in supporting children to become more numerate.

Distinctive features of the LAND approach to numeracy development

The LAND project was based on the premise that attention to both numeracy and educational leadership is needed to bring about sustained improvement in student achievement. Accordingly, the project had two focuses:

- the identification, development and support of effective teaching of mathematics
- the educational leadership exercised by teachers, principals and central office personnel to develop and sustain effective practices in mathematics teaching and numeracy development.

This dual focus meant that participants analysed teaching practices in their school in light of research on the characteristics of effective teaching of mathematics, and considered how leadership capabilities and actions influence effective teaching and improve student achievement in numeracy.

The design and purpose of the LAND project were used to develop a framework (see Figure 2.5). The LAND framework served as a vehicle for studying the major concepts associated with numeracy development at classroom, school and central office level, for planning and evaluating project activity, and as a basis for examining and enacting mathematics teaching and educational leadership.

The logic of the LAND framework is that student numeracy development is a consequence of the effective interaction of certain key elements. For example, teaching practice is understood to have a direct and powerful positive effect on student learning development (Hattie, 2009). Applying the LAND framework, this effect is enhanced by appropriate organisational arrangements and supportive community characteristics that closely align with the vision that the members of the school community share for student numeracy development. The reasoning is similar to that used in research on school improvement (Andrews et al., 2004; Caldwell & Spinks, 2008; Crowther et al., 2002). Student numeracy development, teaching practices, organisational processes and structures, community engagement and vision were hence focus areas for research and development through the LAND project (see Chapter 2 for more detail on the LAND framework and its research base).

Developing each of the framework elements and strengthening the connections between them was the leadership challenge of the LAND project. The leadership components of the professional development workshops were designed to improve the leadership capabilities of principals and teachers to tackle this challenge. LAND school leadership teams were encouraged to develop and maintain the focus on student numeracy development by enhancing their pedagogical content knowledge, engaging with their school community, organising for teaching and learning, and inspiring a shared vision and purpose for numeracy development in their school settings. A set of leadership capabilities were developed and trialled through the project. This work was informed by research on the connection between school leadership behaviour and improvement in student learning outcomes. Each type of capability was linked to an element of the LAND framework and evidenced through specific actions, as shown in Table 10.1.

Table 10.1: LAND framework elements, leadership capabilities and sample actions

LAND framework element	Leadership capability	Sample leadership action
Student numeracy development	Thinking strategically and acting practically to build alignment	Gathering evidence
Teaching	Valuing teaching and professional development	Participating with teachers in professional development
Organisation	Organising curriculum and infrastructure	Managing resources by aligning funds with school numeracy priorities
Community	Engaging the community	Encouraging community support to improve numeracy
Vision	Developing shared purpose to improve numeracy	Developing and exercising teamwork and shared accountability with and among teachers

Evidence from the participant surveys, school visits, LAND school team presentations, and school reports indicates that the leadership challenge was met (see Chapter 4 for more detail). Teachers and principals reported that their participation in the LAND project had developed their capability to lead numeracy development. They also appreciated the practical orientation of the project and the opportunity for principals and teachers to share and develop their pedagogical content knowledge in mathematics and their leadership capabilities as members of a team. One LAND project officer put it this way:

A big element of the LAND project is being involved in action learning. But I think there is another element – that is capacity building of more than just the designated leadership team, being the principal and the APs [assistant principals]. LAND has provided opportunities for other teachers to step up into a leadership position and to form relationships with their principal in terms of whole-school improvement and relationships with the wider school community based on the idea of 'Let's move forward in terms of trying to improve numeracy outcomes'. So I think the relationship side of LAND has been a positive. The LAND school team members fulfil those relationships by working together on a task that they are trying to achieve and an action they are trying to put into place.

Allied with the development of their leadership capability, evidence from the same sources indicated that LAND project participants had enhanced their teaching in various ways. This included their knowledge and implementation of the characteristics of effective mathematics teaching, and their understanding and use of numeracy assessment practices. LAND school team members not only reported higher levels of efficacy in their own teaching ability, but also increasing confidence in working with others in bringing about numeracy development in their schools. Several themes in effective mathematics teaching emerged through the LAND project:

- having a clear, important mathematical focus
- engaging in purposeful tasks
- using teachable moments and making connections
- choosing from a variety of class structures and roles
- building learning communities through interaction
- having high expectations and valuing effort
- reflecting on what is taught and learnt – with students
- gathering evidence
- making and acting on assessment
- believing in mathematics learning and being confident in one's teaching ability
- showing pride and pleasure in student success (Clarke & Clarke, 2004).

LAND schools reported an overall trend of increasing student engagement and achievement in numeracy.

These findings were highlighted in the final project reports of the Western Australia, South Australia and Northern Territory Catholic education authorities to the Department of Education, Employment and Workplace Relations. The common conclusions running through these reports were that the project had resulted in improved student engagement and achievement in numeracy; enhanced pedagogical content knowledge and leadership capability of teachers and principals for developing numeracy in their school communities; and a promising systemic approach for developing numeracy in school communities with a low socioeconomic status.

These outcomes are a consequence of three distinctive features. First, the LAND project was not a predetermined 'package' of content and processes of professional development for teachers and principals designed to remedy presumed deficits in their leadership style or their pedagogical content knowledge and practice related to student numeracy development. Rather, LAND sought to provide school teams of principals and teacher leaders with the understanding and tools to make better use of initiatives currently being adopted or considered in their schools. Moreover, LAND participants were encouraged to consider how the initiatives they already had in place, or were considering, supported the development of whole-school approaches to improving student numeracy achievement. The approach taken in the workshops was to respect and build on participants' existing knowledge and practice in leadership, mathematics curriculum and teaching practice, and invite them to consider educational leadership and numeracy development from a fresh perspective. For teachers, this meant developing their understanding of the need for informed and effective leadership; and for principals, this meant the opportunity to reflect, refresh their thinking, and learn about methods of teaching, assessment and reporting in mathematics.

The second distinctive feature was that the LAND project took a systemic approach by investigating and building alignment between what happens in classrooms, schools and central offices in support of students' numeracy development. A desired outcome of the project was to distil what is required to achieve improved, sustainable student outcomes in numeracy across classrooms, schools and school systems. The approach to studying 'alignment' included working with teachers and principals in LAND school teams, with central office personnel, and with officers from the Department of Education, Employment and Workplace Relations in investigating the causes and effects associated with improving student numeracy in school communities with low socioeconomic status. Different types and combinations of causes and effects were identified by different people working at each of the three levels (school, central office and government), and most of these causes and effects crossed school, central office and government 'boundaries'. For example, the issue of quality mathematics teaching as a cause of numeracy improvement was influenced by what happens in schools (in terms of on-the-job professional learning), in central offices (in terms of industrial awards and professional development programs), and in government (in terms of general recurrent and targeted program funds and related policies on teacher education and professional standards). These findings highlight that policy and program practices targeted at only one (or even two) of the three levels are insufficient to understand the complexity of student numeracy achievement and to take effective action to improve and sustain it. Rather, leadership and associated policy and program action is needed across all three levels to effect worthwhile and lasting improvement.

The third feature was that the LAND project recognised that improving numeracy in school communities with low socioeconomic status can be considered as a 'wicked' problem, and therefore needed to be tackled by agencies (schools, education authority central offices, government, universities) working in partnership, with each being prepared to change. The analysis of improving numeracy achievement as a wicked problem, described in Chapter 8, highlights that those working in different roles in different parts of school systems see the effects and causes of numeracy improvement differently. As a consequence, persisting with an initiative-by-initiative, program-by-program approach to numeracy development, driven from the top and implemented downwards from governments through central office bureaucracies to schools and into classrooms, is pointless. Decades of failed reform tells us that (Sarason, 1990). The findings of the LAND project prove it.

The way to systemic development in numeracy is to deliberately build in the opportunity and the expectation for those in various parts of the system to collaborate and engage in educational change. It is not just about schools doing things differently! It is also about central offices and government considering how they might change their policies and practices to facilitate improvement. Systemic numeracy development is a team effort that requires an effectively functioning partnership among all the agencies involved. The LAND project highlighted the value of school system–government–university partnerships through taking a multi-level, multi-agency perspective in building an evidence base for numeracy development. (See Chapter 7 for more detail on the nature and importance of partnerships in supporting numeracy development and the roles of the various people involved.)

Implementing the LAND approach to numeracy development

Given the outcomes and distinctive features referred to above, the questions are how *transferable* is the LAND approach to other settings and, in particular, how might it work in other schools and school systems. The answer lies in how the LAND approach to numeracy development aligns with a school and a school system's philosophy, policies and programs, and the capacity and willingness of principals, teachers and central office personnel to think strategically and act practically to strengthen such alignment. These various types of alignment are considered in the following sections.

Aligning philosophy on professional learning

The LAND approach works well when it is aligned with school-system philosophies that endorse collaborative professional learning. For example, the LAND approach to professional learning is based on similar premises to those in place in the Western Australia Catholic school system. The concept and function of the professional learning community, with its emphasis on building upon existing pedagogical content knowledge of teachers through informed collaboration, is a central plank of that system's philosophy, and was already well established in the schools when the LAND project commenced. As a consequence, schools' understanding and support of professional learning communities provided an important basis for the LAND school leadership teams to explore and develop numeracy teaching and learning opportunities with their teacher colleagues. This meant that the LAND project was able to add value to existing systemic approaches to professional learning by providing complementary resources and perspectives for schools to consider. This not only helped schools to sustain their curriculum and pedagogical focus in mathematics and numeracy, it also served to validate and strengthen their approach to professional learning in other areas.

Aligning policies and programs in numeracy development

The premise and design of the LAND project in linking mathematics teaching and educational leadership for the purpose of numeracy development means that it can provide the foundation for schools and central offices to consider how other policies and programs, directly and indirectly concerned with student numeracy outcomes, are related to one another. At a school level, this can involve consideration of how, for example, particular numeracy initiatives are linked to a school's Charter for Effective Teaching in Mathematics as well as how they contribute to whole-school development. At central office level, the foundational elements of LAND dealing with the quality of mathematics teaching and the development and exercise of leadership can serve to support related system priorities and programs in school improvement and leadership development. In other words, the way that the LAND approach incorporates these dimensions and develops them collaboratively and in unison can provide a template for how educational leadership and quality teaching can be developed and exercised in other areas of the curriculum – for example, in literacy.

Where the LAND approach was aligned with other policies and programs in numeracy development, it was able to add value to existing school and system initiatives. This was particularly evident when LAND was combined with other programs including specialist mathematics intervention initiatives as well as those being implemented under the Smarter Schools National Partnership umbrella (Commonwealth Department of Education, Employment and Workplace Relations, 2011). The collaborative conversations, mentoring, leadership support and professional learning opportunities provided through LAND carried over to other areas. This, together with the LAND project focus on a whole-school approach to sustaining improvement in numeracy, resulted in more comprehensive planning, more effective use of resources and more searching analyses of student achievement data. As a consequence of their involvement in LAND, principals and teachers were able to better understand how their various school-based numeracy initiatives could be linked and incorporated in their school plans and activities.

At a system level, the foundational dimensions of LAND and how they were being incorporated in school planning and practice provided opportunities for LAND project officers to work more closely with their central office colleagues (school support consultants and the numeracy consultants). This was due to LAND project activity being seen as a component of whole-school development (not only in numeracy) and therefore needing to also be considered by central office personnel responsible for that area. Put another way, the LAND project highlighted the links and strengthened the alignment between local school, central office and government numeracy initiatives and related priorities and programs. This, in turn, helped to ensure that the schools were well supported in their efforts to improve student outcomes, and in school development work more broadly.

Aligning perceptions in numeracy development

Another distinctive feature of the LAND project was the steps taken to ensure that those working in schools, central offices, government and universities understood and appreciated each other's insights, expertise, needs and expectations. The process of causal mapping (described in Chapter 8) proved to be a useful means for bringing assumptions to the surface, and articulating the perceptions of educators working in different parts of school systems. Adopting and sustaining the LAND approach to numeracy development requires that people be open to these types of activities. This means learning to appreciate the viewpoints, contexts and reasoning of others, and being willing to adopt a system mindset.

Aligning teaching practices with school structures, contexts and vision for numeracy development

The logic of the LAND framework is that effective teaching practices need to be recognised, developed and supported through conducive organisational arrangements (including school structures), community engagement (that takes account of school context) and shared vision for numeracy development. Through the LAND project, LAND school leadership team members developed their pedagogical content knowledge in mathematics, a greater awareness of the characteristics of effective mathematics teaching, and confidence in their ability to teach mathematics. They also developed their leadership capability to think strategically and act practically to build better alignment between what happens in classrooms, how the school is organised, how the community is involved and the vision of the school community for numeracy development. This not only involved occasionally challenging preconceptions and 'old school thinking' related to mathematics, but also considering how various school-level factors influence mathematics teaching across a school. One striking example of the leadership of the LAND school leadership teams was the introduction and refinement of dedicated numeracy time, also known as the numeracy block, in many schools. This came about through the leadership teams developing their pedagogical content knowledge and the organisational will and know-how to get things done – in other words, by principals and teacher leaders collaborating and putting research and practice in mathematics teaching and educational leadership together. Having the capacity and willingness to think strategically and act practically to build alignment is an important quality of leadership teams embarking on the LAND approach.

A related feature in building alignment is acknowledging the school context. The LAND project schools were drawn from low socioeconomic status communities in metropolitan, regional and remote areas of Australia. The LAND approach acknowledged each school's context in several ways. For example, schools in regional and remote areas needed to deal with the issue of high staff turnover. The design and implementation of a school charter for teaching mathematics was a powerful way for schools with high turnover to induct new staff regarding their school's vision and beliefs about numeracy development and mathematical teaching practices. The charters were seen to provide the basis for continuity in contexts fraught with changing staff and moving students.

Principles for embedding numeracy development

The LAND project highlighted four principles that are required to embed numeracy development across a school and a school system:

- Build team leadership capacity in numeracy development – at school and central office level.
- Respect the insights, expertise, needs, expectations and context of those working in numeracy development across the school system.
- Build alignment in school system philosophy, policies and programs as well as individual perceptions and practices.
- Have an agreed, consistent and systemic approach to planning and monitoring numeracy development.

Each of these will now be considered in more detail.

Build team leadership capacity in numeracy development – at school and central office level

The composition of the LAND school leadership teams was vitally important in bridging the gap between school administration and classroom mathematics teaching. Having principals and teachers working collaboratively in leading numeracy in their schools had significant benefits (see Chapters 4 and 7). To assist with building team leadership capacity, some schools designated a position of school-based numeracy coordinator. This position may have had allocated time or it may have been performed in conjunction with a teacher's normal teaching role, depending on the funding and structural arrangements of particular schools. In Chapter 3, the roles undertaken by school numeracy coordinators were discussed. These are the salient characteristics of the role drawn from the LAND project experience:

- ability to work as fellow professionals alongside other colleagues to share established practices
  - ◊ confident practitioner without the need to be seen as the 'expert' in all aspects of the role of a mathematics teacher
  - ◊ discernment of good practice, being able to identify and acknowledge effective practice of colleagues
  - ◊ establishing shared discourse in communities of practice
  - ◊ coordinating school-based professional learning activities
- capacity to introduce new practices
  - ◊ this involves reading and interpreting research
  - ◊ application of findings to the specific context of the school
  - ◊ viewed by others as authoritative and therefore can be trusted as a guide
- ability to manage change
- effective administrator, recognising tasks vary from school to school and may involve overseeing assessment processes, data collection, managing resources, record keeping and reporting to parents.

These characteristics reflect those identified in recent research into the role, undertaken by Cheeseman and Clarke (2005, 2006) as well as other researchers (Corbin, McNamara & Williams, 2003).

Team leadership is also important at central office level. The LAND project officers in each of the three education authority central offices were conscious of how the LAND project related to other program areas and system priorities. The extent to which the project officers worked with colleagues in these areas (for example, school improvement, targeted programs, leadership development) varied. Team leadership was more evident and the LAND approach was more likely to be embedded where central offices took deliberate steps to build alignment in their philosophy to professional learning and their policies and programs in numeracy development and related areas.

Respect the insights, expertise, needs, expectations and context of those working in numeracy development across the school system

Everyone has a role to play and something to contribute when it comes to numeracy development. Respecting the expertise, responsibility and contribution of each individual is an important quality of educational leaders (see Chapter 4). It focuses on the relational aspects of leadership and the ability of leaders to engage with their communities. It involves understanding and respecting differences among members of school communities and displaying interest in their work and achievements.

This principle also includes taking a broader view of what constitutes a 'school system' and the importance of having system leaders: that is, people who are willing and able to involve parents, encourage community support, network with other schools and seek advice from others within (and beyond) the school system. These qualities, along with having school-based team leadership capacity, provide the foundation for the third principle.

Foster alignment in school system philosophy, policies and programs as well as individual perceptions and practices

Leading aligned numeracy development is about *things* as well as *people*. It involves both bureaucratic and professional elements where high levels of coordination and clarity about policies, programs and accountabilities coexist with shared understandings and the capacity to recognise and develop people's attitudes, knowledge and skills to deal with new and changing circumstances. The process of causal mapping was found to be a useful tool in bringing to the surface people's understandings about the nature and purpose of various causes of numeracy improvement and how these were related to one another (see Chapter 8 for more detail). In this sense, it can be an important step in building alignment. A related technique for investigating values alignment has been pioneered by Branson (2009, 2010 – see Chapter 4 for more detail).

Develop an agreed, consistent and systemic approach to planning and monitoring numeracy development

One tangible outcome of the principles of building team capacity, respecting others and building alignment is having an agreed, consistent and systemic approach to planning and monitoring numeracy development. The experience of the LAND project was that principals, coordinators and teachers are regularly invited by their central offices, external consultants and others to trial, purchase or adopt various kinds of numeracy interventions. While some interventions adopt a broad strategic approach, many tend to treat particular types of student needs, or year or stage levels, or content areas. Given the importance of mathematics and numeracy and the high stakes involved – particularly for their students – many schools feel the pressure to 'do something' about numeracy and therefore are susceptible to making expedient decisions. Rather than consider and perhaps adopt particular interventions one by one, the findings from the LAND project support the view that it is better for schools to base their decision-making about numeracy development on how specific initiatives or interventions in numeracy align with their charter for effective teaching practice. To do this requires an agreed, consistent and useful approach to planning and monitoring numeracy development – one that is based on professional principles, valid and reliable evidence and relevant indicators of performance. What is involved in planning and monitoring numeracy development is considered in the next section.

Planning and monitoring numeracy development

Sustaining improvement in student numeracy achievement requires an agreed and consistent approach to planning and monitoring numeracy development. It involves adaptations and modifications to teaching strategies, resources and learning environments, as well as to school priorities, organisational arrangements and community relationships. Numeracy development encompasses each of the following three levels (or tiers, see Bryant et al., 2008) but may be more targeted at one level than another depending on the types of initiatives being planned and undertaken:

- *the whole school level* – so that everyone's everyday numeracy experiences are improved (Tier 1)
- *the group level* – so that the numeracy achievement of particular groups of students is raised (Tier 2)
- *the individual level* – so that the numeracy achievement of particular students is improved, perhaps through targeted intervention (Tier 3).

Bryant et al. defined tiers of intervention in this way:

> Tier 1 consists of evidence-based core instruction for all students. Tier 2 includes supplemental intervention and ongoing progress monitoring for identified struggling students. Instructional delivery in Tier 2 is characterized by flexible groupings, informed instructional decision making, and evidence-based interventions. Tier 3 is reserved for those students who are struggling to the

extent that they require intensive intervention, which might include additional instructional time, small instructional grouping, adapted instructional content, and different materials. (2008, p. 20)

Planning and monitoring require leadership. The leadership capabilities and actions of school numeracy teams (comprising principals, numeracy coordinators and teacher leaders) are critical for guiding the planning of activity, implementation and tracking the progress of numeracy development. These capabilities and actions are described in Chapter 4.

Planning numeracy development

A plan is something that someone intends to do. It involves working out in advance *what* is to be done, *why* it is to be done, *how* it is to be done, and *how to assess the value* of what is done. A school numeracy development plan should include the same features:

- the purpose (what)
- the rationale (why)
- a synopsis of activities (how)
- criteria and indicators of success (how to assess the value).

These planning components, along with related questions about monitoring numeracy development and working with teachers, are presented in the framework shown in Figure 10.1.

This framework highlights three key ideas about leading numeracy development:
- *successful numeracy development is achieved with and through teachers.* This means that school leadership teams need to engage their teaching colleagues at

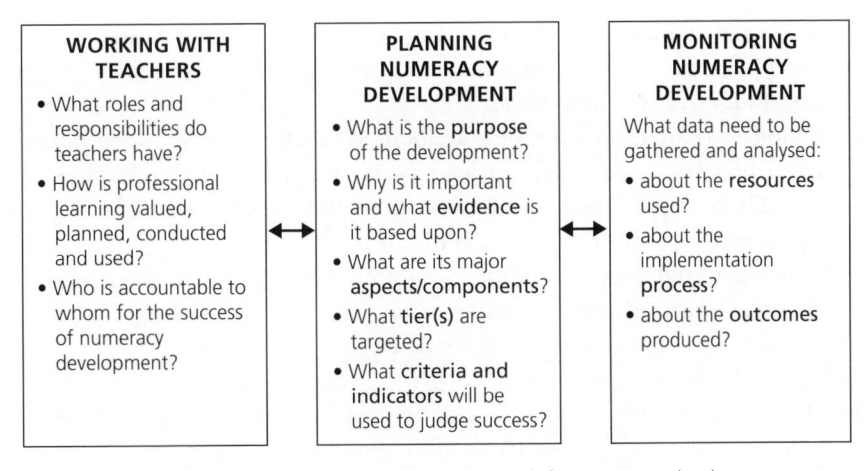

Figure 10.1: Planning and monitoring framework for numeracy development

every step in the process – from conception through the design phase to implementation and evaluation – and support their engagement through professional learning and opportunities to exercise leadership.

- *numeracy development needs to be monitored from start to finish.* Careful thought needs to be put into what types of data need to be gathered and analysed within and across each tier of the intervention. The key message is not to wait until the end to collect the data and draw conclusions!
- *the substance and the connections between each planning component are shaped by the school leadership team.* How the team members develop shared purpose for improvement, value teaching and professional development, organise curriculum and infrastructure, engage the community, and think and act to build alignment between outcomes, purpose, teaching, organisation and community is critical for turning planning intentions into reality.

Things rarely proceed as originally planned. Plans usually need to be refined in light of the data collected during the implementation process. Consequently, school leadership teams need to keep the following questions in mind:

- How are the teachers going? How are they teaching? What concerns do they have?
- How do we know? What data should we be collecting?
- What, if anything, should we do about what the data is telling us?

While plans tend to evolve through implementation and the influence of changing circumstances – within and external to the school and the system – numeracy development plans should contain some basic elements. In essence, a plan should describe what a school or school system is trying to achieve in numeracy; the reasons and evidence to support what is intended to be done; the approach being taken; and what changes are expected: for example, in student achievement and school performance, teaching practice, and parent and/or community support. These are summarised in Table 10.2.

A related part of numeracy development is planning how the process will be led, and how particular types of leadership capability will be developed and exercised. These capabilities, considered in detail in Chapter 4, with sample actions summarised in Table 4.2, are as follows:

- developing shared purpose to improve numeracy
- valuing teaching and professional development
- organising curriculum and infrastructure
- engaging the community
- thinking strategically and acting practically to build alignment between outcomes, vision, teaching, organisation and community.

Table 10.2: A school or school-system plan for numeracy development

Purpose	What is your school/system trying to achieve in numeracy?
Rationale	What are the reasons for this? What evidence is it based upon? How will things be different if your school is successful?
Synopsis	Your approach: • Which students are being targeted: Tier 1, 2 or 3? • What are the strategies and tasks, personnel, timeline and resources for each tier? • What steps are in place for students to move in and out of different tiers?
Success criteria Use as many evidenced-based criteria as you require	Indicators: • Changes in student achievement: whole-school student performance, year level performance, achievement of Tier 1, 2, 3 students, English-as-a-second-language/English-as-a-second-dialect students, students with disability • Changes in teaching practice, teacher pedagogical content knowledge, teacher confidence • Changes in parent and community support

(An appreciation of the significance of team planning for leading numeracy development can be heightened by completing the exercise in Appendix 1.)

Effective planning in numeracy development does not just happen. It requires attention to the basic elements, recognition of the team leadership capabilities and actions that are required, and a willingness and ability to alter course as evidence is collected and circumstances change.

Monitoring numeracy development

Planning and monitoring go together; one should inform the other. Monitoring means gathering and analysing data about resources (or inputs), processes and outcomes for a worthwhile purpose (Dunn, 1981). In the case of the LAND project, the 'worthwhile purpose' is improving students' numeracy achievement. We are therefore interested in gathering and analysing data about the resources used, the implementation processes and the outcomes produced. Some typical resources, processes and outcomes are shown in Table 10.3.

From Table 10.3, it is apparent that data can be gathered about all sorts of things! The key to effective monitoring is having a clear idea of the purpose and means of gathering data. A numeracy monitoring template (see Appendix 1) has been developed to assist anyone facing this task in deciding what data to gather and how to gather it. The template is framed around the two planning elements: the numeracy development plan and the team plan for leading numeracy development.

Table 10.3: Monitoring numeracy development: Sample resources, processes and outcomes

	Resources	Processes	Outcomes
For students	• Student needs, aspirations and abilities • Teaching materials	• Student learning behaviours	• Student engagement • Student achievement
For teachers	• Teacher expertise and sense of efficacy • Professional networks	• Teaching practices • Professional learning and development	• Teacher pedagogical content knowledge • Teacher confidence in teaching mathematics
For principals and school leaders	• Team leadership capability	• Team leadership actions • Principal leadership actions • Teacher leadership actions • Principal and teacher focused discussion, reflection, and goal setting	• Principal leadership capability • Teacher leadership capability • School team leadership capability
For parents and the community	• Parent and local community support	• School community consultation, engagement, and celebration	• Parent and local community support
Other	• Time • Infrastructure (i.e. buildings, equipment) • Education authority policies, programs and personnel • Numeracy and mathematics education specialists and research literature • Numeracy interventions • Funding		

Conclusion: Encouraging numeracy development

Educators are at a crossroads in the way that systemic improvement in student numeracy achievement should be approached. A classroom-by-classroom, school-by-school and initiative-by-initiative road to reform can be followed or something completely different can be tried. The LAND project described in this book took the latter option.

Decades of failed reform resulting from the former option highlight three things. First, top-down approaches decided by governments and central authorities are not sustainable (Sarason, 1990). Rather, systemic change is about cultural shifts rather than implementation of initiatives, and requires buy-in from all concerned: that is, involvement in the design and evaluation as well as the implementation. Second, teaching quality is a shared responsibility of teachers, principals and those working in central offices and government departments. Third, school- and system-wide improvement in student numeracy requires coordinated and complementary leadership at classroom, school, central office and government levels. The LAND project design was based on these three premises.

Recent research on systemic development supports the LAND approach. For example, Fullan (2010, p. 50) argued that successful system-wide reform requires constant communication across all levels, stating that 'it is less about a set of initiatives and more about developing a culture of agreed values, purposes, norms and practices'. He explained that cultural change involves the selection of the 'right kinds of drivers', and warned against selecting drivers that are politically attractive quick fixes enacted through legislation. While recognising that sustaining change depends on continued political support (Levin, 2009), this should not be at the expense of the moral imperatives for the students involved. The right drivers foster intrinsic motivation, engage students and teachers in continuous improvement, inspire teamwork and affect all students and teachers. External accountabilities, including emphasising standards, can work against this if they undermine the culture of learning by distracting attention and increasing isolation among teachers (Fullan, 2010).

On a similar note, related international research (Mourshed et al., 2010) found that improving systems sustain better teaching practices with these approaches:

- collaborative practices that enable teachers to share their skills in teaching practice and peer coaching throughout the school and the system
- a mediating layer between the schools and the central office that provides targeted hands-on support for schools, acts as a communication buffer between the school and the central office, and shares and integrates improvements across schools.

The LAND approach exhibited both of these features, and therefore holds promise for school- and system-wide numeracy development into the future. So, we close with three key messages for teachers, for schools and for systems to encourage numeracy development in schools and school systems.

Teachers

For teachers, the key message is to provide rich tasks that focus on important mathematics, to draw upon a variety of assessment data on individuals and the whole group, to develop flexible lesson structures with an emphasis on engaging students with the content, and to provide substantial time to pull the lesson together.

It is also very important for teachers to plan together, including working through tasks in the role of a student before presenting them to students, discussing likely student responses and common misconceptions.

These features of effective mathematics teaching were emphasised in the LAND project. Principal and teacher participants shared examples of practice. The university team explained the research base and also demonstrated examples of practice. These examples were analysed by workshop groups, then trialled and adapted by the LAND school leadership teams for use in their local school contexts. The results were an increase in teachers' confidence and an enhancement of their mathematics teaching repertoire, as evidenced by the following reflection:

> INTERVIEWER: Is there anything that the LAND project could have done that they didn't?

> LAND SCHOOL LEADERSHIP TEAM MEMBER: No – other than have more LAND projects! I say that in the context that for teachers who aren't, or weren't as passionate about mathematics as myself or others may be, I think it has been very important. I mean my colleague YYY is a classic example. He is now somebody who is really getting interested in mathematics, really looking at how he is teaching it. That can't be stopped, wherever he goes from our school, his involvement in LAND is going to mean that he is going to be a very effective teacher in mathematics somewhere else, and I like that.

Schools

For schools, the key message is to adopt a school charter for teaching mathematics and to develop a shared vision for numeracy, to adjust organisational arrangements, to engage the school community, to think strategically and to act practically to build alignment and to realise student numeracy development.

Leading school-wide development in mathematics teaching and student numeracy achievement is the responsibility of principals and teachers. Teaching and leading in mathematics and numeracy go together. Therefore promote principal and teacher collaborative leadership practice and have respect for where people are in their knowledge, skill and confidence in teaching mathematics.

Systems

For systems, the key message is to sustain development in numeracy through partnerships that involve strategic thinking, focused discussion and practical follow-up action within and across classrooms, schools, education authority central offices and government.

Student numeracy achievement directly depends on the quality of the mathematics teaching, and this depends on teacher pedagogical content knowledge and confidence. These qualities are best developed by teachers, principals and officers from central offices and government working in collaboration, creating new knowledge through partnerships and networks.

Leaders of meaningful educational change work to build an organisation's capacity for developing and exercising leadership, vibrant professional learning communities and the generation of new knowledge. Our hope is that this book has provided some useful insights to assist in leading developments in student numeracy. We encourage you to continue to engage in meaningful numeracy development at school and system level, to create the types of communities and to generate the kinds of knowledge that will enable every child to be numerate. It is their right.

LEADING IMPROVEMENT IN STUDENT NUMERACY: PRACTICAL EXERCISES

Leading improvement in student numeracy requires a team effort. It involves strategic thinking and practical action by teachers, principals, school executive staff and central office personnel *working together*. The following exercise is designed for you to reflect upon your school and school-system context, and to plan for and monitor numeracy improvement. As you reflect upon your team membership and capabilities and discuss the questions and planning elements with colleagues, consider the themes, principles and ideas that have been presented throughout the chapters of this book. As you do, think about how you intend to build alignment in thinking and practice about improving students' engagement with, enjoyment of, and achievement in numeracy.

Reflect on your team membership and leadership capabilities. Describe the strategy you intend to use in leading numeracy development in your school or school system:
- What you are going to do?
- Why you are going to do it?
- How you are going to do it?
- How you will evaluate the success of what you have done?

Consider what leadership capabilities are most important in your context, your team strengths, and what capabilities need to be developed. Adjust your strategy based on these considerations.

Numeracy monitoring template: Numeracy development plan

Table A.1: Numeracy development planning and monitoring template

Numeracy development plan		Useful data to gather*	Useful data-gathering instruments
Purpose rationale		• Teacher participation • Teacher understanding • Teacher agreement	• Teacher survey • Teacher interview • Teacher focus groups
Synopsis	• Students are targeted at tiers 1, 2 and 3 • Strategies and tasks, personnel, timeline and resources for each tier • Steps in place for students to move in and out of different tiers	• Teaching practice • Teaching programs • Professional development • Organisational arrangements (incl. structures and resources)	• Classroom observation • Document analysis • Teacher survey • Teacher interview • Teacher focus groups
Success criteria	Indicators: • Changes in student achievement: whole-school student performance, year level performance, achievement of tier 1, 2 and 3 students, English-as-a-second-language/English-as-a-second-dialect students, students with disability • Changes in teaching: teaching quality, teacher level of use of numeracy intervention, teacher stage of concern about numeracy intervention • Changes in parent and community support		• Those listed above plus: ◊ Student work samples, classroom assessments, NAPLAN ◊ Parent surveys

* Sample data sources and means for collecting data are illustrative only. Actual approaches will depend on the nature of the individual school and school system contexts.

Numeracy monitoring template: Team plan for leading numeracy development

Table A.2: Team planning template for leading numeracy development

Team plan for leading numeracy development	Useful data to gather	Useful data-gathering instruments

Developing shared purpose to improve numeracy	• Student achievement data
	• Teacher* expectations
	• Teacher participation
	• Teacher understanding
	• Teacher agreement
		• Personal professional journal**
		• Document analysis:
		  staff meeting papers
		  ◊ correspondence
		  ◊ school newsletters

Valuing teaching and professional development	Those listed above plus: • Teaching practice • Teacher participation in decision-making • Staff teamwork • Teacher leadership • Professional development (who, when, how, what, with what effect, and what cost)	Those listed above plus: • Teacher survey • Teacher interview • Teacher focus groups • Classroom observation
Organising curriculum and infrastructure	• Teaching programs • Supportive organisational arrangements (incl. timetable, staffing structures and resources) • Resources allocated to improve conditions for learning	Those listed above plus: • School budget priorities and expenditure
Engaging the community	• Parent involvement • Networking with professional colleagues	Those listed above plus: • Parent meeting records and surveys
Thinking strategically and acting practically to build alignment between outcomes, vision, teaching, organisation and community	• Qualitative and quantitative student engagement and achievement data • Teacher, parent and student understanding of the connections between outcomes, vision, teaching, organisation and community	Those listed above plus: • Class- and school-based internal assessment • Systemic external assessment – NAPLAN • School community survey

* While 'teacher' is listed as the data source, it may also be appropriate to gather data from other members of the school community or central office, for example, parents and students, depending on the school or school-system context.

** A personal professional journal is a useful monitoring instrument for tracking one's leadership of numeracy development.

LAND PROJECT SCHOOLS AND PROJECT STAGES

LAND project schools

Northern Territory Catholic Education Office

Santa Teresa – Ltyentye Apurte
Our Lady of the Sacred Heart, Wadeye
St Francis Xavier, Nauiyu, Daly River
Murrupurtiyanuwu Catholic School, Bathurst Island
Xavier Community Education Centre, Bathurst Island

Catholic Education Office South Australia

Immaculate Heart of Mary
St Brigid's School
Whitcfriars
Catherine McAuley School

Catholic Education Office of Western Australia

Banksia Grove
St Vincent's Parmelia
Xavier Catholic College
St. Joseph's Waroona
St Joseph's Kunnunura
St Joseph's Wyndham
Djarindjin Lombadina School
Sacred Heart Beagle Bay

LAND project stages

Stage 1: Project orientation, information gathering and analysis

Stage 1 involved the following steps:
- familiarisation visits by the research team to schools including community consultation
- an orientation workshop with school personnel: principal and other staff for each school cluster
- gathering baseline information about current school and system numeracy practices.

Stage 2: Professional and organisational development

Stage 2 involved the following steps:
- two professional and organisational development workshops. These workshops focused on pedagogy and content knowledge in numeracy; leadership; and school development and alignment.
- visits by the research consultancy team to each project school (at least twice over a 15-month period after the first Stage 2 workshop and before the second. Additional visits made by the central office project officer.
- a mid-project review.

Stage 3: Planning for sustainability

The final stage in the project involved the following steps:
- a final visit to each school in the project
- a planning and evaluation workshop
- a showcase conference involving participants from all LAND schools.

LEADERSHIP REFLECTIONS, COMMITMENTS AND PLANS: LAND PROJECT – WORKSHOP 1

Michael Gaffney, Michael Bezzina, Doug Clarke and Rhonda Faragher

Workshop 1 was based around a series of PowerPoint slides, which are reproduced below.

The following factors are based on the findings from the Leaders Transforming Learning and Learners (LTLL) project by Michael Bezzina, Charles Burford and Patrick Duignan. LTLL is a project researching the ways in which leaders can promote learning in values-based school environments.

Leadership: A process of influencing student numeracy development by:

- encouraging collaboration
- using evidence
- promoting professional learning
- shaping the culture of the school community
- working with change
- networking
- planning for sustainability
- building capacity.

Leadership: A process of influencing student learning in numeracy

Read your description(s).

As a group consider each factor in turn by:

- explaining your factor description to colleagues
- inviting colleagues to rate and record their thoughts about the evidence of the factor in their school setting.

Rating and reflecting

[Participants were shown a traffic light symbol and asked to rate their reflections according to the colours of the lights]

- RED: No evidence
- YELLOW: Some evidence
- GREEN: Lots of evidence

Reflect on your rating. Why have you selected that colour and what are some examples?

Leadership through collaboration

Supporting staff to *work in partnership* when making decisions about teaching and learning – recognising that all have a leadership contribution to make.

An effective school:

- has an explicit and agreed educational purpose
- has a shared view of what constitutes good teaching and learning
- promotes a sense of staff efficacy and competence
- empowers staff to make decisions that are in tune with the school's educational purpose
- has agreed standards for performance
- engages in collaborative professional learning
- promotes team-based initiatives
- trials innovative practices
- demonstrates collective responsibility for outcomes.

Leadership based on evidence

- Building teachers' capacity to collect and analyse relevant data to inform their planning and actions
- Encouraging teachers to take a 'research stance' in their work

An effective school:
- identifies the types of evidence relevant for improving teaching quality and student learning
- has valid and reliable procedures for collecting and analysing relevant evidence
- acts on the results
- develops teachers' capabilities for evidence-based practice.

Leadership promoting professional learning
- Developing the professional learning community
- Encouraging shared understandings and principles of practice

An effective school:
- values professional learning
- supports team-based learning through school structures and procedures
- encourages professional conversation based on experience and expertise, as well as authoritative literature and research
- evaluates the impact of professional learning on teaching practice and student outcomes.

Leadership shaping the culture of the school community
- Recognising that every school has an organisational culture and that 'community' is at the heart of the Catholic school
- Shaping school culture to influence the ways people think, feel and act to improve outcomes for students

An effective school:
- has an explicit, shared vision and purpose grounded in its identity
- uses clear, shared language to describe its vision and core activities
- has an accepted set of norms for behaviour
- celebrates key events and achievements as a community
- lives out shared values in behaviour, word, ritual and symbol.

Leadership in working with change
- Initiating and responding to change driven from within the school community
- Influencing and responding to change driven from outside the school community, i.e. from central office, governments

An effective school:
- works with change because of the moral purpose – to improve outcomes for students

- engages those affected by change
- develops procedures sharing knowledge and learning from change
- uses change to bring vision, teaching, community characteristics, organisation and outcomes into closer alignment
- embodies enthusiasm, hope and energy in the leadership of change.

Leadership through networking

- Working in partnership with parents and the local community
- Building constructive alliances with other partners in the education enterprise

An effective school:
- works in partnership with parents, focusing on two-way communication about the needs of individual students
- develops networks with other schools within and beyond its local system
- engages actively with other education providers in targeted programs
- encourages staff membership of professional associations.

Leadership for sustainability

- Planning for sustainable improvement
- Developing sustainable leadership

An effective school:
- plans 'strategically' for sustainable improvement
- supports those in leadership roles
- encourages and develops members of the school community to be leaders.

Leadership building capability

- Assisting staff to integrate knowledge, skills, personal qualities and understanding . . . (thereby)
- Developing staff capacity to respond to changing circumstances

An effective school:
- recognises the capabilities of its people
- appreciates the complexity of building capability
- provides opportunities for staff to develop their capabilities
- builds a climate of trust, mutual support and development.

Leading Improvements in Student Numeracy. Published by ACER Press.

LAND school leadership team reflections on numeracy

What are our school's areas of strength?
What are our school's areas of weakness and possibility?

LAND school leadership team member commitments

The personal dimension: Myself

As a consequence of my start in the LAND project, I commit, in the next month, to take on this personal challenge:

by:

The professional dimension: Me and my class

As a consequence of my start in the LAND project, I commit, in the next two months, to implement new numeracy practices in the following area(s) in my classroom:

The peer leadership dimension: Me and my colleague(s)

As a consequence of my start in the LAND project, I commit, in the next month, to share my learning about:

with:

Leadership in the school dimension: Us and our school

Our LAND school leadership team will commit to work with colleagues and community members across the school community to bring about change in the following area(s) of numeracy:

LAND school action plan

What's in an action plan?

- *Focus*: what are we trying to do?
- *People*: who will be directly affected? Who else might be interested?
- *Resistance*: who or what will get in the way/oppose/block?
- *Assistance*: who or what will be able to support us?
- *Our learning*: what have we learned that we can use?
- *Possible strategies*: what strategies can we think of? Which will we use?

Action plan

We want to make this change:

_____

_____

We are conscious that these people will be affected:

_____

_____

These are the steps in our plan:

Step	By whom?	By when?

Action plan critique

How well do you think the plan has:

- identified helping and constraining factors?
- developed ways for dealing with these?
- made use of the material presented in the workshop?

What would improve your plan?

APPENDIX 4

ACHIEVING VALUES ALIGNMENT
Chris Branson and Michael Gaffney

How are teachers' attitudes and behaviour influenced by the psychological relationship between their school and them?

This is referred to as having an 'affective organizational commitment' (Gautam, Van Dick & Wagner, 2004). In other words, teachers have an emotional attachment to, identification with and positive involvement in the school (Van Knippenberg & Sleebos, 2006, p. 573).

This attachment results from the achievement of 'organisational values alignment' where the personal values of the employee are aligned with the values of the organisation. This implies that everyone participating in the change process would share the same values.

Organisational values alignment is not a naturally occurring or simple outcome to achieve. Values are specific to an individual and only reside in the mind of that person. Often, within organisations, the people hold many different and sometimes incompatible beliefs and values based on assumptions they individually hold about their own personal entitlements, constraints and preferred courses of action. When people come together in an organisation, they each bring their own personality and set of values. The organisation hence does not possess a set of values unless the individuals in the organisation personally and authentically embrace each value within the proposed set.

Successful educational change has a deliberate and comprehensive organisational values clarification and alignment process. This process has two elements:

- a values clarification procedure designed to cooperatively discern the essential values that need to characterise the school
- a means by which each person is encouraged to support the application of these values in their everyday endeavours.

Leading Improvements in Student Numeracy. Published by ACER Press.

Figure A.1 shows a framework designed to guide the values clarification and application. The key components of the framework are elaborated in the next section.

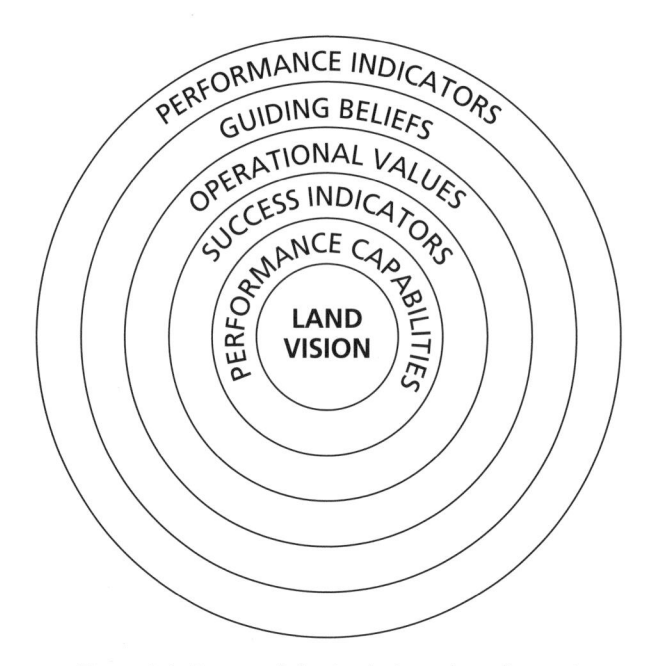

Figure A.1: Framework for developing values alignment

Framework for developing values alignment

LAND project vision

Project vision is what the group is striving to achieve through the LAND project. It describes what the group needs to do and, as such, it is distinct from, but related to, the school vision. The project vision is a single sentence that describes not only what is seen as the core business of the group but also the manner and means for achieving it.

For example: 'Our LAND project vision is to [state core business and aspirations] by [describe ways of achieving it]'.

As a controlling insight, the project vision is a source of potential school values in the minds of those involved. These values have meaning since each individual understands them and therefore is in a better position to support and adopt them.

These points act as guidelines for defining project vision:
- What are we trying to achieve as the school LAND team?
- What unique outcomes are required to distinguish our work from that of others aiming to achieve a similar expectation but in a different context?
- What are the key roles and responsibilities of this group in achieving these expectations?
- Whom do we serve and what do they want or expect from us?
- Create a one-sentence vision statement that captures these insights.

Performance capabilities

Performance capabilities are the strengths and weaknesses of the group and each individual with respect to the achievement of the project vision. Discussion builds confidence by reinforcing strengths and finding ways to overcome weaknesses: for example, through targeted professional development. The transparency of the process clarifies what is valued and why it is valued. In this way, the meaning of the values is reinforced in the minds of the group members.

These points act as guidelines for defining performance capabilities:
- What are the real strengths of our school LAND team?
- How can these strengths be maximised?
- What personal strengths do I contribute to this group?
- What are our clear weaknesses and how can they be overcome?
- What personal weakness can I attend to so as to enhance the strengths of our team?

Success indicators

Success indicators are the perceived logical consequences achieved as the group realises its vision. Having the group develop the indicators of success builds commitment and motivates individuals to become engaged in project activities, and clarify and share group values.

These points act as guidelines for defining success indicators:
- How will we know when we are achieving our vision? What are our *success indicators*? What will we see, hear and feel to be happening when we are achieving our vision?
- What is our most critical *success indicator*?

Operational values

Operational values are the values arising from the preceding components and the ones that are required to realise the vision. The group needs to prioritise the most important values. Having too many values diffuses commitment.

These points act as guidelines for defining operational values:

- What are the possible values that would help to achieve all the outcomes that have been previously discussed? (See the final section for a list of possible values.)
- Of these values, which are more important for achieving success?

The next step is to engage in a collaborative prioritisation process:

- From the full list of possible values chosen by the group, each individual selects and prioritises their own top five, and gives the most important value a rating of 10, and the least important value a rating of 1.
- Collate all of the individual ratings.
- Determine the top five values and place a tick adjacent to the value to indicate its acceptance as a preferred value for the group. In the event of several values having the same score, giving a total of more than five top values, further discussion should take place to determine the top five accepted values.

See Table A.3 for an example.

Table A.3: Sample collation and determination of operational values

Nominated value	Group rating	Accepted
Respect	6	✓
Trust	6	✓
Communication	6	✓
Honesty	5	
Loyalty	4	
Courtesy	4	
Achievement	1	
Reliability	4	
Responsibility	5	
Understanding	3	
Empathy	4	
Cooperation	7	✓
Harmony	3	
Encouragement	2	
Collegiality	1	
Professionalism	7	✓

Guiding beliefs

Guiding beliefs are the agreed guidelines arising from the operational values.
Henderson and Thompson stated:

> Every time we have worked through this process with a group, people have
> commented on how powerful the experience was. To feel a group of people
> align on a single and unanimously agreed belief about a value is unifying and
> empowering. It also has an added benefit of being a wonderful team-building
> experience. (2003, p. 109)

Guiding beliefs are created by converting each value to a belief by asking the group
to complete the following sentence with each value: 'We value [insert nominated
value] because . . .'

Here are some examples:

'We value COOPERATION – because we are a team and a team works together.'

'We value PROFESSIONALISM – because we have confidence in each other's
specialist skills and knowledge.'

Performance indicators

Performance indicators are the behavioural outcomes expected to be seen enacted
by a person authentically living out these beliefs and values. Having the group
identify behaviour and outcomes that logically result from living out the values not
only makes it quite clear what is expected, but each person also knows that others
will be able to judge their personal commitment to these values by their behaviour.
In this way, it is more likely that each person will commit to these beliefs and
values.

These points act as guidelines for defining performance indicators.

- If the team is performing in accordance with these values and beliefs, what
  would each member be doing?
- Draw up a personal plan for the next five days that states four things that you
  will do to contribute to the team's agreed vision.

Each of these aspects involved in aligning values builds meaning for the individuals
involved. Synergy is achieved by working through each aspect. The whole becomes
greater than the sum of the parts.

As a consequence, individuals are able to better align their values with the
organisation's values while also sensing heightened workplace meaningfulness
and fulfilment.

Possible values

Abiding by the law; accepting others; accountability; achievement; adaptability; adventurous; affirmation; alignment; altruism; approval; authenticity; authority; balance; belonging; candour; caring; Catholic; caution; Christian; cohesiveness; collaboration; collegiality; comfort; commitment; communication; community; community involvement; community orientation; community support; companionship; compassion; competition; compliance; concern for others; confidence; confidentiality; congruence; consideration; consistency; control; cooperation; courage; courtesy; creativity; credentials; credibility; curiosity; dedication; deference; delight; dependability; dependency; developing others; dignity; diligence; diplomacy; discernment; discretion; diversity; effectiveness; efficiency; empathy; empowerment; encouragement; enthusiasm; equality; ethics; evangelising; excellence; expediency; faith; fellowship; flexibility; freedom; friendship; fulfilment; generosity; genuineness; giving; glory; hard work; harmony; health; honesty; honour; humility; humour; imagination; improvement; inclusiveness; independence; influence; initiative; innovation; integrity; intelligence; interdependence; intuition; involvement; justice; kindness; love; loyalty; material possessions; mentoring; merit; morality; mutual interests; networking; perseverance; politeness; popularity; prestige; productivity; professionalism; progress; obedience; openness; opportunity; optimism; order; organisational orientation; originality; ownership; participation; partnering; patience; peace; quality; recognition; reliability; respect; responsibility; responsiveness; results; risk-taking; routine; security; self-control; self-discipline; self-interest; seniority; service; sincerity; situational ethics; speed; spirituality; spontaneity; stability; status; status quo; subservience; success; support; synergism; tact; teamwork; territory; tolerance; tradition; trust; trustworthiness; truth; understanding; winning; wisdom; witness to faith

APPENDIX 5

PROCESS AND STAGES OF ANALYSIS IN THE LAND CAUSAL MAPPING STUDY

Craig Ashhurst

LAND project participants (LAND school leadership team members, central office personnel and officers from the Department of Education, Employment and Workplace Relations) were invited to respond to an initial survey that posed the question: What in your experience are the significant causes of improvement in student achievement in numeracy? The responses to this question were combined to create an 'original' cluster causal map.

Each map represented an initial collection of perceived causes required to improve numeracy in the participants' specific context (school, central office, government department). For ease of comparison, causes were grouped according to the LAND framework. If causes were linked in the survey responses, this was shown on the map by a line with an arrow. An example of an original cluster causal map is shown in Figure A.2.

Each cluster map was printed and presented to the related cluster group at Workshop 3 in the series of LAND project workshops. This provided a means by which an individual's originally identified causes were combined with those of their colleagues and reflected back to them in visual form as a representation of their collective thinking. Two 90-minute sessions in Workshop 3 functioned as the first round of work on causal mapping. In the first session, participants were asked to reflect on their map in school groups during the workshop, making any modifications that they considered necessary. School groups were then asked to discuss the following questions:

- Is there anything we need to remove from the map?
- Is there anything missing that should be added?

Each group's response was reported back to the whole cluster.

Groups were then asked to nominate the top three causes essential for improving numeracy in their schools, give their reasons and report back to cluster group.

At the planning and evaluation workshop (Workshop 4 in Stage 3), the revised maps, based on the Workshop 3 feedback, were presented to the cluster groups. Participants were then asked to comment and also to discuss a series of questions relating to their maps.

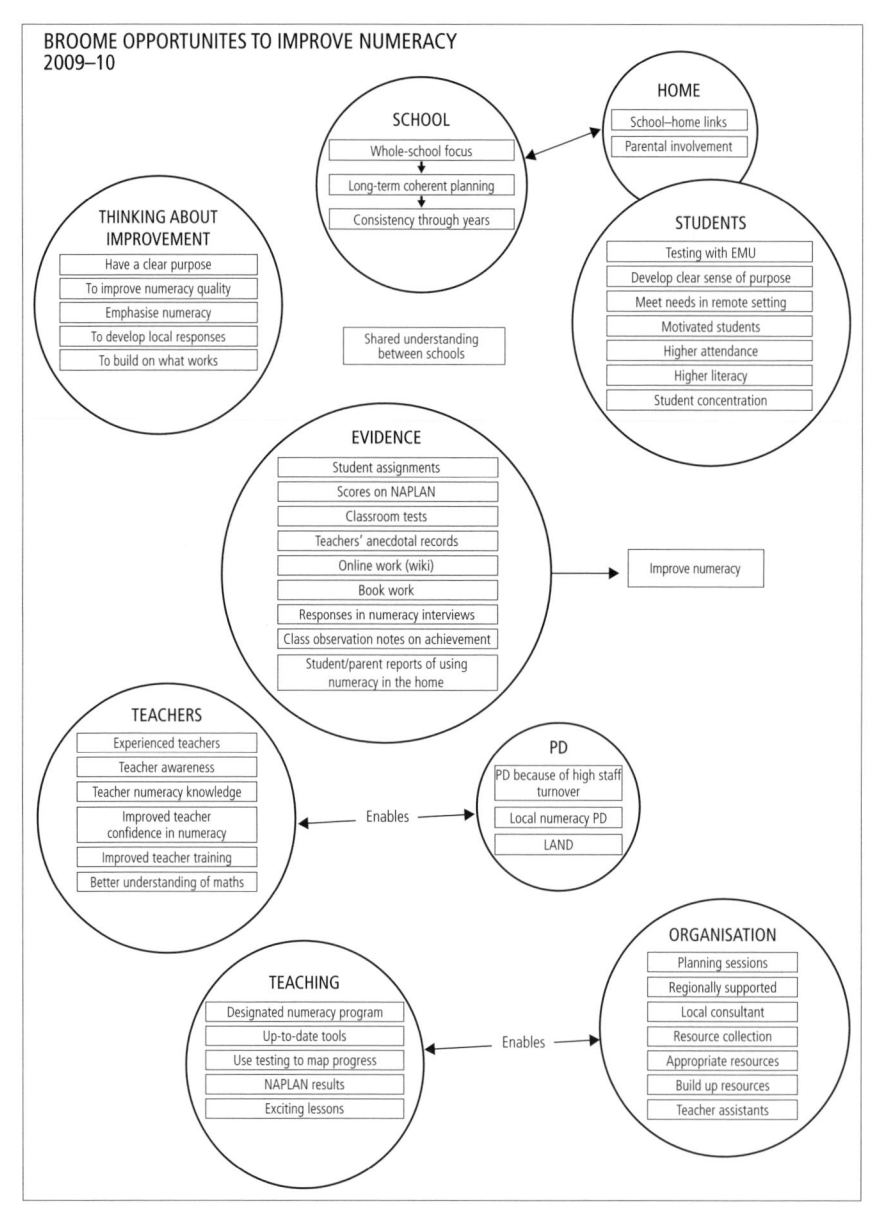

Figure A.2: Original causal map – Broome (Kimberley) school cluster

REFERENCES

Akkerman, S. F., & Bakker, A. (2011). Boundary crossing and boundary objects. *Review of Educational Research, 81*(2), 132–169.

Andrews, D. J., Conway, M., Dawson, M., Lewis, J., McMaster, A., & Morgan, H. (2004). *School revitalisation: The IDEAS way*. ACEL Monograph Series, Number 34. Winmalee, NSW: Australian Council for Educational Leaders.

Ashhurst, C. (2012). *Taming to tackling: Addressing numeracy achievement in low SES schools as a wicked problem* (Masters thesis). Australian Catholic University, Canberra.

Askew, M. (2004). Learning together: Effective teaching of numeracy. In A. McIntosh & L. Sparrow (Eds.), *Beyond written computation* (pp. 171–181). Perth: Mathematics, Science and Technology Education Centre.

Askew, M., Brown, M., Rhodes, V., Johnson, D., & Wiliam, D. (1997). *Effective teachers of numeracy: Final report*. London: King's College.

Askew, M., Hodgen, J., Hossain, S., & Bretscher, N. (2010). *Values and variables: Mathematics education in high-performing countries*. London: Nuffield Foundation.

Atweh, W., & Goos, W. (2011). The Australian mathematics curriculum: A move forward or back ot the future? *Australian Journal of Education, 55*(3), 214–228.

Australian Academy of Science (AAS). (2006). *Mathematics and statistics: Critical skills for Australia's future*. Melbourne: AAS.

Australian Association of Mathematics Teachers (AAMT). (1985). *Joint policy statement on maths, families and teachers*. Adelaide: AAMT.

Australian Association of Mathematics Teachers (AAMT). (1997). *Numeracy = everyone's business*. The Report of the Numeracy Education Strategy Development Conference, May 1997. Adelaide: AAMT.

Australian Association of Mathematics Teachers (AAMT). (2002). *Standards for excellence in teaching mathematics in Australian schools*. Adelaide: AAMT.

Australian Association of Mathematics Teachers (AAMT). (2006). *Standards for excellence in teaching mathematics in Australian schools*. Retrieved from http://www.aamt.edu.au/Activities-and-projects/Standards

Australian Catholic University Flagship for Creative and Authentic Leadership (ACUFCAL). (2007). *System leadership framework*. Strathfield, NSW: Australian Catholic University.

Australian Council for Educational Leaders. (2010). *ACEL leadership capability framework*. Retrieved from http://www.acelleadership.org.au/acel-leadership-capability-framework%C2%A9

Australian Council for Educational Research (ACER). (2003). *Investigation of effective mathematics teaching and learning in Australian secondary schools*. Report to Commonwealth Department of Education, Science and Training. Camberwell, Vic.: ACER.

References

Australian Council of Deans of Science (ACDS). (2006). *The preparation of mathematics teachers in Australia.* Melbourne: ACDS.

Australian Curriculum, Assessment and Reporting Authority (ACARA). (2011). *NAPLAN: National assessment program.* Retrieved from http://www.nap.edu.au/naplan/naplan.html

Australian Curriculum, Assessment and Reporting Authority (ACARA). (2013). *My school.* Retrieved from http://www.myschool.edu.au

Australian Curriculum, Assessment and Reporting Authority (ACARA). (n.d.). *Australian Curriculum: Mathematics.* Retrieved from http://www.australiancurriculum.edu.au/Mathematics/Rationale

Australian Institute for Teaching and School Leadership. (2012a). *Australian professional standard for principals.* Carlton South, Vic.: Education Services Australia.

Australian Institute for Teaching and School Leadership. (2012b). *Australian professional standards for teachers.* Carlton South, Vic.: Education Services Australia.

Australian Public Service Commission (ASPC). (2007). *Tackling wicked problems: A public policy perspective.* Canberra: ASPC. Retrieved from http://www.apsc.gov.au/__data/assets/pdf_file/0005/6386/wickedproblems.pdf

Barber, M. (1997). *The learning game: Arguments for an education revolution.* London: Indigo.

Barber, M., & Mourshed, M. (2007). *How the world's best-performing school systems come out on top.* London: McKinsey.

Begle, E. (1979). *Critical variables in mathematics education: Findings from a survey of the empirical literature.* Washington, DC: Mathematical Association of America and the National Council of Teachers of Mathematics.

Bezzina, M. (2007, August). *Moral purpose and shared leadership: The leaders transforming learning and learners pilot study.* Paper presented at the The Leadership Challenge: Improving learning in schools, Melbourne.

Bezzina, M. (2008). We do make a difference: Shared moral purpose and shared leadership in the pursuit of learning. *Leading and Managing, 14*(1), 38–59.

Bezzina, M., & Burford, C. (2010). Leaders transforming learning and learners: An Australian innovation in leadership, learning and moral purpose. In A. H. Normore (Ed.), *Global perspectives on educational leadership reform: The development and preparation of leaders of learning and learners of leadership.* (Vol. 11, pp. 201–211). Bingley, UK: Emerald.

Branson, C. M. (2009). *Leadership for an age of wisdom.* Dordrecht, Netherlands: Springer Educational Publishing.

Branson, C. M. (2010). *Leading educational change wisely.* Rotterdam, Netherlands: Sense Publishers.

Brophy, J. E., & Good, T. L. (1986). Teacher behavior and student achievement. In M. C. Wittrock (Ed.), *Handbook of research on teaching* (3rd ed., pp. 328–375). New York: Macmillan.

Brown, M. (1998). *Raising standards in school mathematics and science: How can we achieve significant improvement?* Unpublished manuscript.

Brown, M. (1999). Is more whole class teaching the answer? *Mathematics Teaching, 169,* 5–7.

Bruce, C. D., Esmonde, I., Ross, J., Dookie, L., & Beatty, R. (2010). The effects of sustained classroom-embedded teacher professional learning on teacher efficacy and related student achievement. *Teaching and Teacher Education, 26*(8), 1598–1608.

Bryant, D. P., Bryant, B. R., Gersten, R., Scammacca, N., & Chavez, M. M. (2008). Mathematics intervention for first-and second-grade students with mathematics difficulties. The effects of tier 2 intervention delivered as booster lessons. *Remedial and Special Education, 29*(1), 20–32.

Caldwell, B. J. (2007). *Alignment.* London: Specialist Schools and Academies Trust.

Caldwell, B. J., & Spinks, J. M. (2008). *Raising the stakes: From improvement to transformation in the reform of schools.* London: Routledge.

Cheeseman, J., & Clarke, D. (2005). Early numeracy coordinators in Victorian primary schools: Components of the role, highlights and challenges. In P. Clarkson, A. Downton, D. Gronn, M. Horne, A. McDonough, R. Pierce & A. Roche (Eds.), *Building connections: Theory, research and practice* (pp. 225–232). Melbourne: Mathematics Education Research Group of Australasia.

Cheeseman, J., & Clarke, D. M. (2006). Examining the changed role of numeracy coordinators. In P. Grootenboer, R. Zevenbergen & M. Chinnappan (Eds.), *Identities cultures and learning spaces.* Proceedings of the 29th annual conference of the Mathematics Education Research Group of Australasia (pp. 123–130). Adelaide: MERGA.

Clarke, B. A., & Clarke, D. M. (1996). A compulsory mathematics unit for primary preservice teachers: Content, pedagogy and assessment. In R. Zevenbergen (Ed.), *Mathematics education in changing times: Reactive or proactive. Proceedings of the Mathematics Education Lecturer's Association Conference* (pp. 27–36). Melbourne: MELA.

Clarke, D. J. (1988). *Assessment alternative in mathematics.* Melbourne: Curriculum Corporation.

Clarke, D. M. (1997). The changing role of the mathematics teacher. *Journal for Research in Mathematics Education, 28*(3), 1–31.

Clarke, D. M. (2001). Understanding, assessing and developing young children's mathematical thinking: Research as powerful tool for professional growth. In J. Bobis, B. Perry & M. Mitchelmore (Eds.), *Numeracy and beyond. Proceedings of the 24th Annual Conference of the Mathematics Education Research Group of Australasia* (Vol. 1, pp. 9–26). Sydney: MERGA.

Clarke, D. M., & Clarke, B. A. (2002). *Using rich assessment tasks in mathematics to engage students and inform teaching.* Background paper for seminar for upper secondary teachers, Stockholm, September 2002. Retrieved from http://www.arm.catholic.edu.au/educational-resources/curriculum/pd-items/assessment_paper_rich%20tasks.pdf

Clarke, D. M., & Clarke, B. A. (2004). Mathematics teaching in Grades K–2: Painting a picture of challenging, supportive, and effective classrooms. In R. N. Rubenstein & G. W. Bright (Eds.), *Perspectives on the teaching of mathematics: 66th Yearbook of the National Council of Teachers of Mathematics* (pp. 67–81). Reston, VA: National Council of Teachers of Mathematics.

Clements, M. A., & Ellerton, N. (1995). Assessing the effectiveness of pencil-and-paper tests for school mathematics. In B. Atweh & S. Flavel (Eds.), *Galtha: MERGA 18. Proceedings of the 18th Annual Conference of the Mathematics Education Research Group of Australasia* (pp. 184–188). Darwin, NT: University of the Northern Territory.

Coleman, J. (1966). *Equality of educational opportunity study. (Coleman study)*. Ann Arbor, MI: Inter-university Consortium for Political and Social Research.

Coleman, J. (1987). Families and schools. *Educational Researcher, 16*(6), 32–38.

Commonwealth Department of Education, Employment and Workplace Relations (DEEWR). (2008). *National action plan for literacy and numeracy*. Canberra: DEEWR.

Commonwealth Department of Education, Employment and Workplace Relations (DEEWR). (2011). *Smarter schools*. Retrieved from http://smarterschools.gov.au

Commonwealth Department of Education, Science and Training. (2004). *Teachers enhancing numeracy*. Canberra: Australian Government.

Commonwealth Department of the Prime Minister and Cabinet. (2012). *A national plan for school improvement, speech to National Press Club, Canberra (Prime Minister, Julia Gillard)*. Canberra: Australian Government. Retrieved from http://pmtranscripts.dpmc.gov.au/

Corbin, B., McNamara, O., & Williams, J. (2003). Numeracy coordinators: 'Brokering' change within and between communities of practice? *British Journal of Educational Studies, 51*(4), 344–368.

Council of Australian Governments. (2008a). *National numeracy review report*. Commissioned by the Human Capital Working Group, Council of Australian Government. Canberra: Commonwealth of Australia.

Council of Australian Governments. (2008b). *National partnership on literacy and numeracy*. Canberra: Commonwealth of Australia.

Crowther, F. (2012). *From school improvement to sustained capacity*. Moorabbin, Vic.: Hawker Brownlow Education.

Crowther, F., Andrews, D., Morgan, A., & O'Neill, S. (2012). Hitting the bullseye of school improvement: The IDEAS Project at work in a successful school system. *Leading and Managing, 18*(2), 1–34.

Crowther, F. S., Kaagan, M., Ferguson, M., & Hann, L. (2002). *Developing teacher leaders: How teacher leadership enhances school success*. Thousand Oaks, CA: Corwin Press.

Davies, J. (2004). *Wiki brainstorming and problems with wiki*. Retrieved from http://www.jonathan-davies.co.uk/portfolio/wiki.php

Dawson, L., Faragher, R., & Gaffney, M. (2012). *Leading numeracy teaching learning and assessment*. Core Unit 3: Literacy and Numeracy Leadership Program. Unpublished manuscript. Centre for School Leadership Learning and Development, Charles Darwin University.

Dempster, N., Konza, D., Robson, G., Gaffney, M., Lock, G., & McKennariey, K. (2012). *Principals as literacy leaders: Confident, credible and connected*. Kingston, ACT: Australian Primary Principals Association.

Dempster, N., Robson, G., & Gaffney, M. (2011). Leadership for learning: Research findings and frontiers from down under. In T. Townsend & J. MacBeath (Eds.), *International Handbook of Leadership for Learning* (pp. 143–164). London: Springer.

Department for Education and Employment (UK). (1999). *The national numeracy strategy: Framework for teaching mathematics from reception to year 6*. London: DEE.

Dewey, J. (1916). *Democracy and education: An introduction to the philosophy of education*. New York: Macmillan.

Downton, A., Knight, R., Clarke, D., & Lewis, G. (2006). *Mathematics assessment for learning: Rich tasks and work samples.* Melbourne: Australian Catholic University.

DuFour, R. (2004). What is a professional learning community? *Educational Leadership, 61*(8), 6–11.

Duignan, P. (2006). *Educational leadership: Key challenges and ethical tensions.* Cambridge, UK: Cambridge University Press.

Dunn, W. N. (1981). *Public policy analysis: An introduction.* Englewood Cliffs, NJ: Prentice-Hall.

Eden, C., & Ackermann, F. (1992). The analysis of cause maps. *Journal of Management Studies, 29*(3), 309–324.

Education Services Australia. (2010). *Maths300: Supporting excellence in mathematics teaching.* Retrieved from http://www.maths300.esa.edu.au

Elmore, R. F. (2004) *School reform from the inside out.* Cambridge, MA: Harvard Education Press.

Faragher, R. M. (2011). Thinking mathematically. In D. Siemon, K. Beswick, K. Brady, J. Clark, R. M. Faragher & E. Warren (Eds.), *Teaching mathematics: Foundations to middle years* (pp. 68–82). Melbourne: Oxford University Press.

Faragher, R. (2014). Learning mathematics in the secondary school: Possibilities for students with Down syndrome. In B. Clarke & R. Faragher (Eds.), *Educating learners with Down syndrome: Research and practice for children and adolescents* (pp. 174–191). London: Taylor Francis.

Fink, E., & Resnick, L. B. (2001). Developing principals as instructional leaders. *Phi Delta Kappan, 82,* 598–606. Retrieved from http://www.kappanmagazine.org/content/82/8/598.abstract

Fullan, M. (2002). Moral purpose writ large. *School Administrator, 59*(8), 14–17.

Fullan, M. (2005). *Leadership and sustainability: System thinkers in action.* London: Corwin Press.

Fullan, M. (2009). *The challenge of change.* Ontario, CA: Corwin Press.

Fullan, M. (2010). *All systems go: The change imperative for whole school system reform.* Ontario, CA: Corwin Press.

Fullan, M., & Barber, M. (2005). Tri-level development: It's the system. *Education Week.* Retrieved from http://www.edweek.org/ew/articles/2005/03/02/25fullan.h24.html

Fulton, K., & Britton, T. (2011). *STEM teachers in professional learning communities: From good teachers to great teaching. Report for the National Commission on Teaching and America's Future (NCTAF).* Washington, DC: NCTAF.

Gaffney, M. (2010, May–June). *Leading networked school communities.* Developer, facilitator and presenter. Australia Institute for Teaching and School Leadership master class (workshop) series, held in Adelaide, Melbourne, Albury, Perth, Bunbury, Sydney, Brisbane and Cairns.

Gaffney, M. (2012). Leadership capabilities for developing numeracy. *Australian Educational Leader, 34*(2), 30–35.

Gaffney, M. (in press). *Leading school system development,* Camberwell, Vic.: ACER Press.

Gardner, H. (1993). *Frames of mind: The theory of multiple intelligences*, London: Fontana.

Garmston, R., & Wellman, B. (2009). *The adaptive school: A sourcebook for developing collaborative groups* (2nd ed.). Norwood, MA: Christopher Gordon.

Gautam, T., Van Dick, R., Wagner, U. (2004). Organizational identification and organizational commitment: Distinct aspects of two related concepts. *Asian Journal of Social Psychology, 7*(3), 301–315.

Hargreaves, A., & Fullan, M. (2012). *Professional capital: Transforming teaching in every school.* New York: Teachers College Press.

Hargreaves, D. (2008). *Leading System Redesign 1.* London: Specialist Schools and Academies Trust.

Harris, A. (2010). Leading system transformation, *School Leadership and Management, 30*(3), 197–207.

Harris, A., & Chrispeels, J. (Eds.) (2008). *International perspectives on school improvement.* London: Routledge.

Hattie, J. (2009). *Visible learning: A synthesis of meta-analyses relating to achievement.* New York: Routledge.

Henderson, M., & Thomson, D. (2003). *Values at work: The invisible threads between people, performance and profit.* Auckland, New Zealand: HarperCollins Publishers.

Hiebert, J., Carpenter, T. P., Fennema, E., Fuson, K. C., Wearne, D., Murray, H., Olivier, A., & Human, P. (1997). *Making sense: Teaching and learning mathematics with understanding.* Portsmouth, NH: Heinemann.

Hiebert, J., & Grouws, D. A. (2007). The effects of classroom mathematics teaching on students' learning. In F. K. Lester (Ed.), *Second handbook of research on mathematics teaching and learning* (pp. 371–404). Charlotte, NC: National Council of Teachers of Mathematics and Information Age Publishing.

Hollingsworth, H., Lokan, J., & McCrae, B. (2003). *Teaching mathematics in Australia: Results from the TIMSS video study.* TIMSS Australia Monograph No. 5. Camberwell, Vic.: Australian Council for Educational Research.

Hopkins, D. (2008). *Every school a great school.* London: Open University Press.

Hopkins, D., Munro, J., & Craig, W. (2011) *Powerful learning: A strategy for systemic educational improvement.* Camberwell, Vic.: ACER Press.

Horn, R. E., & Weber, R. P. (2007). *New tools for resolving wicked problems: Mess mapping and resolution mapping processes.* Retrieved from http://www.strategykinetics.com//New_Tools_For_Resolving_Wicked_Problems.pdf

InPraxis Group. (2006). *Professional learning communities: An exploration.* Edmonton, Canada: Alberta Education.

Jensen, E. (2009). *Teaching with poverty in mind: What being poor does to kids' brains and what schools can do about it.* Alexandria, VA: Association for Supervision and Curriculum Development.

Kieren, T. E. (1997). Theories for the classroom: Connections between research and practice. *For the Learning of Mathematics, 17*(2), 31–33.

Kilpatrick, J., & Silver, E. A. (2000). Unfinished business: Challenges for mathematics educators in the next decades. In M. J. Burke & F. R. Curcio (Eds.), *Learning mathematics for a new century. Yearbook of the National Council of Teachers of Mathematics* (pp. 223–235). Reston, VA: National Council of Teachers of Mathematics.

Kraut, R. E., Gergle, D., & Fussell, S. R. (2002, November). *The use of visual information in shared visual spaces: Informing the development of virtual co-presence.* Paper presented at the 2002 ACM Conference in Computer Supported Cooperative Work, New Orleans, LA.

Kyriacou, C., & Issitt, J. (2008). *What characterizes effective teacher-initiated teacher-pupil dialogue to promote conceptual understanding in mathematics lessons in England in Key Stages 2 and 3?* London: EPPI Centre, University of London.

Langfield-Smith, K. (1992). Exploring the need for a shared cognitive map. *Journal of Management Studies, 29*(3), 349–368.

Leithwood, K., Louis, K., Anderson, S., & Wahlstrom, K. (2004). *How leadership influences student learning.* New York: The Wallace Foundation.

Levin, B. (2009). *How to change 5000 schools.* Cambridge, MA: Harvard Education Press.

Levin, B., & Fullan, M. (2008). Learning about system renewal. *Educational Management, Administration & Leadership, 36*(2), 289–303.

McDonough, A., & Clarke, D. (2003). Describing the practice of effective teachers of mathematics in the early years. In N. A. Pateman, B. J. Dougherty & J. T. Zilliox (Eds.), *Proceedings of the 2003 joint meeting of the International Group for the Psychology of Mathematics Education and the Psychology of Mathematics Education Group of North America* (Vol. 3, pp. 119–139). Honolulu, HI: University of Hawaii.

Marzano, R. J. (2003). *What works in schools: Translating research into action.* Alexandria, VA: Association for Supervision and Curriculum Development.

Marzano, R., Waters, T., & McNulty, B. A. (2005). *School leadership that works.* Alexandria, VA: Association for Supervision and Curriculum Development.

Mason, J., Burton, L., & Stacey, K. (2010). *Thinking mathematically* (2nd ed.). London: Addison-Wesley.

Masters, G. (2012). *Enhancing the quality of teaching and learning in Australian schools. Submission to the senate inquiry on teaching and learning.* Retrieved from http://research.acer.edu.au/tll_misc/16/

Milburn, C., & Hall, B. (2012, 18 June). Numbers adding up in literacy and numeracy campaign. *Sydney Morning Herald.* Retrieved from http://www.smh.com.au/national/education/numbers-adding-up-in-literacy-and-numeracy-campaign-20120615-20f7l.html#ixzz1z3NNPX3k

Millett, A., & Bibby, T. (2004). The context for change: A model for discussion. In A.Millett, M. Brown & M. Askew (Eds.), *Primary mathematics and the developing professional* (pp. 1–17). Netherlands: Kluwer Academic Publishers.

Ministerial Council for Education, Employment, Training and Youth Affairs (MCEETYA). (1997). *National report on schooling in Australia.* Canberra: Commonwealth Government.

Ministerial Council on Education, Employment, Training and Youth Affairs (MCEETYA). (2008a). *Numeracy non-calculator test: Year 7, 2008.* Canberra: Commonwealth Government.

Ministerial Council on Education, Employment, Training and Youth Affairs (MCEETYA). (2008b). *Background paper on the Australian Government National Literacy and Numeracy Pilots*. Canberra: DEEWR.

Mintzberg, H. (2009). *Managing*. San Francisco: Berrett-Koehler.

Mourshed, M., Chijioke, C,. & Barber, M. (2010). *How the world's most improved school systems keep getting better*. London: McKinsey & Company. Retrieved from http://mckinseyonsociety.com/how-the-worlds-most-improved-school-systems-keep-getting-better/

Muyskens, P., & Ysseldyke, J. E. (1998). Student academic responding time as a function of classroom ecology and time of day. *Journal of Special Education, 31*(4), 411–424. doi: 10.1177/002246699803100401

The New International Webster's Dictionary and Thesaurus (2000). (Encyclopedic Ed.). Winnepeg, MAN: Trident Press International.

New South Wales Department of Education and Training, the Catholic Education Commission New South Wales, and the Association of Independent Schools of New South Wales. (2004). *What's making the difference? Achieving outstanding numeracy outcomes in NSW primary schools*. Canberra: Commonwealth of Australia.

Newmann, F. M. & Associates. (1996). *Authentic achievement: Restructuring schools for intellectual quality*. San Francisco: Jossey-Bass.

Ney, S. (2009). *Resolving messy policy problems: Handling conflict in environmental, transport, health and ageing policy*. London: Earthscan.

Novak, J., & Cañas, A. (2008). *The theory underlying concept maps and how to construct and use them*. Pensacola, FI: Florida Institute for Human and Machine Cognition.

Ontario Ministry of Education. (2009). *Leadership framework*. Toronto: OME.

Pettit, P. (2010). From data-informed to data-led? School leadership within the context of external testing. *Leading and Managing, 16*(2), 90–107.

Pont, B., Nusche, D., & Moorman, H. (2008). *Improving school leadership: Policy and practice*. Paris: OECD.

Reeves, D. (2005). Six principles of effective accountability: Accountability-based reforms should lead to better teaching and learning – period. *Harvard Education Letter, 18*(2). Retrieved from http://hepg.org/hel/article/208

Rittel, H., & Webber, M. (1973). Dilemmas in a general theory of planning. *Policy Sciences, 4*(2), 155–169.

Robinson, I. (1983). Unpublished work on parental participation in Victorian schools.

Robinson, K. (2011). *Out of our minds: Learning to be creative*. West Sussex, UK: Capstone.

Robinson, K. (2013). *Leading a learning revolution* [video recording]. Learning without Frontiers Series. Retrieved from http://www.youtube.com/watch?v=-XTCSTW24Ss

Robinson, V. (2007). *School leadership and student outcomes: Identifying what works and why*. ACEL Monograph Series, 41 (October). Winmalee, NSW: Australian Council for Educational Leaders.

Robinson, V., Hohepa, M., & Lloyd, C. (2009). *School leadership and student outcomes: Identifying what works and why: Best evidence synthesis iteration (BES)*. Wellington, New Zealand: Ministry of Education.

Rowley, G., & Horne, M. (2000, December). *Validation of an interview schedule for identifying growth points in early numeracy.* Paper presented to the Australian Association for Research in Education Annual Conference, University of Sydney, New South Wales.

Sarason, S. B. (1990). *The predictable failure of educational reform: Can we change course before it's too late?* San Francisco: Jossey-Bass.

Scavarda, A., Bouzdine-Chameeva, T., Meyer Goldstein, S., Hays, J. M., & Hill, A. (2004, April/May). *A review of the causal mapping practice and research literature.* Paper presented at the Second World Conference on POM and 15th Annual POM Conference, Cancun, Mexico.

Senge, P. (1990). *The fifth discipline: The art and practice of the learning organization.* New York: Doubleday/Currency.

Siemon, D., Beswick, K., Brady, K., Clark, J., Faragher, R., & Warren, E. (Eds.). (2011). *Teaching mathematics. Foundations to middle years.* Melbourne: Oxford University Press.

Skemp, R. R. (1976). Relational understanding and instrumental understanding. *Arithmetic Teacher, 26*(3), 9–15.

Sparks, D. (2002). *Designing powerful professional development for teachers and principals.* Oxford, OH: National Staff Development Council.

Stein, M. K., Smith, M. S., Henningsen, M. A., & Silver, E. A. (2009). *Implementing standards-based mathematics instruction* (2nd ed.). New York: Teachers College Press and National Council of Teachers of Mathematics.

Stenmark, J. K., Thompson, V., & Cossey, R. (1986). *Family math.* San Francisco: Lawrence Hall of Science.

Stigler, J. W., & Baranes, R. (1988). Culture and mathematics learning. In E. Z. Rothkopf (Ed.), *Review of research in education* (pp. 253–306). Washington, DC: American Educational Research Association.

Stigler, J. W., & Stevenson, H. W. (1991). How Asian teachers polish each lesson to perfection. *American Educator, 15*(1), 12, 14–20, 43–47.

Sullivan, P., Mousley, J., & Zevenbergen, R. (2006). Teacher actions to maximize mathematics learning opportunities in heterogeneous classrooms. *International Journal of Science and Mathematics Education, 4,* 117–143.

Tegarden, D. P., Tegarden, L. F., & Sheetz, S. D. (2007). Cognitive factions in a top management team: Surfacing and analyzing cognitive diversity using causal maps. *Group Decision and Negotiation, 18*(6), 537–566.

Thomas, J. (1986). *Number ≠ Maths.* Melbourne: Child Migrant Education Services, Ministry of Education, Victoria.

Thomson, S. (2011). Challenges for Australian education. *Research Developments, 25,* 2–7.

Thomson, S., & Buckley, S. (2009). *Informing mathematics pedagogy: TIMSS 2007.* Camberwell, Vic.: ACER.

Thomson, S., De Bortoli, L., & Buckley, S. (2013). *PISA in Brief. Highlights from the full Australian report: PISA 2013: How Australia measures up.* Retrieved from http://www.acer.edu.au/documents/PISA-2012-In-Brief.pdf

Thomson, S., Hillman, K., Wernert, N., Schmid, M., Buckley, S., & Munene, A. (2012). *Highlights from TIMSS & PIRLS 2011 from Australia's perspective.* Retrieved from http://www.acer.edu.au/documents/TIMSS-PIRLS_Australian-Highlights.pdf

Van Knippenberg, D., & Sleebos, E. (2006). Organizational identification versus organizational commitment: Self definition, social exchange, and job attitudes. *Journal of Organizational Behavior, 27*(5), 571–584.

Vo, H. V., Poole, M. S., & Courtney, J. F. (2005). An empirical comparison of collective causal mapping approaches. In V. Narayanan (Ed.), *Causal mapping for research in information technology* (pp. 142–171). London: Idea Group Publishing.

Webb, N. L. (1992). Assessment of students' knowledge of mathematics: Steps towards a theory. In D. Grouws (Ed.), *Handbook of research on mathematics teaching and learning* (pp. 661–683). New York: Macmillan.

Webster-Wright, A. (2009). Reframing professional development through understanding authentic professional learning. *Review of Educational Research, 79*(2), 702–739. doi: 10.3102/0034654308330970

Willis, S. (1992, October). *Being numerate: Whose right? Who's left?* Keynote address at the Conference of the Australian Council of Adult Literacy, Sydney.

Zevenbergen, R., & Flavel, S. (2007). Undertaking an archaeological dig in search of pedagogical relay. *Montana Mathematics Enthusiast*, Monograph 1, 63–74.

INDEX